Library of Gender and Popular Culture

From *Mad Men* to gaming culture, performance art to steampunk fashion, the presentation and representation of gender continues to saturate popular media. This series seeks to explore the intersection of gender and popular culture, engaging with a variety of texts – drawn primarily from Art, Fashion, TV, Cinema, Cultural Studies and Media Studies – as a way of considering various models for understanding the complementary relationship between 'gender identities' and 'popular culture'. By considering race, ethnicity, class and sexual identities across a range of cultural forms, each book in the series adopts a critical stance towards issues surrounding the development of gender identities and popular and mass cultural 'products'.

For further information or enquiries, please contact the library series editors:

Claire Nally: claire.nally@northumbria.ac.uk
Angela Smith: angela.smith@sunderland.ac.uk

Published and forthcoming titles:

The Aesthetics of Camp: Post-Queer Gender and Popular Culture, by Anna Malinowska

Ageing Femininity on Screen: The Older Woman in Contemporary Cinema, by Niall Richardson

All-American TV Crime Drama: Feminism and Identity Politics in Law and Order: Special Victims Unit, by Sujata Moorti and Lisa Cuklanz

Are You Not Entertained?: Mapping the Gladiator Across Visual Media, by Lindsay Steenberg

Bad Girls, Dirty Bodies: Sex, Performance and Safe Femininity, by Gemma Commane

Beyoncé: Celebrity Feminism in the Age of Social Media, by Kirsty Fairclough-Isaacs

Conflicting Masculinities: Men in Television Period Drama, edited by Katherine Byrne, Julie Anne Taddeo and James Leggott

Fat on Film: Gender, Race and Body Size in Contemporary Hollywood Cinema, by Barbara Plotz

Fathers on Film: Paternity and Masculinity in 1990s Hollywood, by Katie Barnett

Feel-Bad Postfeminism: Impasse, Resilience and Female Subjectivity in Popular Culture, by Catherine McDermott

Film Bodies: Queer Feminist Encounters with Gender and Sexuality in Cinema, by Katharina Lindner

From the Margins to the Mainstream: Women in Film and Television, edited by Marianne Kac-Vergne and Julie Assouly

Gay Pornography: Representations of Sexuality and Masculinity, by John Mercer

Gender and Austerity in Popular Culture: Femininity, Masculinity and Recession in Film and Television, edited by Helen Davies and Claire O'Callaghan

Gender and Early television: Mapping Women's Role in Emerging US and British Media, 1850–1950, by Sarah Arnold

The Gendered Motorcycle: Representations in Society, Media and Popular Culture, by Esperanza Miyake

Gendering History on Screen: Women Filmmakers and Historical Films, by Julia Erhart

Girls Like This, Boys Like That: The Reproduction of Gender in Contemporary Youth Cultures, by Victoria Cann

'Guilty Pleasures': European Audiences and Contemporary Hollywood Romantic Comedy, by Alice Guilluy

The Gypsy Woman: Representations in Literature and Visual Culture, by Jodie Matthews

Love Wars: Television Romantic Comedy, by Mary Irwin

Male and Female Violence in Popular Media, by Elisa Giomi and Sveva Magaraggia

Masculinity in Contemporary Science Fiction Cinema: Cyborgs, Troopers and Other Men of the Future, by Marianne Kac-Vergne

Paradoxical Pleasures: Female Submission in Popular and Erotic Fiction, by Anna Watz

Positive Images: Gay Men and HIV/AIDS in the Culture of ' Post-Crisis', by Dion Kagan

Postfeminism and Contemporary Vampire Romance: Representations of Gender and Sexuality in Film and Television, by Lea Gerhards

Queer Horror Film and Television: Sexuality and Masculinity at the Margins, by Darren Elliott-Smith

Queer Sexualities in Early Film: Cinema and Male-Male Intimacy, by Shane Brown

Screening Queer Memory: LGBTQ Pasts in Contemporary Film and Television, by Anamarija Horvat

Steampunk: Gender and the Neo-Victorian, by Claire Nally

Television Comedy and Femininity: Queering Gender, by Rosie White

Tweenhood: Femininity and Celebrity in Tween Popular Culture, by Melanie Kennedy

Women Who Kill: Gender and Sexuality in Film and Series of the post-Feminist Era, edited by David Roche and Cristelle Maury

Wonder Woman: Feminism, Culture and the Body, by Joan Ormrod

Young Women, Girls and Postfeminism in Contemporary British Film, by Sarah Hill

From the Margins to the Mainstream

Women in Film and Television

Edited by
Marianne Kac-Vergne and Julie Assouly

BLOOMSBURY ACADEMIC
LONDON • NEW YORK • OXFORD • NEW DELHI • SYDNEY

BLOOMSBURY ACADEMIC
Bloomsbury Publishing Plc
50 Bedford Square, London, WC1B 3DP, UK
1385 Broadway, New York, NY 10018, USA
29 Earlsfort Terrace, Dublin 2, Ireland

BLOOMSBURY, BLOOMSBURY ACADEMIC and the Diana logo are trademarks of Bloomsbury Publishing Plc

First published in Great Britain 2022

Cover design: Charlotte Daniels
Cover image: Gal Gadot in *Wonder Woman* (2017)
directed by Patty Jenkins
(© Warner Bros / Photofest NYC)

A catalogue record for this book is available from the British Library.

A catalog record for this book is available from the Library of Congress.

ISBN: HB: 978-1-7883-1267-7
ePDF: 978-1-3501-2017-4
eBook: 978-1-3501-2018-1

Series: Library of Gender and Popular Culture

Typeset by Newgen KnowledgeWorks Pvt. Ltd., Chennai, India
Printed and bound in Great Britain

To find out more about our authors and books visit www.bloomsbury.com and sign up for our newsletters.

Contents

Figures

Series editors' foreword

The place of women in the media industry is one that has concerned several authors in this library. For example, Sarah Arnold's *Gender and Early Television* (2021) explores the role of women behind TV cameras in the United States and UK up to the 1950s. In *From the Margins to the Mainstream*, Marianne Kac-Vergne and Julie Assouly have drawn together researchers who have explored the trajectory of women as they appear on screen and behind the cameras in both film and television. They take as a starting point the 2017 film, *Wonder Woman*, which starred Gal Gadot and was directed by Patty Jenkins. The commercial success of this film is therefore held as an example of a high-grossing woman-produced film, in which the central female character is allowed to be feminine, seeing the world from a female point of view.

The character of Wonder Woman is one who has a whole book dedicated to her in this Library: Joan Ormrod's *Wonder Woman: The Female Body and Popular Culture* (2020) explores the shifts in the way this character has developed to reflect key changes in the wider social context of women's increasing empowerment and choice. As both books argue, the more recent appearances of Wonder Woman can be considered emblematic of the new strands of feminism that are characterized as 'fourth wave'. However, this film is not the only example of female empowerment in front of and behind the camera, as Kac-Vergne and Assouly's edited collection shows, including chapters featuring female directors such as Sofia Coppola's *Marie Antoinette* (2006) as well as women protagonists in mainstream television such as *Sex and the City* (HBO, 1998–2004) and *Stranger Things* (Netflix, 2016–). They show how films directed by women from the 1970s and 1980s usually failed to make it to the mainstream, but also that female filmmaking actually thrived in the 'indie', low-budget sector. By comparison, mainstream television offers a more dynamic place to explore female protagonists. The book also includes an interview with filmmaker Vivienne Dick, who chose to work from the margins of the film industry rather than the mainstream in an attempt to retain a subjective voice and tell a story from a female perspective.

The essays show that there continues to be a tension between what it is assumed audiences want – more of the same – and what can be offered by a different, feminine view. This tension is something we find embedded in culture, as Victoria Cann's *Girls Like This, Boys Like That* (2018) has demonstrated elsewhere in this library. In this way, Kac-Vergne and Assouly's collection shows that there is slow progress for women in the film and television industries but joins other books in this library to show that there is hope that films such as *Wonder Woman* are not one-offs, and that there can be a place for women in the media industry alongside more established patterns of male-led production.

Claire Nally and Angela Smith

Acknowledgements

We would like to start by thanking the authors for their patience and willingness to revise and rewrite their chapters. This collected volume started as the three-day annual Film Studies Society SERCIA conference held in September 2015 at the Université d'Artois (Arras, France). The conference was funded by our two university research groups: Textes et Cultures (UR 4028) at Université d'Artois and CORPUS (UR 4295) at the Université de Picardie Jules Verne. We would like to thank the SERCIA board members for helping with the organization of the conference, especially Jean-François Baillon, SERCIA President at the time, Nathalie Cabiran, administrative coordinator at Université d'Artois, and Céline Murillo, SERCIA Treasurer. We would also like to thank all the conference participants, who created a warm and stimulating atmosphere, and we apologize to those whose contributions could not be included in this volume. Thanks finally to those who helped us review the chapters and improve the book: Jean-François Baillon, Patricia Caillé, Anne Crémieux, Celestino Deleyto, Claire Dutriaux, Gilles Menegaldo, Elizabeth Mullen, David Roche and Jeffrey K. Ruoff.

Introduction

Marianne Kac-Vergne and Julie Assouly

From the Margins to the Mainstream: Women in Film and Television is a collective volume which considers how women's status has progressively evolved within the film industry using independent films as a stepping stone to new career and representational possibilities, thus paving the way for changes within mainstream productions. The book logically follows the same trajectory. It opens with an interview with emblematic experimental director Vivienne Dick and then examines the ways in which female directors, critics, actors and characters gradually opened the male-dominated mainstream industry to new perspectives on gender, behind and in front of the camera. As a result, we have recently witnessed the feminization of traditionally masculine mainstream genres like superhero films, with the glass-ceiling-shattering release of *Wonder Woman*, directed by female director Patty Jenkins. This introductory chapter proposes to analyse this movement towards the mainstream via the specific case of *Wonder Woman* which also closes this volume.

The release of *Wonder Woman* in 2017 seemed to signal that women had finally made it into the heart of mainstream Hollywood: the industry was at last bringing to the screen the most famous comic book heroine and releasing a female-led "superheroine" movie directed by a woman (Patty Jenkins). Until then, superhero films (always directed by men) featured women mainly as love interests or in ensemble casts, even in the post 9/11 wave of superhero blockbusters triggered by the success of Sam Raimi's *Spider-Man* trilogy (2002, 2004, 2007) and the *X-Men* franchise. While Mary Jane (Kirsten Dunst) remains a typical damsel in distress in *Spider-Man*, the women in the *X-Men*'s ensemble cast were sidelined in a series that pitted two white male leaders against one another and developed a spin-off to focus on the quintessentially muscular white male who had become the main protagonist of the films, Wolverine (*X-Men Origins: Wolverine*, 2009; *The Wolverine*, 2013; *Logan*, 2017). Characteristically, it took ten *X-Men* films to finally focus on Jean Grey, in *X-Men: Dark Phoenix* (Kinberg, 2019), but the film mainly emphasized her destructive power and became the least profitable film of the series, supporting the thesis that superheroines are more often than not 'box office poison', as evidenced by the relative failures of *Catwoman* (Pitof, 2004) and *Elektra* (Bowman, 2005).

By contrast, *Wonder Woman* was a major box office success, ranking third in the domestic box office results of 2017 after two other female-led blockbusters (*Star Wars: the Last Jedi* and *Beauty and the Beast*) and becoming the highest-grossing superhero origin film. In 2017, it was the highest-grossing woman-directed film, until it was topped by *Captain Marvel* in 2019, the first superheroine movie in the Marvel universe, co-directed by a woman (Anna Boden with Ryan Fleck) with female screenwriters (Anna Boden and Geneva Robertson-Dworet) and a female composer (Pinar Toprack). *Wonder Woman* can thus be seen as a major advance in women's presence both on screen and behind the camera, since Patty Jenkins was only the second woman to direct a film budgeted at over $100 million (after Kathryn Bigelow's *K-19: The Widowmaker*, 2002) (Smyth, 2017). The film also drew in many more female spectators than the average superhero movie, reaching unprecedented parity between male and female viewers as early as its third opening week (McNary, 2017). But can such an example of women entering the commercial mainstream be seen as a feminist victory?

On a textual level, *Wonder Woman* has been mostly celebrated for its challenge to male domination anchored in an exploration of feminine subjectivity. Even if the film was criticized for its casting of a supermodel, revealing costumes and heteronormative approach, it does provide a still-too-rare example of a dominant female gaze (Zitzer-Comfort and

Rodríguez, 2019), adopting Diana's (Gal Gadot) point of view on a world dominated by men that arouse, in turn, her curiosity, indignation and empathy. The female gaze is especially apparent in the only nudity scene of the film, where it is actually the male protagonist who appears naked, closely scrutinized by Diana, who debunks the phallic mystique by bringing attention, through her insistent and questioning gaze, to the embodied and corporeal nature of the penis. The dialogue further detaches women's sexual pleasure from male intervention, so that the all-female matriarchy Diana grew up in appears as a self-contained haven of peace where men are neither needed nor desired. Furthermore, not only does the film reverse the gendered expectations of superhero fare by having a woman lead men into battle, but the love interest who repeatedly needs saving is now male, turning the damsel-in-distress trope into a stale cliché from the past. Yet, Diana is not masculinized as other action heroines have been, like Ripley and Sarah Connor, so that, in Jeffrey A. Brown's words, she 'provides a legitimate example of female heroism' (2004: 47). Indeed, *Wonder Woman* draws on traditionally feminine qualities like compassion, ability to express love and capacity for dialogue that, in Leigh Singer's words, 'avoids macho, fanboy-driven triumphalism' (2018) and makes Diana 'relatable for many women', according to Kathleen Rowe Karlyn (2017).

Reviewers indeed highlighted the film's 'feminist ethos' (Bastien, 2017), spurred by the actor's 'feminist fire' (Travers, 2017), as well as its focus on female empowerment,[1] while Gal Gadot unabashedly identified as a feminist in a *Rolling Stone* interview: 'People always ask me, "Are you a feminist?" And I find the question surprising, because I think, "Yes, of course ... Because whoever is not a feminist is a sexist"' (Morris, 2017). The film can thus be seen as an exemplar of what Sarah Banet-Weiser (2018) calls 'popular feminism', referring to the contemporary visibility of feminism in popular and commercial media, turning it into a fashionable trend as well as a contested terrain. While feminism came to have negative connotations in the post-feminist 1990s–2000s, with many women reluctant to identify with the term,[2] many celebrities embraced feminism in the 2010s and incorporated it into their star image, be it Beyoncé sampling Chimamanda Ngozie Adichie's 'We should all be feminists' TED talk in 'Flawless' (2013) and performing at the Video Music Awards in front of a screen emblazoned with the word 'FEMINIST' in 2014, or Emma Watson launching the HeforShe movement as UN Women Goodwill Ambassador in 2014. This new-found visibility has gone hand in hand with what some have seen as the emergence of a 'fourth wave' of feminism as early as 2012, thanks to social media activism around such issues as sexual harassment and rape culture,[3] which gained broad recognition and cultural momentum after the Weinstein scandal of 2017 and the global traction it gave the #MeToo movement. In film, Valerie Estelle Frankel identifies *The Hunger Games* (Ross, 2012) as a (somewhat early) triggering point for 'a new type of story' that has brought 'a new awareness and a desire to be more inclusive', engaging with fourth wave feminism through strong female protagonists and a more diverse cast, with *Wonder Woman* as its epitome (2019: 4).

Wonder Woman can be considered as emblematic of these new strands of feminism not only because it represents the acme of commercial visibility for women but also because it remains a site of struggle. Indeed, the film challenges the boys' club of Hollywood superhero productions by proving that female-led productions can widen the market with their specific appeal to female spectators – women-only screenings of *Wonder Woman* were organized in many US cities and sold out, despite the outcry (*The Guardian*, 2017). It participates in a wider transformation of the homogenized male-dominated film industry through the feminization of big-budget blockbusters and franchises as do *Star Wars: The Force Awakens* (Abrams, 2015), *Mad Max: Fury Road* (Miller, 2015) and *Ghostbusters* (Feig, 2016). Indeed, both Warner Bros. and Disney are respectively expanding the DC and Marvel universes through female-led and female-directed productions: *Wonder Woman 1984* (Jenkins, 2020), *Birds of Prey* (Yan, 2020) and *Black Widow* (Shortland, 2021). Yet women's entry into the commercial mainstream has not come without struggle: only in 2008 did the first woman receive an Oscar for Best Picture and Best Director (Kathryn Bigelow for the very male-centred *The Hurt Locker*), and the more recent feminization of famous male-centred franchises such as *Star Wars*, *Mad Max* and *Ghostbusters* has met with intensely sexist backlash. There is a growing polarization between openly feminist celebrities and a vocally anti-feminist manosphere that directs vitriolic attacks on social media against films or events seen as hostile to men,[4] including the women's-only screenings of *Wonder Woman*.

An exemplar of 'popular feminism', *Wonder Woman* is indeed contested terrain and has sparked many debates that highlight the tensions and contradictions between different strands of feminism. The first issue that can and has been raised is that of Wonder Woman's hypersexualization. While Gal Gadot's armoured outfit in the film is less tight-fitting and revealing than the original comic book heroine's costume worn so iconically by Lynda Carter in the television series (CBS, 1975–9), critics like Kyle D. Killian highlight the fact that her beauty is commented on by all the characters in the movie (2018: 59) and that she is repeatedly presented as a sexy woman who arouses men, be it Steve (Chris Pine), his friend Sameer (Said Taghmaoui) or the nefarious German general she seeks to eliminate. Gal Gadot was in fact a model who was crowned Miss Israel in 2004 and had a limited acting career before being cast as Wonder Woman, suggesting that her looks were more important than her acting experience. Wonder Woman's objectification raised further controversy after James Cameron denounced the character as 'an objectified icon' – as opposed to the more masculine Sarah Connor he featured in *Terminator 2* (Cameron, 1991), calling the film 'a step backward'.

Jenkins's reply suggesting that Cameron did not understand the appeal of the character because he is a man and that women should be allowed to be powerful while being attractive can be linked to the tensions that have continually run through feminist debates on the compatibility between femininity and feminism, glamour and empowerment, as well as who is allowed to speak in the name of women, as Jenkins nods to 'the massive female audience who made the film a hit' and 'can surely choose and judge their own icons of progress' (Lopez, 2017). By describing her protagonist as 'loving', Jenkins addresses another criticism directed at the film, the fact that it follows a traditional narrative of heteronormative romance (a central element of the franchise since it is reprised in *Wonder Woman 1984*). Furthermore, after leaving behind the matriarchal island of Themyschira, *Wonder Woman* is set in a world of men where the only other female characters are a fleeting secretary and Dr Maru, an evil disfigured mastermind, while Diana's ultimate power comes from her father, a God. The film thus does not break free from the dominant heteronormative patriarchal ideology. Yet, as Karlyn argues (2017), glamour and romance are typically enjoyed by female audiences so 'why should they be guilty pleasures?' Women's mainstreaming thus raises questions about what is acceptably feminist, bringing to the fore issues raised already during the 1990s and the 'Third Wave' of feminism by young feminist activists like Rebecca Walker (1995) and Naomi Wolf (1993), who rejected what they saw as the Second Wave's 'victim feminism' in favour of 'power feminism' and celebrated women's sexuality, insisting that feminists could be feminine and should use the media to their advantage. However, *Wonder Woman* did not heed the call of the Third Wave for more intersectional representation, since the unnamed women of colour on Themyscira are given only a few lines and then vanish from the rest of the film. The lesbianism long associated with the character and the island also disappears, leaving Diana as a lone empowered woman during the second half of the film, where female solidarity is replaced by antagonistic relations with Dr Maru. The film could thus be seen as post-feminist, as it promotes individual female success and empowerment through a narrative of choice[5] – Diana's individual choices are repeatedly underlined throughout the film, when she decides to leave the island to help mankind or cross the No Man's Land to stop German fire, for instance.

Discourses of individual success also characterize the trajectory of female filmmakers like Patty Jenkins, whose box office hit was received with wonder from the general and industry press,[6] as it went against the industry 'lore' according to which female directors cannot direct big budget productions (Donoghue, 2019: 4–6). Courtney Brannon Donoghue emphasizes the 'superhero expectations' placed on female filmmakers' shoulders, as they are expected to break the glass ceiling not only for themselves but also for others, while gendered obstacles in Hollywood are constantly played down in favour of narratives of individual female confidence and ambition (10). This type of exceptionalist feminism puts forward a narrative of trickle-down empowerment, as if one successful female director or female-led film could break Hollywood's glass ceiling. In fact, there are very few female star directors like Kathryn Bigelow or Sofia Coppola, and many independent female directors struggle to make it – in 2017, women directed 34 per cent of films screened at Sundance (Erbland, 2017) but only 11 per cent of the 250 top-grossing films (Lauzen, 2018). One may hope that independent filmmaker Chloé Zhao's recent Best Director and Best Picture Oscar wins for *Nomadland* in 2021 will pave the way for others, but her victories are as exceptional as they are rare. Indeed, in the 2010s, Kathryn Bigelow's victory in 2010 did not lead to more awards being given to female directors since women were excluded even from nominations – only one female director was included in the decade's Oscar nominations (Greta Gerwig in 2017). Several years (2018 and 2019) featured no women at all in the Best Director nominations for the Oscars, Golden Globes and BAFTAS. Moreover, the issue of the gender pay gap has not been resolved, with female stars still being paid less than males. According to a study reported in *The Guardian* (2019), male Hollywood stars earn $1.1 million more per film than their similarly experienced female co-stars, with the gap being almost the same in 2015 as it was in 1980. Even in 2019, Scarlett Johansson received an estimated total of $56 million, while Dwayne 'The Rock' Johnson was paid $89.4 million; he topped the list of best-paid actors again in 2020 with $87.5 million, while the best-paid female actor, Sofia Vergara, earned only $43 million.[7] So if *Wonder Woman* helped Gal Gadot reach third place on the Forbes list of highest-paid actresses in 2020, the visibility and credit it gave to women as directors, actors as well as spectators may have been short-lived. As Donoghue argues, while *Wonder Woman* was acclaimed as the film that would save Warner Bros.'s floundering DC Extended Universe (Kelley, 2017), 'a pattern of recognition, celebration and forgetting emerges' (Donoghue, 2019: 11) in the trade coverage when it comes to the box office weight of women. While *Wonder Woman* has proved that women can make it into the mainstream and be commercially successful, it remains to be seen whether it will open wide the doors of Hollywood blockbusters to women or whether the film is yet another instance of an 'exceptional' (in every sense of the word) female-driven success.

As a specifically feminist enterprise, the film has its limits, although it does work towards some of the historic goals of the feminist struggle for visibility and institutional change. It has revived an icon of female empowerment and attracted a large mixed audience to see a woman challenge a century-old Hollywood tradition of absenting, punishing or sidelining physically active women and femmes fatales, as Mary Ann Doane underscored in her seminal work (1991). Superheroines are now firmly on the map. Indeed, the film defies and counters industry prejudice against trusting women with big-budget productions and franchises. Despite *Wonder Woman 1984*'s disappointing box office results in its domestic opening weekend in December 2020, Warner Bros. still green-lighted a threequel pairing Gal Gadot and Patty Jenkins yet again (Lee, 2020), developing the first female-directed superheroine franchise. In the aftermath of the Time's Up movement and the pressure for gender parity, Warner Media also became the first major studio in September 2018 to announce a policy to address diversity and in September 2019 released the first studio report on diversity and inclusion in its corporate operations, as well as in the films, television series and digital content created by its various properties (Ramos, 2019).

The case of *Wonder Woman* can thus help us examine what can be gained and what has been lost when women leave the margins for the mainstream. Jenkins herself exemplifies such a career move. She achieved considerable success with a semi-independent, relatively low-budget ($8 million) production, *Monster* (2003), which delivered a strong feminist message and an outstanding performance by Charlize Theron. Despite the film's critical acclaim and relative success at the box office (the film reached #85 in the 2003 worldwide box office with $64.2 million), Jenkins was only able to find work in television, and it took more than ten years for her to be hired to helm a big-budget Hollywood blockbuster, thus achieving fame and recognition in the mainstream. Yet, does *Wonder Woman*'s huge box office success ($822.3 million worldwide) mean that Jenkins's feminist message has become more widespread? Are blockbusters more likely to spread feminist messages than independent films or are they inherently constrained by conservative industry forces? What do women, as not only directors and actors but also spectators, have to gain (or lose) from going mainstream?

A collective book, *From the Margins to the Mainstream: Women in Film and Television* proposes to address these questions by following in Teresa de Lauretis's footsteps and 'traversing the space' between the 'oppositional terms', '"mainstream" (Hollywood and derivatives) and "non-mainstream" (political-aesthetic avant-garde)' and 'mapping it otherwise' (1987: 59). It adopts a diachronic structure, first considering films directed by women in the 'political-aesthetic avant-garde' during the 1970s and 1980s, who were often reluctant to move into the mainstream. It then examines how 'indie' productions offered a bridge for female directors and actors and ends by investigating how women are represented in mainstream productions, whether on television or in Hollywood. The book thus sets out to explore the tensions between the possibilities offered by the margins and the constraints placed by the mainstream, bringing new and varied perspectives to explore the trade-offs between speaking from the margins and entering the commercial mainstream. Contrary to other collective volumes like *Doing Women's Film History: Reframing Cinemas, Past and Future* (Gledhill and Knight, 2015), *Women Who Kill: Gender and Sexuality in Film and Series of the Post-Feminist Era* (Roche and Maury, 2020) and *Independent Women: from Film to Television* (Perkins and Schreiber, 2021), *From the Margins to the Mainstream* applies a gender approach to topics that are less widely present in feminist film studies like the position of film critics, cosmopolitanism and the use of voice-over in TV series. The project of the book, to reprise de Lauretis's words, is 'not so much "to make visible the invisible" … as to construct another (object of) vision and the conditions of visibility for a different social subject' (1987: 67). The collective volume explores women's increased visibility off screen and especially on screen in American and British film and television since the late 1970s without ever forgetting that, in Peggy Phelan's words, 'if representational visibility equals power, then almost-naked young white women should be running Western culture. The ubiquity of their image, however, has hardly brought them political or economic power' (1993: 10).

Indeed, women's mainstreaming also has drawbacks. By adhering to the requirements of the industry, women run the risk of losing their subjective voice and their ability to tell a different story, which drove filmmakers like Vivienne Dick to work from the margins rather than enter the mainstream. In the interview that opens this volume, Dick indeed states that she has been trying 'to imagine a different way of telling stories', outside of narrative cinema. Her 'anti-cinema aesthetic' (Foster, 1995: 29) heeds the calls voiced by Claire Johnston (1973) and Laura Mulvey (1975) to break with conventional storytelling for a more radical feminist cinema to emerge. As Céline Murillo explains in the first chapter of this volume, *Guerillere Talks* (Dick, 1978) and, to a lesser extent, *Born in Flames* (Borden, 1983), can be linked to feminist guerrilla warfare in the way they challenge narrative conventions built up by Hollywood cinema in particular, where women are conceptualized as objects and parts of a unified story. Discontinuity and decentring are also used by filmmakers Michelle Citron, Su Friedrich and Sarah Polley to transform the patriarchal genre of home movies, as argued by Nicole Cloarec in the second chapter. Filming from the margins can thus help focus on what is around or outside the patriarchal narrative, spotlighting, for instance, the bonds of sisterhood (or motherhood) that tend to disappear from more mainstream productions, as exemplified by Hélène Charlery's analysis of *Strange Days* (Bigelow,

1995) in Chapter 4, Anne Sweet's Chapter 9 on action-drama TV female heroes and Charles-Antoine Courcoux's examination of female-led blockbusters such as *Star Wars: The Force Awakens* in Chapter 10. Finally, the costs of reaching the apex of the commercial mainstream are explored by Sara Pesce in her examination of *Marie Antoinette* (Coppola, 2006) in the context of the development of a specifically feminine celebrity culture (Chapter 7).

From the Margins to the Mainstream: Women in Film and Television seeks to shed new light on some of the issues raised by feminist film theory through the prism of different methodological and theoretical approaches. The question raised, for instance, by E. Ann Kaplan in *Feminism and Film* (2000: 20) of whether women directors make films that are obviously different from those of male directors is tackled by Murillo and Cloarec through formal analyses that highlight the aesthetic singularity of female-directed films, while Charlery, Pesce and Yvonne Tasker (in her last chapter on *Wonder Woman*) highlight their respective female directors' engagement with debates that could be seen as specific to women – the male gaze, the trendsetting power of stardom, the meaning of glamour – but actually have a much wider impact on society at large, in a move from the personal to the political. This can be linked to the issue of women's spectatorial pleasure, which is raised directly by Anne Hurault-Paupe's chapter on female film critic Molly Haskell and connects with one of the paradoxes of feminist film theorists, who 'need films that construct women as the spectator yet do not offer repressive identifications' and are 'wary' about the fact that 'women can take pleasure in the objectification of women' (Kaplan, 2000: 124). Identification and its limits are at the core of many of the chapters of this book, notably Celestino Deleyto's analysis of *It's a Free World…* (Loach, 2001) through the prism of our 'engagement' (Smith, 1995: 82) with a female protagonist who rises through the objectification of others. Deleyto's chapter highlights one of the current stakes in feminist film theory, that of intersectionality (Crenshaw, 1989). *From the Margins to the Mainstream* pays specific attention to long-neglected intersections, that of gender and race, of course, which is at the heart of

David Roche's chapter on Pam Grier in *Jackie Brown* (Tarantino, 1997), as well as Charlery's chapter on *Strange Days*, where she highlights the implications of whiteness as well as Blackness. Yet, the book also focuses on the intersectionality of gender and class, remedying the lack of consideration given to working-class women's perspective thanks to Deleyto's chapter on *It's a Free World…* and Roche's on *Jackie Brown*, but also the gap on upper-class female status thanks to Pesce's analysis of *Marie Antoinette*. Finally, this volume takes into account the need for a relational approach; in effect, disrupting the gender order is only possible if both masculinity and femininity are reworked in tandem. The resulting fluidity can help transform media representations as a whole, as Anais Lefevre-Berthelot shows in her analysis of the influence of female voice-overs on male ones in television series.

The volume starts by examining women speaking from the margins as filmmakers and critics and their relationship with the commercial mainstream, whether they seek to challenge dominant patriarchal forms or/and create their own voice and aesthetics. An interview with filmmaker Vivienne Dick explores her journey as an experimental female filmmaker from the No Wave scene of 1970s New York to the art world of Ireland, her vision of women, as well as her relationship with feminism and her constant excitement at finding new connections that make up a voice of her own.

Céline Murillo further examines Dick's work through a comparison between Dick's *Guerillere Talks* (1978) and Lizzie Borden's *Born in Flames* (1983), two No Wave films based on Monique Wittig's *Les Guérillères* (1969) that challenge mainstream Hollywood conventions and the construction of woman as an object to be looked at. Both films depict characters looking, reappropriating the (male) gaze as a source of power for women. Both also deploy an aesthetics of fragmentation to deconstruct the patriarchal narrative and the 'visual pleasures' (Mulvey, 1975) afforded by the unified, transparent style of mainstream cinema while highlighting women's diversity in an intersectional approach.

Finding a new voice within a reworking of classical narrative tropes is also a common feature of the home movies analysed by Nicole

Cloarec: Michelle Citron's *Daughter Rite* (1978), Su Friedrich's *The Ties that Bind* (1986) and *Sink or Swim* (1990), and Sarah Polley's *Stories We Tell* (2012). These 'daughters behind the camera' reclaim their place behind the camera, replacing their fathers, in an effort to find a voice of their own by exploring their lineage and questioning the gender roles traditionally inscribed in the genre. Like the No Wave films discussed by Murillo, these home movies emphasize discontinuity rather than control of the words and images, seeking to accommodate a plurality of voices in a hybrid form and exploring the meaning and limits of subjective filmmaking.

Anne Hurault-Paupe's chapter examines Molly Haskell's position as a feminist critic outside of academic film criticism from the 1970s to the 1990s. While often dismissed by the emergent feminist film criticism of the 1970s in Great Britain, with its psychoanalytical framework and focus on identification and the 'male gaze', Haskell was nonetheless key in bolstering the status of the woman's film, women directors and 'woman's directors', bringing European cinephiliac tastes to American audiences. While Haskell can be criticized for her lack of attention to racial issues, Hurault-Paupe interestingly demonstrates how she created a feminist persona in her writings that enabled her to speak to a female spectator, countering Mulvey's much-discussed emphasis on the male spectator.

The second part of the book moves into the mainstream as it centres on independent, semi-independent or 'indiewood' (King, 2009) films of the 1990s–2000s directed by men and women but featuring strong female protagonists. It focuses on four case studies: *Strange Days*, *Jackie Brown*, *It's a Free World…* and *Marie Antoinette*.

Hélène Charlery analyses *Strange Days* from an intersectional perspective that takes into account race to highlight the differences in the treatment of the white and Black female bodies, both in James Cameron and Jay Cocks's script and Kathryn Bigelow's directorial approach, and how those bodies can be seen as sites of resistance to their construction as visual objects. She argues that Bigelow moves away from the script to build female characters as subjects, independent from the white male objectifying gaze. While the white female body appears exposed and passive, its artificiality highlights the fragility and instability of the male gaze, from which the active Black female body escapes almost entirely.

Intersectionality is at the heart of David Roche's analysis of Pam Grier's star image in *Jackie Brown*, which he relates to her Blaxploitation heritage but also more generally to the image of African-American women in American cinema and culture. While Tarantino's film obviously references Grier's past successes such as *Coffy* (Hill, 1973) and *Foxy Brown* (Hill, 1974), as well as other Blaxploitation hits like *Super Fly* (Parks, 1972), it also reinvents the star by revising the genre's conventions, especially when it concerns Black women and their relationships with men. By dramatizing the working-class Black heroine's reinvention of herself within a certain number of social constraints, the film reflexively draws attention to the lack of opportunity Grier has had, trapped both by the gendered and racialized terms of her star image, and thus to the difficulty for a talented Black actor to achieve and/or maintain star status.

Celestino Deleyto's chapter on Ken Loach's strong independent standpoint in *It's a Free World...* also adopts an intersectional approach that focuses this time on gender, class and migration from a cosmopolitan perspective. Deleyto underlines how the film represents a move away from national cinema towards a cosmopolitan standpoint that takes into account borders and those who cross them; it is also a rare occurrence of female agency and point of view in Loach's filmography that enables Deleyto to fill the gender gap often left open by cosmopolitan theory. Indeed, the film's heroine, Angie (Kierston Wareing), offers a point of view from the border not only because she performs 'borderwork', hiring and exploiting foreign immigrants, but also because she herself is frustrated with her marginalized status as a working-class woman with limited opportunities of social mobility in a globalized and male-dominated labour market.

Women's access to power in a neoliberal economy marked by inequality and the search for fame is examined by Sara Pesce, who analyses Sofia Coppola's *Marie Antoinette* as a metaphor for the

Hollywood dream of stellar acclaim in the new millennium. She draws a parallel between the fame accrued by the last queen of France, notably through her trendsetting fashion statements, as well as her vilification, and the cult of celebrity that has spread across the media from fashion blogs to reality TV shows. The film explores the contradictions of this cult, emphasizing not only the privileges and power afforded to women by celebrity through access to leisure, luxury and high fashion but also the constraints of being constantly in the public eye. Yet the film's linking of celebrity with high caste and its elitist imagery reflect contemporary mixed feelings about the dissemination of celebrity cults to the detriment of the Hollywood elite to which Coppola squarely belongs.

The third part of the book focuses on women protagonists in mainstream productions, be it television series like *Sex and the City* (HBO, 1998–2004), *Xena: Warrior Princess* (Syndicated, 1995–2001), *Bones* (Fox, 2005–17) and *Stranger Things* (Netflix, 2016–), or blockbusters like *Star Wars: The Force Awakens* and, finally, our starting point for this volume, *Wonder Woman* (Jenkins, 2017).

Anais Lefevre-Berthelot examines the recent rise of female voice-overs in television series. Indeed, female voices were deemed unsuitable for broadcasting in the 1920s and 1930s and television shows resorted to male voice-overs until the 1980s to provide an omniscient narrator, 'a voice of God' who sees and knows all. Even in more recent television series, Lefevre-Berthelot draws a contrast between male voice-overs that are invested with experience and authority, and female voice-overs that are more personal and intimate, in the tradition of the autobiographical literary tradition, from the pioneering *My So-Called Life* (ABC, 1994–5) all the way to *Sex and the City*. However, Lefevre-Berthelot highlights the influence of feminine representations on men, since the turn of the twenty-first century has seen the rise of first-person male voice-overs that convey the thoughts and feelings of their heroes, making them more ambiguous for the audience.

Anne Sweet also focuses on gender conventions in television series of the 1990s–2000s, addressing the issue of motherhood in female-led action dramas. Sweet first shows how, until the 1990s, pregnancy on television was considered a delicate and sometimes controversial matter, notably by producers, yet she stresses that women's reproductive and maternal functions continue to be represented in a negative light. Pregnancy is still rare, and when it occurs in a series, it is shown as disempowering for action-drama heroines, sometimes for comedic effect, as unruly heroines lose control of their bodies. More often it has horrific consequences, with childbirth being described as traumatic, depicted using tropes of the horror film that change the heroines into figures of the 'monstrous-feminine' described by Barbara Creed (1993). Women cannot 'have it all' and, in an exaggerated version of the difficult work/life balance many women face, being a woman of action seems incompatible with being a mother.

A similar strategy of containment of female action heroines through tropes of the 'monstrous-feminine' can be found in the films examined by Charles-Antoine Courcoux, who considers the recurrence of the motif of the 'vagina dentata' from a psychoanalytical perspective in contemporary films and television series like *Star Wars: The Force Awakens*, *Evil Dead* (Alvarez, 2013) and *Stranger Things*. The toothed vagina functions as the externalized expression of sexuality to be repressed and can be seen as a repeated discursive concession that counterbalances the supplement of agency given to female heroes. Indeed, this agency is articulated with signs of the abject female body in order to signal the lethal potential of an autonomous femininity in terms of sexuality.

Finally, women's entry into the mainstream seemed complete with the release of *Wonder Woman* in 2017 after decades of waiting for the most famous female comic book character to be given her own film. Yvonne Tasker stresses how groundbreaking the film was since it showed that a 'superheroine film' where women are not mere supporting characters could be a box office success. Comparing Wonder Woman with Marvel's Thor, she also underlines that the two mythical figures draw on classical imagery in different ways: whereas the *Thor* films follow the rather conventional script of what it means to become a man,

Wonder Woman addresses the issues of power and engagement with more earnestness and melodramatic intensity. Drawing on multiple intertexts, the film nevertheless builds a new model of femininity that does not depend on sexualized glamour or self-reflexivity, in a move away from the characteristics associated with post-feminism (Genz and Brabon, 2009).

Tasker's chapter thus concludes this diachronic study of women's movement from the margins to the mainstream by spotlighting the female takeover of a highly masculine, mainstream film genre. Considering this movement as part of a global tendency, one cannot fail but notice that today, the mainstream is more than ever before used to foreground what had remained marginalized, with box office success. Countless films and TV series, largely distributed in theatres, but even more pervasively by on-demand platforms, participate in the mainstreaming of long-marginalized characters and subjects (e.g. Black and Latino superheroes in *Spider-Man: Into the Spider-Verse* (Persichetti, Ramsey and Rothman, 2018), *Black Panther* (Coogler, 2018) and *Watchmen* (HBO, 2019–), teenage gay sex and more in *Sex Education* (Netflix, 2019–) or the African-American transgender underground scene in *Pose* (FX, 2018–21)). Throughout this book, the authors not only question the place of women in the film/TV industry on and off screen but also the industry as a norm-maker, inviting further reflection on the intrinsic relationship between film and society.

Notes

1 Sheri Linden (2017) talks about the 'female empowerment mix' in her review of *Wonder Woman* in the *Hollywood Reporter*; Diana is an 'agent of power' according to *Variety* (Barker, 2017) and 'she totally kicks ass' according to Justin Chang (2017) for the *LA Times*.

2 There are notable exceptions of course, with, for instance, the launching in 2004 of the Geena Davis Institute on Gender and Media to push for more equal representation of women in the media.

3 https://www.britannica.com/topic/feminism/The-fourth-wave-of-feminism. See also Chamberlain (2017).
4 See e.g. Mullen (2020) and Kac-Vergne (2021).
5 See McRobbie (2009: 11).
6 See e.g. Cavna (2017).
7 According to the Forbes lists of highest-paid actors and actresses in 2019 and 2020: https://www.forbes.com/sites/maddieberg/2019/08/27/top-earning-actresses/?sh=1ad7d0d15b79; https://www.forbes.com/stories/arts-entertainment/the-highest-paid-actors-2019/; https://www.forbes.com/stories/celebrities/the-10-highest-paid-actresses-2020/; https://www.forbes.com/stories/the-10-highest-paid-actors-2020/ (all accessed 23 December 2020).

Works cited

Banet-Weiser, Sarah (2018), *Empowered: Popular Feminism and Popular Misogyny*, Durham, NC: Duke University Press.

Barker, Andrew (2017), 'Film review: "Wonder Woman"', *Variety*, 29 May. Available online: https://variety.com/2017/film/reviews/film-review-wonder-woman-1202446320/ (accessed 13 July 2021).

Bastien, Angelica Jade (2017), 'Reviews: *Wonder Woman*', RogerEbert.com, 2 June. Available online: https://www.rogerebert.com/reviews/wonder-woman-2017 (accessed 13 July 2021).

Brown, Jeffrey A. (2004), 'Gender, sexuality and toughness: The bad girls of action films and comic books', in Sherrie A. Inness (ed.), *Action Chicks: New Images of Tough Women in Popular Culture*, 47–74, New York: Palgrave Macmillan.

Cavna, Michael (2017), 'How Wonder Woman director Patty Jenkins cracked the superhero-movie glass ceiling', *Washington Post*, 31 May. Available online: https://www.washingtonpost.com/news/comic-riffs/wp/2017/05/31/how-wonder-woman-director-patty-jenkins-cracked-the-superhero-movie-glass-ceiling/ (accessed 24 December 2021).

Chamberlain, Prudence (2017), *The Feminist Fourth Wave: Affective Temporality*, Basingstoke: Palgrave Macmillan.

Chang, Justin (2017), 'Review: The stirring "Wonder Woman" comes to the rescue of the DC Comics universe', *LA Times*, 31 May. Available online: https://www.latimes.com/entertainment/movies/la-et-mn-wonder-woman-review-20170531-story.html (accessed 13 July 2021).

Creed, Barbara (1993), *The Monstrous-Feminine: Film, Feminism, and Psychoanalysis*, London: Routledge.

Crenshaw, Kimberlé (1989), 'Demarginalizing the intersection of race and sex: A Black feminist critique of antidiscrimination doctrine, feminist theory, and antiracist politics', *University of Chicago Legal Forum*, 1989.8: 57–80. Available online: https://chicagounbound.uchicago.edu/uclf/vol1989/iss1/8 (accessed 13 April 2020).

De Lauretis, Teresa (1987), *Alice Doesn't: Feminism, Semiotics, Cinema*, London: Macmillan Press.

Doane, Mary Ann (1991), *Femmes Fatales: Feminism, Film Theory, Psychoanalysis*, New York: Routledge.

Donoghue, Courtney Brannon (2019), 'Gendered expectations for female-driven films: Risk and rescue narratives around Warner Bros.' Wonder Woman', *Feminist Media Studies*: 1–17.

Erbland, Kate (2017), 'One-third of the Films at Sundance were directed by women, but that shouldn't be confused with the real world', *IndieWire*, 30 January. Available online: https://www.indiewire.com/2017/01/sundance-2017-female-filmmakers-inclusion-diversity-1201775242/ (accessed 24 December 2021).

Foster, Gwendolyn Audrey (1995), *Women Film Directors: An International Bio-Critical Dictionary*, Westport, CT: Greenwood.

Frankel, Valerie Estelle (ed.) (2019), *Fourth Wave Feminism in Science Fiction and Fantasy*, vol. 1, Jefferson: McFarland.

Genz, Stephanie, and Benjamin A. Brabon (2009), *Postfeminism: Cultural Texts and Theories*, Edinburgh: Edinburgh University Press.

Gledhill, Christine, and Julia Knight (2015), *Doing Women's Film History: Reframing Cinemas, Past and Future*, Urbana: University of Illinois Press.

Johnston, Claire (1973), 'Women's cinema as counter-cinema', in Claire Johnston (ed.), *Notes on Women's Cinema*, 24–31, London: Society for Education in Film and Television.

Kac-Vergne, Marianne (2021), 'Le féminisme au secours des franchises de science-fiction: le cas de *Mad Max: Fury Road* (2015) et *Ghostbusters* (2016)', *Res Futurae*, 17. Available online: https://journals.openedition.org/resf/9419 (accessed 10 January 2022).

Kaplan, E. Ann (2000), *Feminism and Film*, Oxford: Oxford University Press.

Karlyn, Kathleen Rowe (2017), 'Wonder women: Women's tears, and why they matter', *Jump Cut*, 58, Winter 2017–18. Available online: https://www.ejumpcut.org/archive/jc58.2018/karlynWonderWoman/index.html (accessed 13 July 2021).

Kelley, Seth (2017), 'Wonder Woman: How Patty Jenkins saved the DC Extended Universe', *Variety*, 4 June. Available online: http://variety.com/2017/film/news/wonder-woman-box-officeanalysis-patty-jenkins-warner-bros-1202453504/ (accessed 22 July 2021).

Killian, Kyle D. (2018), 'How *Wonder Woman* is, and is not, a feminist superheroine movie', *Journal of Feminist Family Therapy*, 31.1: 59–61.

King, Geoff (2009), *Indiewood, USA: Where Hollywood Meets Independent Cinema*, London: I.B. Tauris.

Lauzen, Martha (2018), 'It's time for action, not promises, to get more women in filmmaking', *Variety*, 4 May. Available online: https://variety.com/2018/voices/columns/women-filmmakers-1202796124/ (accessed 21 July 2021).

Lee, Chris (2020), '*Wonder Woman 1984* earns highest box-office opening of the pandemic era', *Vulture*, 28 December. Available online: https://www.vulture.com/2020/12/wonder-woman-1984-highest-box-office-opening-of-pandemic.html (accessed 21 July 2021).

Linden, Sheri (2017), '"Wonder Woman": Film review', *Hollywood Reporter*, 29 May. Available online: https://www.hollywoodreporter.com/review/wonder-woman-review-1005711 (accessed 13 July 2021).

Lopez, Ricardo (2017), 'Patty Jenkins fires back at James Cameron over "Wonder Woman" criticism', *Variety*, 24 August. Available online: https://variety.com/2017/film/news/patty-jenkins-james-cameron-wonder-woman-1202538790/ (accessed 21 July 2021).

McNary, Dave (2017), '*Wonder Woman*: Female and older moviegoers powered box office, new study shows', *Variety*, 6 July. Available online: https://variety.com/2017/film/news/wonder-woman-study-box-office-1202488262/ (accessed 13 July 2021).

McRobbie, Angela (2009), *The Aftermath of Feminism: Gender, Culture and Social Change*, Los Angeles: Sage.

Morris, Alex (2017), 'Gal Gadot on becoming Wonder Woman, the biggest action hero of the year', *Rolling Stone*, 24 August. Available online: https://www.rollingstone.com/movies/movie-features/gal-gadot-on-becoming-wonder-woman-the-biggest-action-hero-of-the-year-113568/ (accessed 13 July 2021).

Mullen, Elizabeth (2020), 'Licensed to kill? Arming and disarming female killers in action film and parody in *Mad Max: Fury Road* and *Spy*', in David Roche and Cristelle Maury (eds), *Women Who Kill: Gender and Sexuality in Film and Series of the Post-Feminist Era*, 189–208, London: Bloomsbury.

Mulvey, Laura (1975), 'Visual pleasure and narrative cinema', *Screen* 16.3: 6–18.

Perkins, Claire, and Schreiber, Michele (2021), *Independent Women: From Film to Television*, London: Routledge.

Phelan, Peggy (1993), *Unmarked: The Politics of Performance*, New York: Routledge.

Ramos, Dino-Ray (2019), 'WarnerMedia diversity and inclusion interim report reveals workforce close to gender parity, representation for people of color in film & tv needs improvement', *Deadline*, 26 September. Available online: https://deadline.com/2019/09/warnermedia-diversity-and-inclusion-report-women-people-of-color-representation-1202745057/ (accessed 21 July 2021).

Roche, David, and Cristelle Maury (eds) (2020), *Women Who Kill: Gender and Sexuality in Film and Series of the Post-Feminist Era*, London: Bloomsbury.

Singer, Leigh (2018), 'Blockbusters and franchises', *Sight & Sound*, 28.1 (January).

Smith, Murray (1995), *Engaging Characters: Fiction, Emotion, and the Cinema*, Oxford: Oxford University Press.

Smyth, Lucinda (2017), 'Female directors and the progress myth', *Prospect*, 23 June 23. Available online: https://www.prospectmagazine.co.uk/arts-and-books/female-directors-and-the-progress-myth-wonder-woman (accessed 13 July 2021).

The Guardian (2017), 'Women-only Wonder Woman showings sell out despite outcry', 27 May. Available online: https://www.theguardian.com/film/2017/may/27/women-only-screenings-wonder-woman (accessed 21 July 2021).

The Guardian (2019), 'Hollywood's gender pay gap revealed: Male stars earn $1m more per film than women', 15 September. Available online: https://www.theguardian.com/world/2019/sep/15/hollywoods-gender-pay-gap-revealed-male-stars-earn-1m-more-per-film-than-women (accessed 21 July 2021).

Travers, Peter (2017), '"Wonder Woman" review: Gal Gadot brings comics' original riot girl to life', *Rolling Stone*, 30 May. Available online: https://www.rollingstone.com/movies/movie-reviews/wonder-woman-review-gal-gadot-brings-comics-original-riot-girl-to-life-196786/ (accessed 13 July 2021).

Walker, Rebecca (1995), *To Be Real: Telling the Truth and Changing the Face of Feminism*, New York: Anchor Books.

Wolf, Naomi (1993), *Fire with Fire*, New York: Random House.

Zitzer-Comfort, Carol, and José I. Rodríguez (2019), 'Riding the waves of feminism in *Wonder Woman*: A shock heard 'round the world', in Valerie Estelle Frankel (ed.), *Fourth Wave Feminism in Science Fiction and Fantasy*, vol. 1, 184–93, Jefferson, NC: McFarland.

Part One

Women speaking from the margins

Interview with Vivienne Dick

Marianne Kac-Vergne: On the MUBI platform, there is a beautiful quote that is attributed to you and I was wondering if it is actually yours. 'All my life, I've been looking at films which foreground men and I wanted to make films where men are peripheral, in the background, the way women usually are.'

Vivienne Dick: That's right.

MKV: Your films all feature mostly women and sometimes only women. What interests you about filming women?

Vivienne Dick: I was interested from the very beginning in the fact that women in our culture are not full and equal subjects. Now, at that time I didn't use that word 'subject', but that's what it was. I felt that the way women were represented in society was biased and limited. So I decided, well, I'm not going to be adding to all this kind of material. I'm going to just make films about women. I'm a woman. I'm interested in women, and so I'll make films about women. It's as simple as that. So I have men sometimes come in on the edge of the frame and that's fine.

Céline Murillo: The women you're filming are so different. In *Guerillere Talks* (1978), Lydia Lunch is all curves and hyperfeminine, while the other extreme is the very lean and twiggy Pat Place.

Vivienne Dick: Lydia is feminine, but she's strong and tough. She's feminine, but she's like a demon as well. She's not a pushover by any means. She has the power. She's got the control always. Pat is more passive, and very androgynous looking, which is interesting to me. The woman who is the dancer at the beginning of *Red Moon Rising* (2015) also looks amazing.

CM: But did you cast Pat Place and Lydia Lunch because they were so different?

Vivienne Dick: I wasn't thinking about casting when I was making *Guerillere Talks*. I was just interested in both of them. I'd seen Lydia perform in the No Wave band Teenage Jesus and the Jerks and I'd never seen such a creature. Listening to this music, it seemed wild to me. And then seeing these women I'd never come across before was fresh and different. So I just gravitated towards them and some others – like Adele Bertei and Anya Phillips. I simply approached Lydia, for example, and asked if I could film with her. And that was a way to get to know her.

CM: In New York, there were a lot of women in the No Wave groups.

Vivienne Dick: That was what was really exciting for me when I moved to New York and when I discovered the music scene and its incredible energy. Many of the women were involved in that scene not just as singers, but playing instruments and even having their own bands. This was replicated elsewhere too, in other kinds of music and in other arts; there were photographers, women involved with theatre, female choreographers and dancers, this incredible array of women doing all kinds of creative work, the likes of which I had never experienced before. It was very exciting.

CM: Why do you think that there were so many women in these groups and that there was no difference between cinema and the other arts in terms of the participation of women?

Vivienne Dick: New York in the late 1970s was going through a highly creative period. There were a lot of women involved in the arts, in performance art as well, like Yvonne Rainer, who was a filmmaker, a dancer and a performance artist, for example. I used to attend Anthology Film Archives and saw quite a lot of American experimental films made by women, which was new to me. Then there were other women who were highly successful, in dance, too, such as Twyla Tharp, Trisha Brown and Lucinda Childs. And Meredith Monk was very interesting as well. I'd never seen any performer like her before in the way she used the voice in theatre.

MKV: Were you attracted to the No Wave style because there were so many women?

Vivienne Dick: No, I was attracted to the music, particularly to the very avant-garde, experimental noise bands which I found very exciting.

MKV: Were there links between the No Wave bands and arts collectives and the feminist movements of the 1960s and 1970s?

Vivienne Dick: A number of the women who were involved in the music scene at the time, people like Pat Place or Adele Bertei, were lesbian or queer. They and others, like Lydia Lunch, were very strong and a type of woman that I had not encountered before. So I was intrigued by that: that's what made me want to film them in the very first film, *Guerillere Talks*.

MKV: Were there official or institutionalized links with more feminist or more political groups?

Vivienne Dick: There wasn't any really, but I knew Claire Pajaczkowska, who lives and works in London now as a professor at the Royal College of Art, and who was involved at the time in a feminist magazine called the Heresies Collective that produced really interesting work on art and politics. The magazine was quite radical in content and layout and the work was very collective. We used to have meetings on my rooftop to discuss feminism and possible collaborative work in film, and

Claire was the theoretical person in the group. That's where the title *Guerillere Talks* comes from (we had been reading Monique Wittig's book, *Les Guérillères*). Claire encouraged me to continue making films. Some of the feminists at that time were suspicious of the women who were involved in the music scene because of the way they dressed and used makeup. Many feminists at the time dressed down and were opposed to wearing sexy clothes or whatever, but on the punk scene, women dressed to please themselves, sexy or otherwise.

MKV: Going back to what you said about many of the members of the scene being lesbians, the feminist movements of the 1960s especially and some of the 1970s have been criticized for being quite hostile to lesbianism. And they've also been criticized for being quite white-centred, not necessarily including very many women of colour. What do you think of that? Was this also true in the No Wave movement with women of colour?

Vivienne Dick: There weren't many women of colour on the scene, apart from a very good friend of mine called Felice Rosser, who was one of the few who was around at that time. She's a musician and she's featured in my last film [*New York Our Time* (2020)]. New York has always been segregated. But then something changed when hip hop came downtown. Some filmmaker friends of mine were hanging out in the Bronx and Charlie Ahearn started working with the very early hip hop people. Michael Holman, who used to play with Jean-Michel Basquiat in a band called Gray, was the person who first brought the bands downtown, very close to where I was living in fact, to a small basement club called Negril. I went along to some of those early performances. It was really exciting to be there at the very beginning of hip hop.

CM: But did it really change something in the multi-racial makeup of the neighbourhood, or was there just one place that had hip hop and all the rest was punk?

Vivienne Dick: It did not change the racial makeup of the neighbourhood but it did become more diverse with more Black, white and gay people mixing in some clubs – and new, larger venues opening all the time. People were very excited about the new rhythms of hip hop. Blondie, for example, had been listening to hip hop and she brought out a song called Rapture that was influenced by that sound. The thing is, the music was changing all the time. You had this avant-garde, austere kind of music, and you had the very simple Ramones-style punk music. There was a cross-pollination between minimalist music (Rhys Chatham, Glenn Branca) and punk, and this led to a lot of guitar sound – Sonic Youth, for example. And then after a few years, it became more rhythmical, with a more African influence, especially from Nigeria, Fela Kuti for example. Reggae had always been around and the music was becoming what they call 'postpunk'. Bands like Konk and a very popular band that Pat was in, the Bush Tetras, were using a more funky kind of sound.

MKV: In an interview, you mentioned the community gardens in New York with many Puerto Ricans or Hispanics. Was there any interaction between artistic groups and the community garden movement?

Vivienne Dick: There were plenty of Puerto Rican and Caribbean people around the Lower East Side but a lot more in Brooklyn. Interaction was limited although it developed later on, especially in the larger gay clubs, and also when the graffiti artists who worked on the subways began to be shown in downtown galleries and become well-known. Early on, I was teaching English in a Central American school on 14th Street. So I knew loads of people from the Dominican Republic and they brought me to some merenque or salsa events in social clubs.

MKV: But the links were mainly musical rather than through film?

Vivienne Dick: Yes. I only know of one Hispanic filmmaker from that time – Manual DeLanda – in fact he is from Mexico.

CM: The ABC No Rio building was right in the centre of the Hispanic neighbourhood. Was there any participation from the Hispanic community?

Vivienne Dick: There probably was over time. But I really do not know much about that. I do know that Charlie Ahearn and Robert Cooney and his friend Jorge Mendez spent a lot of time in the South Bronx exploring the hip hop scene. Robert was a filmmaker and an anarchist. They made beautiful silk screen posters, Charlie made his well-known film *Wildstyle* (1983) with the rappers, graffiti artists and breakdancers from there.

MKV: The title of this book is *From the Margins to the Mainstream: Women in Film and Television*. Do you think that actually applies, that women have gone from the margins to the mainstream, or not? Would you say that women have been able to enter the mainstream?

Vivienne Dick: It depends on what you want. Not everyone wants to make mainstream films. I am not sure I fit into a mainstream model. I don't even work with scripts, by choice.

But there are more women around now who are successful filmmakers and who work in the mainstream. It is a complicated issue as I feel that it is still very hard for women to get support for their films, but it is better than it was before. Women as well as men are more conscious of these difficulties. Personally, I have to be true to myself and make the kind of work that feels authentic to me whether that is going to be mainstream or not. But it's extraordinary to me how work that I made many years ago, that was so low budget and so visceral, is still being shown in places like the Museum of Modern Art here in Dublin, who bought two of the works. When the work is shown today and I meet young people who come along from art colleges and film schools and who tell me that they can relate to this work, that is really interesting to me.

CM: Where are your new films released now, in art shows or in the cinema?

Vivienne Dick: I prefer to show my work in the cinema but sometimes it works well in a gallery or museum too – it depends how it is installed. They are distributed by LUX UK and The Filmmakers Coop in New York City.

CM: Do you think of having them online on a platform like MUBI?

Vivienne Dick: Yes, I would be interested in that.

MKV: The book actually ends with a chapter on Wonder Woman. So here we're talking about a strong female protagonist.

Vivienne Dick: Oh, I always loved Wonder Woman, a very inspirational icon. There is that wonderful video made by Dara Birnbaum called 'Technology/ Transformation'. It's an iconic work. I showed it when I curated a show in Galway a few years ago.

CM: How has being a woman affected your career, your way of making films?

Vivienne Dick: The only way I could possibly have made films was the way I did it, which was very low budget. And anyway, I needed to find my own voice unimpeded by funding organizations. Working in the traditional way would never have worked for me, so I was feeling my way with the early films and over the years I have grown more confident in making proposals. But I still work with the Arts Council rather than with Screen Ireland, although someday that might change. Anyway, Screen Ireland only partly fund films, you also have to get matching funding from elsewhere, which I know to be a very long journey. The Arts Council provides quite a substantial budget now for experimental work, it's a lot easier to work with them to raise money. It's really difficult to raise money commercially for experimental work or even for work that isn't experimental.

MKV: In an interview, you said that for women it can be much harder to get their films funded. Has this been the case for you as a woman?

Vivienne Dick: The Arts Council have been very supportive of my films. When I returned to Ireland in the 1980s it was not easy for me to get funding from the Arts Council as everything depended on a finished script. I went to the UK and was able to get funding there. These days it is different. Today Screen Ireland have become very pro gender equality when it comes to funding. This is all since Waking the Feminists, a theatre revolt for gender equality in the Abbey Theatre, made such a noise in 2015. There is hope that Screen Ireland will begin to take a chance with more diverse filmmaking styles in the future.

MKV: I was wondering what might be specific about the stories that women have to tell or about what you have to say about women.

Vivienne Dick: There are women who make terrific narrative films. I am a big fan of Jane Campion, Claire Denis and Marta Meszaros for example. But there are different ways to make films. Generally, my work has been process-led. I like to connect disparate elements; that is the way my brain works, hopping from one thing to the next. Somehow or another, magically, there is a connection there between disparate elements that seem totally alien. It's always such a joy to make something coherent with elements that seem so different, through editing, for instance. The brain does it anyway: we're always looking for connections. I do what I do and I'm sure not everyone likes it, but I can only make films that feel right to me.

We all make different kinds of work and not everyone's going to like everything. I think it's a huge mistake to make films to please others.

MKV: Would you consider yourself to be a feminist filmmaker? How so?

Vivienne Dick: I would definitely consider myself a feminist filmmaker. Feminism stands in for every 'other'. There isn't one story, or one way of telling it – whether you are white, Black, gay trans or whatever. A world defined and controlled by the White Western Male is over.

MKV: So I'm guessing that you've never really considered working in the more commercial film industry.

Vivienne Dick: It's important that I stick with what I want to make myself. I have nothing against making films for a wider audience. I am just not willing to make work I do not believe in.

MKV: We now have some questions about your involvement with the No Wave movement. Some film critics have called you the quintessential No Wave filmmaker. I was wondering if you agreed with this definition.

Vivienne Dick: I think it was Jim Hoberman who said that. He was very supportive of my work from the very beginning, as was Amy Taubin. I thought they wrote really well on my work. I was a very raw sort of filmmaker. I hadn't been to film school and I was working in a very intuitive way at the time, and it was astonishing to me to get this feedback.

MKV: Do you still see yourself as No Wave?

Vivienne Dick: The early work is associated with that period and maybe I would never have begun to make films if I had not gone to New York at that particular time. I still like to work with a mixture of documentary, performance and fiction. The later films are different and that is to do with the technology and access to funding. The newer digital cameras didn't allow for the hand-held movements I used before. I began to get interested in the long take and the still frame.

MKV: What elements would you say have remained from the No Wave era?

Vivienne Dick: I am still interested in gender issues and sexuality and just what it means to be human. There's always a very subjective element to my work. I think there's a kind of messiness about my work, but I think it's very controlled at the same time, it's both messy and controlled.

MKV: Your later work seems much more controlled than your older films.

Vivienne Dick: I suppose editing skills improve with time. I now work with editing in a much more granular way. I enjoy editing very much, but I've always liked the disruption in the flow and unexpected shots, so you don't know what's coming next. I like for there to be an element of risk, of play, and a space for the unexpected. This was always the case and I hope, continues to be there in films I make today.

CM: You said at some point that you were scared of professionalism. And now you talk about technique and editing. Do you still have this opinion about professionalism?

Vivienne Dick: If you work with a larger budget and you decide to work with a crew, you have to work in a different way, obviously. It's much more organized in terms of time. But I always like to leave room within that process for something unexpected. There's a kind of battle to work out how you can work with a crew and still make the sort of films I make. The last feature film I made is possibly more mainstream. It was shot in just two weeks. But it is possibly aimed at a different kind of audience. It had a very small crew since it was a documentary.

CM: We were wondering also about the budget for these last films, *New York Our Time* and *Red Moon Rising*, where the lighting is so sophisticated.

Vivienne Dick: Both films were funded by the Irish Arts Council. The first was funded by the Reel Art Scheme and the second through a Film Project Award. I love lighting and I was so excited to have the opportunity to work with lighting and be able to experiment in the woods [in *Red Moon Rising*] and play with colour. I am an older filmmaker now. I am grateful I still have the desire to make films, that I still want to take risks, that I am still trying to 'speak' through film. What is essential is that there is a fine balance between having control and not having control. And that is where the best work comes from, I think.

MKV: So would you say that your recent films have benefited from higher budgets than the previous ones?

Vivienne Dick: In some ways, if you're making films when you're in your twenties and you're just exploring the medium, the sort of work you make forty years later is bound to have changed, because you're a different kind of person. My early work was self-funded, the equipment was crude and the shooting ratio was tiny. With more recent films and with the advantage of higher budgets I've been able to collaborate with other people. That's really important to me, to work with interesting composers or interesting dancers or performers.

CM: Can you tell us a little more about your latest film, *New York Our Time*?

Vivienne Dick: The period I spent in New York hugely marked me. It got me started making films. It was a university of life for me. I was introduced to so many different ideas, so many different people. It was a culture shock, it was exhilarating – the music, the cinema, art, dance – so different from what I grew up with. I have friends from that time who are still living there. So I decided to make this film and put the proposal to the Arts Council. I've also got a lot of archive footage from the time that I've never used. It was fun exploring what I had and what I could use for this film. It was also interesting finding music because it's very difficult to get music for a film, you have to get permission and it's a lot of work.

The film, *New York Our Time* is about two strata of time: now and a period in the late 1970s. But it's not a nostalgia fest, it's about the strangeness of time passing, how strange it is that we get old and we're going to die. It's a philosophical film as well as a film that looks at this period when we were all young. I just think that time is so strange, everything's changing all the time, but it's changing so slowly that we don't notice it. But when you look back at a period in the past and you see the fabric of it, the clothes, the way people moved, everything that makes up reality, it's preserved in the film. I've always been interested in time that reaches right back to the ice age, to prehistoric time, partly maybe because many years ago, when I went to university, my subject of study was archaeology and particularly the Paleolithic period. I'm not just interested in what is a woman, but what is a human. In this new Anthropocene period we're going to have to learn how to respect nature and how to relate to the other. In our history, the relationship to the other has always been based on dominating the other, whereas I think it's more interesting to think that we *are* the other as well. I think of it in terms of reciprocity, we're different from the other, but we're also part of the other.

MKV: One of your films is actually entitled *The Irreducible Difference of the Other* (2013). What did you mean by that title?

Vivienne Dick: I mean that we're not the same. We are different and we're separate. In the history of philosophy, woman is not understood as being separate, she's collapsed into the man. I was very influenced by Irigaray's writings on all of that and her very beautiful way of using words.

MKV: Has feminist film criticism or feminist writings in general influenced your work as a filmmaker?

Vivienne Dick: Absolutely. I have been influenced by film writers like Mary Ann Doane, E. Ann Kaplan, Barbara Creed, and philosophers like Irigaray, Butler, Grosz. I read those a while ago. Now I am interested in what it means to be a human and our relationship to the world and to nature. I have been reading books by Harari, Timothy Morton and Jane Bennett.

MKV: You seem to film mainly with people you know or friends. So we were wondering if you saw any links between your filmmaking and home movies.

Vivienne Dick: You could say my films have some relationship to home movies in the documentary side of things and the fact that I often work with people around me. I don't script films. I very occasionally work with actors, such as Olwen Fouéré in *The Irreducible Difference of the Other*. I mostly work with people I know and I am interested in. I'm interested in everyday things and people as well. If they trust you, they can reveal things that you don't see in a lot in films. I'm interested in the material between the shots. There is an element of performance. It's a little like what a lot of young people are doing today with selfies or TikTok. There's much less rehearsal involved, it's not polished and there's always a space there for something to intrude. And that was always the exciting thing about working with Super 8, which had live sound. Something that was happening in the street would suddenly become an element in the film. A space for chance to shape the work. I would like to keep that as much as possible.

MKV: You said that your latest work is maybe more mainstream?

Vivienne Dick: It's definitely designed for a wider audience, but it still has the same elements and features that you can see in the older work. I'm sure the film I make after this will be completely different. I hope it is.

MKV: So before talking to you, I had a question which was: given an unlimited budget, what would you do with it? But I get the impression that budgets are actually not that important to you.

Vivienne Dick: It is not like I feel I'm held back because I don't have this big budget. I'd rather have an idea first and then think about the budget. Of course, when you have a budget you can start thinking about possibilities that otherwise are impossible. Managing a budget is very interesting because there's always a limit, with any budget. You've got to manage it so it doesn't get out of hand. It's very easy for that to happen. I have learned that working with budgets, even very low budgets, is managing people's energy. You have to be ready for people when they come. You can't keep them hanging around endlessly because they lose interest, especially if they're not actors. There is a balance between managing this enterprise that you're setting out to do, which has to be meticulously planned, and then leaving space for unexpected or improvised things to happen. It is most important to know when you have what you need, without knowing how it's all going to be put together. Often I collect material, I don't know where it's going to come into the film, but it's something I want. I collect all kinds of little pieces of material and some of it is abandoned or not used. But then you find something interesting that is working. For example, if you take *Red Moon Rising*, I was shooting a lot in the countryside, and it was quite banal stuff in many ways. And then one morning I made myself go out and film at eight o'clock in the morning. I was in the country with the camera not knowing what I was looking for and not knowing where I was going. There was fog everywhere, I found the signpost pointing down to the lake and went down to the water. And then I got this amazing footage with the trees and the fog and the reflections: it just came about, there's no way you could plan that. When I found that, I knew immediately I would be using it in the film. I always know when I have something that's stronger and that I'm going to be able to use. That experience was really lovely, it was very loose and felt like going fishing. You can't do that all the time, you'd be exhausted. But here the footage shot in the forest was more or less planned, except the performances, which were very free. In general, with a larger budget you work with a producer, it is much more of a team effort and then the film is made within a set period. The right team and good planning: this is how we worked on the last few films.

MKV: What's the latest film that you've enjoyed or found inspirational?

Vivienne Dick: I recently saw *Hive* – a Kosovan film I liked. I also like much of Aldomovar's work as well as Wong Kar-wai's early work. *In the Mood for Love* is such a beautiful film for me. I love the production design and the way he uses music. I love that kind of film: it's not really a story film. It is a story, but a very, very simple story.

MKV: I can see the links with your work. Do you have any further plans after your film on New York, anything that you're working on?

Vivienne Dick: I made a short three-screen work recently which was for a group show at Temple Bar Gallery. The show was called Wayward Eye. It was two screens in sync in the space and one silent tiny screen the size of an ipad which filled a tiny window to the street outside. It was all about being in the city during Covid. And I had a retrospective last November at Jeu de Paume in Paris which also included music and performance in the lobby.

MKV: Were you able to shoot outside with Covid?

Vivienne Dick: Using very simple equipment, yes. I was using just my own camera. It was a small production. Which is nice, for a change, to be working by myself.

MKV: I read in an interview that you wanted your films to be revolutionary. It was an old interview, but I was wondering if you still had that wish.

Vivienne Dick: I really want to hold onto that. You have to remind yourself sometimes of what your early aims were. That's what I'm doing right now. I finished this New York film and I can make anything I want now in a way, I can make something completely different. It's about having the energy and the desire.

MKV: Well, we're looking forward to the next revolution.

Vivienne Dick: Oh, thank you. We'll see what happens!

1

Lizzie Borden and Vivienne Dick: Fighting for female filmmaking

Céline Murillo

The women affirm in triumph that all action is overthrow.

Monica Wittig, *Les Guérillères*

This chapter compares two films made in New York at the same moment by two female filmmakers who were both part of 'The Downtown Scene' (Yokobosky, 2006: 126), a group which included a number of female filmmakers who shared a concern about female representation and spectatorship, yet with different stylistic approaches, such as Ericka Beckman, Bette Gordon, Beth B., Tina L'Hotsky, Clara Perlman, Vivienne Dick and Lizzie Borden. We will focus here on works by the last two filmmakers.

Borden's *Born in Flames* (1983) takes place at an unknown date, ten years after a socialist revolution has transformed the United States into a country where the government's mission is to protect workers through a policy called 'workfare'. However, the 'workfare' policy does not sufficiently take women's rights into account; as a consequence, female activists gather to create a women's army. They take up arms and resort to violence to obtain power over the media and express themselves. More than a 'utopian-dystopian' (Willse and Spade, 2013: 1) world, this fiction is better described as an *altertopia* as it presents neither an ideal future as in a utopia nor a gloomy one as in a dystopia: it appears in retrospect as an alternative, unexpected vision of the future.

Guerillere Talks (Dick, 1978) is an experimental film made up of five episodes. It was shot with a super-8 camera by the filmmaker herself. While the initial idea was to have women wear a small microphone and talk to the camera, in the finished film, not all of them do so: the women perform varied activities, some of which are akin to a parody of traditional masculinity. Some talk to the camera or aggressively stare at it; others silently take pictures of the filmmaker, read letters or pretend to do jobs around the house.

Although the two films seem at first to be quite different – the first one is based on linear traditional storytelling while the second has a non-linear *quasi* non-narrative structure – they have much in common. In addition to the common place and time of their production by two female filmmakers with a limited budget, both are linked to Monique Wittig's novel, *Les Guérillères* (1969). The novel centres on a large group of women designated by the French feminine plural pronoun '*Elles*', which makes them a unified group yet signifies that they are female – which would not be the case with the English pronoun 'they'. The women, the '*Elles*', are fighting a war against men. Men are referred to as '*Ils*' or '*Il*', the French masculine pronouns. The singular here shows men as either scattered individuals (looking less dangerous since they are isolated) or as an abstract patriarchal power. The women are a mass of true warriors, who are 'joyfully aggressive' (Jean, 1970). Their fight is comparable to the one the women's army is waging in *Born in Flames*.

Born in Flames and *Les Guérillères* both deliberately make their fiction feel unreal. Wittig's story takes place in a mythical temporality and can be read as an epic. Borden turns away from realism by depicting the future. Her film is not overtly inspired by Wittig's text, which she does not quote in the film or mention in interviews, but common points are so obvious that the film was distributed in France under the title *Guérillères*. As for *Guerillere Talks*, its links with Wittig's text begin with its very title. Dick's neologism, meaning female *guerrilla* warriors, is also the name of a feminist group she founded:

> We had a group going on in New York, Les Guerilleres. We met several times, we were a group of women (lesbian and non-lesbian) and we were reading Monique Wittig's *Les Guérillères* and felt a connection to it. (Dick and O'Brien, 2011: 19)

Both films also share their filmmakers' feminist commitment, which appears in their films and interviews. Dick has an 'anti-patriarchal stance': she attacks the stifling effects of patriarchal power on women in her interviews. Her 'cool punk feminism is grounded in strata of rage and grief' (Hoberman, 1980: 93, 92) that is both personal and finds representation in her films such as *Beauty Becomes the Beast* (1979). She sees the source of the problem in the balance of power attached to the gender binary: 'It's just proof that the whole male-female thing is so fucked-up' (Dick and MacDonald, 1982: 88). She also screens 'female macho' attitudes (Hoberman, 1980: 91), where women act like men who perform masculinity, thus creating a loop that exposes gendered behaviour: 'I'm interested in how women could switch the power around. How they can make men feel uncomfortable in the way that men make women feel uncomfortable' (Dick interviewed by Amy Taubin, quoted in Hoberman, 1980: 94).

Borden, who sees herself as a 'proud feminist' (Grayson, 2020), wanted to rekindle the feminist movement that had been losing impetus since the seventies (Lane, 2000: 126). But while Dick targeted the gender binary first and foremost and was not at all concerned by race issues, Borden regretted that 'women of different races and classes [had] been very alienated from each other' and wanted to create a fiction 'in which all these different subgroups were brought together' (Sussler, 1983). Her film depicts female activists coming from varied racial groups, although they are mainly African American. It thus emphasizes intersectionality, representing how two categories – here being Black and being a woman – overlap while their interests may or may not be similar, making one's position in society difficult to find and maintain. The term had not yet been coined at the time,[1] but the concern has been central to Black female activism from at least 1978. For example, in the Combahee River Collective Statement, systems of oppression including race and gender are seen as 'interlocking'.[2]

In this chapter, I contend that both films, with different feminist approaches, endeavour to change the representation of women on film so that women are able to be at the centre of their own lives, as subjects. The films will be compared along three lines. Attention will first be paid to how the films allow women to regain the gaze, that is to say, appropriate the gaze as a source of power. Then I will examine the filmic narration and its fragmentation, and finally how the films try to invent a world centred on a female voice. The analysis will be grounded in a feminist and psychoanalytical framework, including Laura Mulvey's first version of 'Visual Pleasure and Narrative Cinema' (1975) as well as the writings of Teresa de Lauretis, especially *Technologies of Gender* (1987).

Reclaiming the gaze

According to Mulvey, long-standing mainstream visual patterns foster patriarchal values and visually position woman as an object of male desire. Man is the active bearer of the gaze both as character and as spectator. Meanwhile, the woman on screen receives the gaze; she is mere spectacle: 'Woman displayed as sexual object is the leitmotif of erotic spectacle: from pin-ups to striptease, from Ziegfeld to Busby Berkeley, she holds the look, plays to and signifies male desire' (1975: 9). Because of the gaze that has fallen on her, she is in a state of 'to-be-looked-at-ness', which has gendered consequences on spectator identification:

> As the spectator identifies with the main male protagonist, he projects his look onto that of his like, his screen surrogate, so that the power of the male protagonist as he controls events coincides with the active power of the erotic look. (Ibid.)

In Mulvey's original article, 'the female spectator seems inevitably to be wedged into the male subject position and thereby forced to participate in the sadistic victimisation of the female characters' (Hollinger, 1987: 19). In a later text, Mulvey addresses this question saying that 'women from early on have the habit of transsexual identification as a second nature, but it is a nature that does not sit easily and shifts restlessly in its borrowed transvestite clothes' (Mulvey, 1981: 12). De Lauretis in turn worries about what female spectators might experience: 'Are women constituted as masculine subjects of vision by the apparatus of cinema, or are they lured by narcissistic identification to the side of the image, to the position of object of the gaze?' (1987: 100). She obliquely points to the need for women's 'safety' (ibid.) in creating a female, or feminist, subject of vision.

To go against the mainstream patriarchal visual pleasures as they have been defined by Mulvey, one strategy consists in representing female protagonists who are active bearers of the gaze. In *Born in Flames*, when Zella Wylie watches the New York City mayor's broadcast on TV, she is first shown in a medium shot, where we only see her from the shoulders up since the back of the TV set blocks the bottom of the frame and creates an embedded frame that puts her face exactly at the centre of the image – a composition very similar to the shots where the mayor speaks. Zella is sitting very still, listening attentively, and wearing jewellery and a white headscarf: she looks as formal as the mayor does; there is nothing relaxed in her attitude or her appearance: nothing tells us she is at home. For all we know, she could be in the same room with the mayor, getting ready to speak. Thanks to a cut-in, we get closer to Zella's face and her reactions become visible: she rolls her eyeballs and moves her head from side to side, suggesting impatience and disapproval. Her gaze is active: the mayor and his speech are the object, while she appears as a female watching subject.

Guerillere Talks is more playful with the concept of 'to-be-looked-at-ness'. In the third episode, a young Asian woman is presented in a series of extreme close-ups displaying parts of her body with a rather slow editing pace: for a few moments, she gives herself up to the active and hermeneutic, even haptic, gaze of the camera. We are so close we can see the texture of her skin and of the fabric of her garments. The gaze of the camera is 'like a hand that searches and gropes its way' (Levinas, 1990: 181). It mimics 'the way vision itself can be tactile, as though one were touching the film with one's eyes' (Marks and Polan, 2000: 85). Later as the woman moves, she is seen in a long shot. Playfully active and free, she fights the state of 'being-looked-at-ness' through lithe movements. She may escape from the frame and even from the gaze of the movie camera. At some point, she grabs a small camera herself. We see her in a closer shot where she literally returns the cinematographer's gaze that is now bouncing back and forth between the two women and the two cameras. The scene results in a double empowerment of the female gaze, both the filmmaker's and the actor's. As we can identify with both the camera and the character, both suggest that we free our own gaze. This is made possible by Dick's approach: 'I think I am interested in this "looking at" and "being looked at" thing. I, as cameraperson, am also being looked at' (Dick and O'Brien, 2011: 56).

In the last episode, Anya Phillips, who had an important role in the No Wave scene as the manager of various stars such as James Chance and Lydia Lunch, as well as being a fashion designer for people like Debbie Harry (Reynolds, 2010: 136–7), silently sits and smokes a cigarette. She is self-consciously posing and composing her appearance, with sophisticated gestures and make-up. Heavy lipstick lacquers her lips. On her cheeks, shiny red and golden make-up enhances the shape of her cheekbones. Her eyelids are entirely covered by two hues of shimmering eyeshadow. Even if make-up is a traditional female art, she reclaims it on the side of feminism, since she uses colours in an idiosyncratic way, in a subversion of traditional femininity that was common for members of the punk scene, as Charles Mueller explains about Susan Janet Ballion, the lead singer of the band Souxsie and the Banshees, who donned special costumes and make-up as part of her Souxsie persona:

> It violated the masculine preoccupation with clarity and positivist logic, made traditional ideals of feminine beauty seem strange and unsafe, and disrupted the notion that feminine identity can be reduced to a positivist truth. (Mueller, 2017)

Anya, following Charles Baudelaire's suggestion, recreates the order of the world on her face, she lets her makeup 'display itself ... with frankness and honesty' (Baudelaire, 2010: 24) without paying respect to the dominant patriarchal order. Her gestures are slow, sensuous, both self-absorbed and calculated. She delicately lights a cigarette; she runs her fingers through her short jet-black hair; she moves her head from side to side. The camera zooms in and accompanies Anya's extreme care for her cigarette, her interest in her hair and her heavily painted eyelids. Anya's attitude seems to mimic noir actresses smoking on screen, for example, Lauren Bacall in *To Have and Have Not* (Hawks, 1944). Yet there is none of the elaborate three-point lighting or subtle chiaroscuro the studios used in those films. Here, Dick shoots Anya with two crude lights, one coming from the left, the other from the right; these create large shadows on the wall behind Anya and reveal the shiny, almost wet, texture of her skin and make-up. The extreme close-ups of her eyes and hair offer a very different vision than the pared-down style of film noir and Bacall's aloofness. Here, on the contrary, the camera is as if magnetically attracted, fascinated by Anya's face and body. Her plump arms and her exposed cleavage, as well as her lips, imply closeness, the possibility of touching that is in contradiction with her self-absorption and defiant gaze. Contrary to what happens in the Asian photographer sequence, here haptic visuality is not mainly exploratory but also sensuous. Anya's performance is akin to a Warholian 'screen test',[3] but here instead of submitting to Andy Warhol's rules, she sets them for herself. Her gaze, looks, gestures and beautifying actions are all turned into ways of transforming to-be-looked-at-ness into activity, as if turning a glove inside out. With the extreme close-ups, the narration gives in to the fascination she has created for her face, hair or body. These shots are interrupted (as if the spectators had been caught red-handed)

Figure 1.1 Anya Philips returning the gaze in *Guerillere Talks* directed by Vivienne Dick © 1978.

by medium shots where Anya looks back, sideways or from below, returning the gaze with a vengeance (Figure 1.1).

Both films successfully reclaim the gaze on the side of women both as embedded spectators and as characters. *Born in Flames* does it very literally by having women as active and effective bearers of the gaze. It is also quite literal in *Guerrillere Talks*, as participants play with who holds the camera or provocatively stare at it. Additionally, the latter film tackles the ambiguous seductive power of the woman who stops the narration by attracting the gaze and returning it, reclaiming the concept of 'to-be-looked-at-ness' for a female subject.

Narration versus fragmentation

Having women as active bearers of the gaze would not be enough to do away with the 'visual pleasures' Mulvey denounces, if the films respected the mainstream convention of a gapless fictional world and a plot-led narration. According to Mulvey (1975), the spectator feels 'free to command the stage' where he directs the gaze and 'creates the action'. Regardless of who is the 'bearer of the gaze', these pleasurable film-viewing habits require a unified space without perceptible limits. In other words, Mulvey's gendered pattern is inscribed in the conventions of the transparent style of classical Hollywood (Bordwell, Staiger and Thompson, 1988). Thanks to well-defined reverse-angle editing and frequent use of match-on-action editing, the classic style makes film space fluid. It sutures all gaps, so that the imagined off-screen space turns progressively into on-screen space (Heath, 1977: 65). Both films under study reject this style by undoing space and narration through fragmentation, which appears in Wittig's *Les Guérillères* in the form of a gap:

> They say, the language you speak is made up of signs that rightly speaking designate what men have appropriated. Whatever they have not laid hands on, whatever they have not pounced on like many-eyed birds of prey, does not appear in the language you speak. This is apparent precisely in the intervals that your masters have not been able to fill with their words of proprietors and possessors, this can be found in the gaps, in all that which is not a continuation of their discourse, in the zero, the O, the perfect circle that you invent to imprison them and to overthrow them. (Wittig, 1971: 114)

In this quote, 'gaps' represent the unnamed part of the world. Wittig here says that naming is the same as appropriating, as a conqueror or colonist would. Men seem to commandeer 'the right to signify' (Bhabha, 1992: 49). The quote by Wittig is ambivalent regarding its nominalist or non-nominalist perspective. First, it seems to go from things to words but then it goes in the opposite direction when the unnamed gaps proved inexistent in the masters' topography. The gaps do not appear as patches of uncharted territory or wilderness as could be found in nineteenth-century maps. So naming is a source of power, what is unnamed in the gaps can be grabbed or grasped by the 'guerilleres'.

When they name these possible contents, even with the void sign or the zero sign, the gaps become apparent as cracks that may fragment the masters' world that up to then was a unified whole. Appropriating the gaps works first as a weapon: expressing what is *in the gaps* will disarm men, who will be faced by what they believe to be unthinkable, threatening their intellect. Second, it works as a tool: the obliterated parts of the world, or of experience, can be used as building blocks for a new language that will belong to women.

From a Lacanian perspective, the gaps are parts of the masters' real (Lacan, 2005) since they defy all representations, both linguistic and imaginary, and thus have no *ex-sistence* – they cannot be projected outside one's inner life and psyche. Through a shift, the masters' real (the gaps) become women's symbolic order (what they can represent with words) (Trinh, 1992: 173). This shift is quite a revolution, as the 'guerilleres' try to create chaos or din to increase the intervals and eventually take apart the well-ordered patriarchal system that restrains women: 'they say they foster disorder in all its forms' (Wittig, 1971: 93).

On screen, these concerns lead to diverse modes of fragmentation. *Born in Flames* breaks up space and narration as a dispersive prism would. Narration is separated into numerous threads that the spectator can put together to form a narrative argument. The film's first thirty minutes create a fictional world by juxtaposing a plethora of sequences or autonomous shots mixing central characters with extras. The film is narrated from various sources, offering us diverging versions of the fictional world. For example, a woman is on the verge of being raped by two men; first, she is shot in medium close-up with a circling camera and Latino dancing music, until a squad of bike-riding women rescue her. Following a high-angle shot that puts us in the position of an omniscient narrator, the scene cuts to a new version of the same event seen through TV news footage where the presenter tells us that women attack men who *may* have attacked women in the first place. Later in the film, a voice-over, which will later be identified as an FBI investigator's voice, will give yet another version denouncing the violence these women are wielding: 'I would not call them terrorists, although they are responsible for those bicycle incidents; what bothers me is the vigilante sensibility.' Eventually, an African American woman discusses the matter with a friend and rejects the bicycle actions as childish: 'You know what the army did ... bicycles ... This army is not mature enough to hang out with me.' The event is thus unstable and infinitely open to reassessment and redescription.[4]

For each type of protagonist there is a different quality of image. For example, at the very beginning of the film, the first presenter appears in an image so contrasted that it is barely possible to identify shapes and characters. The black parts of his outfit seem to merge with the background and lack depth and relief. On the contrary, Caucasian punk radio DJ Isobel speaks on the microphone among warm colours with delicate contrasts, allowing us to perceive the shape of her body and face, as if touching it. This coloured atmosphere is found further in a montage sequence where we see various women at social events accompanied by mellow reggae music. As for the voice-over of an FBI agent, it is heard as we see a slide show that includes archival stills.

With a framing narrative conveyed through five or six groups of characters, four sources of secondary narration coming from diegetic media, found footage and slide shows of diverse stills, spectators are overwhelmed by an audiovisual flow that prevents them from reflecting on what they are experiencing. The overabundance of images makes them difficult to understand, and the soundtrack can also be confusing. Very often, the film uses music in a playful contrapuntal[5] way. The songs are related to the image and to fictional noises although they do not systematically stick to them through their rhythm or volume. For example, in the rape scene, a joyful tune is first heard, then it is suppressed by the woman's screams that blend into the high-pitched whistles of the cyclists. All the sounds give us contradictory mood cues: are we supposed to be happy when something potentially terrible is happening? Are we supposed to be alarmed by the screaming and relieved by the whistles? The confusion, by not enabling us to connect felt sensations, knowledge or affects linked to the event, is frightening: we experience, in a minimal way, a traumatic perception;

indeed, 'at its most basic, the psychoanalytic concept of trauma insists on this ambiguous coupling between affect and event, feeling and knowing: trauma names a happening about which one never fully knows how to feel, or feels how to know' (Elmer, 1998: 5).

Fragmentation as dispersion is also conveyed through the representation of a wide range of women who offer obvious differences. According to de Lauretis's discussion of *Born in Flames*, it allows us 'to see difference differently' (1987: 136). In other words, it enables us to see more differences amongst women than between men and women (ibid., 137). Probably due to the charismatic performance of star lawyer Florynce Kennedy, cast as the mentor of the feminist group at the centre of the film, it has often been said that *Born in Flames* was mainly about Black lesbian feminism – a statement I will refute here. For example, Lucas Hilderbrand mentions that the film ends on a 'climactic progressive Black lesbian terrorist attack on the World Trade Center' (2013: 10), which is erroneous since the bomb on the media transmitter is planted by a Caucasian girl whose sexual orientation is unknown. In general, the film shows as many white women as Black women – not to mention the many Hispanic and Asian women in the group. There are women who are in the construction industry, women who perform menial jobs, elegant women, sporty women, DJs (both Black and white), younger women, older women, Black political leaders and white journalists to name but a few (Figure 1.2). This variety of women in terms of race and class and age is important: the film is about heterogeneous women, women who cannot be unified by one qualifier. According to de Lauretis, it allows to avoid gendered 'interpellation':

> There is no one-to-one match between the film's discursive heterogeneity and the discursive boundaries of anyone spectator. We are both invited in and held at a distance, addressed intermittently and only insofar as we are able to occupy the position of addressee; for example, when Honey, the Phoenix Radio disc jockey, addresses to the audience the words: 'Black women, be ready. White women, get ready. Red women, stay ready, for this is our time and all must realize it.' Which individual member of the audience, male or female,

Figure 1.2 DJ Honey talking on the radio in *Born in Flames* directed by Lizzie Borden © 1983.

> can feel singly interpellated as spectator-subject or, in other words, unequivocally addressed? (1987: 143)

As a result of its heterogeneity, the film creates a more personal space for a woman spectator: 'through an erotic engagement with the film' that is not a gendered interpellation, but something more personal, 'a recognition, unmistakable and unprecedented' (ibid., 142).

In the diegetic discourse, this dispersive principle is explained and justified by Florynce Kennedy's character herself, Zella Wylie. Flo(rynce) Kennedy was an early Black feminist who protested the interlocking oppression brought about by race, class and gender and became the leader of the National Black Feminist Organization. She was central in the fight for abortion rights in the state of New York. A charismatic figure, she used the trial courts as a platform and the media to her advantage, just as her character does. As in the film, in real life she mentored younger feminists (Randolph, 2015: 136–60). In the fiction, her protégée is Adelaide Norris, one of the leaders of the Women's Army. As the latter complains that the march organized by the

Army was not unified, Zella replies by defending dispersion, scattering, as more valuable than unity to advance the women's cause. She says,

> If you were the army, and the school, and the head of the health institutions, and the head of the government, and each of you had guns, which would you rather see coming through the door? Would you have rather one lion (unified) or five hundred mice? My answer is five hundred mice can do a lot of damage and disruption. (*Born in Flames*, 33:20)

As the film moves on, dispersion will prove useful after Adelaide dies in prison. Because the Women's Army has many leaders, it will not disappear once its leader is dead; it will survive and be led by another member very easily. Indeed, the Women's Army does not have a top-down hierarchical structure, but a cloud-like one where leadership goes from member to member and where many people are in a position to act as leader at any time, as an FBI agent explains in the film: 'That's the problem: we don't know at any given time who is in charge.'[6] The decentralized structure is also highlighted when the Women's Army radio stations continue broadcasting even after their studios have been destroyed, since they have replaced a fixed location by transmission from a van driving around town. Here again the radio waves are dispersed as if from a prism, and they are instrumental in the success of the Women's Army's fight.

Guerillere Talks provides a different type of fragmentation. First, dispersion stems from the episodic structure of the film. Each episode features a new active female protagonist and fragmentation depends on a 'propensity to detail' (Dick and O'Brien, 2011: 12). Bodies are cut into incongruous body parts through framing, whether it be a lingering shot of a foot swathed in thick material, or the same actor's (Pat Place) crotch covered in long johns whose woolly texture make the image tactile while concealing the texture of her skin. Body parts are made so unfamiliar that we struggle to understand what we are looking at, rendering them more fascinating. Elsewhere, the filmmaker seems to be forced to shoot only body parts as there is not enough distance between her camera and her subject. As mentioned previously, the young Asian girl in the third episode swirls, jumps and continuously escapes. Her fragmented body (the nape of her neck, her ankle, hips or face) is the result of the cinematographer's efforts to hold the girl in the frame of her handheld camera. The body parts are juxtaposed back-to-back in an experimental attempt at portraying somebody – some body – by reinventing film narration, dumping continuity and opening the image to gaps. *Guerillere Talks* builds space through snippets, without any reverse shots, the most common tool to give the spectator the feel of an open and unified world. The fictional world of *Guerillere Talks* never unfolds as if through an open window.

In *Born in Flames*, reverse shots are replaced by very short scenes and juxtapositions. The method becomes especially striking in scenes that call for a reverse shot, such as the moment when Zella and Adelaide watch the New York City mayor on television. At first, it is hard to understand Zella's location in relation to Adelaide. Instead of cutting back and forth between the viewers and the TV screen, the camera pans fluidly and slowly from Zella to Adelaide, suddenly revealing that they are sitting close together in the space of the room, underlining their tight friendship.

Finally, fragmentation affects the narration of both films, but not in the same way. *Guerillere Talks* rejects narration almost totally. Its episodes are not linked by causality, nor do they progress through this principle; rather, they are based on a structural protocol and on performance. Each episode introduces a performer who is both actor and character. Dick's ambition is to make films that are different (Dick and MacDonald, 1982: 87) and are said to have an 'anti-cinema aesthetic' (Foster, 1995: 29), rendering them barely fit to be shown in theatres. On the contrary, Borden maintains a rather traditional three-part narrative: first, the film depicts the economic situation in New York ten years after the socialist revolution; then it shows how women converge into an army, leading to the assassination of a character turned heroine, Adelaide; and finally, it closes with revenge through action (the Women's Army takes over the media). Because of fragmentation, the narration is difficult to follow at the beginning of the film. But after the turning point of Adelaide's death, the narration becomes denser and causality leads the film, even creating a form of suspense.

For spectators, *Born in Flames* requires a great deal of effort, since we are always trying to piece together what is happening. For example, there is a series of sequences that deal with legislation removing women from protected jobs in construction. The series begins with a news sequence showing protests by 'young men in their twenties' who think that too many jobs are given to minorities (including women) under the 'workfare' programme. The news sequence includes some hard-to-identify archival footage of a riot; the next sequence shows Adelaide being fired from a construction job; it segues into a montage sequence where we see women's hands performing various tasks while the soundtrack features the film's main song 'Born in Flames' (The Red Krayola, 1980). Next, Adelaide stands by a small group of protesting women asking for jobs; there follow many close-ups of Adelaide's dreamy face and medium close-ups of the protesters while Adelaide hands out Women's Army pamphlets. This very short sequence seems to purposefully confuse spectators as we cannot tell whether it focuses on the role of a leader or the action of a group.

The ensuing sequence stages the editors of the *Youth Socialist Review* working at their office while we hear them in voice-over stating their opinion: women should not defend their interests – here getting more jobs – because this would be 'separatist'. In a contrapuntal way, we hear and see Zella saying, 'We have a right to violence,' followed by a montage sequence where an FBI agent reveals Zella's background as a seasoned lawyer and activist, and describes her derogatively as being both aggressive and 'a walking loony bin'. In the last sequence of this segment, women in construction jobs attempt a lockout on a construction site – as if trying to implement their 'right to violence'. Retrospectively these sequences can be taken together as a segment dealing with the question of jobs for women. The juxtaposition of sequences outlines the problem, gives various opinions and shows different actions. The frequent jumping between different groups of characters makes it difficult to follow the narration and gives the segment a very analytical quality (Brody, 2016).

These sequences mesh together different groups (Women's Army members and *Youth Socialist Review* editors) and outline questions of leadership, with Zella's character blending with Flo Kennedy's public persona. They also dramatize the issue of violence, since the dense interwoven images play with extra-diegetic events from the late 1960s such as the protests against the Vietnam War and for gay rights – events frequently met with police brutality. For example, images of protests may refer to the Stonewall riots in 1969. We can also link them with New York's violent environment when the city was close to bankruptcy[7] and with the wave of home-grown terrorist attacks led by left-wing groups such as FALN or the Weather Underground that planted bombs but caused few casualties – the fact that a large number of them were detonated at night (Burrough, 2016) shows that terrorists wilfully avoided making casualties the same way the Women's Army deliberately avoids killing people in Borden's film (they do not bomb the World Trade Center buildings but only its transmitter). The complexity of all this information requires a very alert spectator.

In contrast, *Guerillere Talks* can be either pleasant or boring to watch. Once viewers accept that nothing will *happen*, they may quit the hermeneutic posture that here cannot help them assemble information and let themselves be carried away by the sensorial quality of the images and sounds. Indeed, the first episode completely annihilates whatever expectations we may have of a causal story. A girl with short hair, a bulky black outfit and safety pins dangling from her ears concentrates on a pinball game. She smokes and talks to people around her. She plays in a very self-possessed manner: she does not thrust her hips at the machine to control the ball, as men are often seen doing. She completely desexualizes the game. People passing by carelessly put their hands in front of the camera lens. The episode surprises us not at all through suspense but through the unexpected depiction of a female pinball player, as well as through the offhand way the scene is filmed. We start watching the next episode with this pattern in mind, and nothing else happens by way of narrative; the same goes for the other episodes. The film draws our attention because each episode breaks both gender and stylistic conventions. It can be a totally unexpected camera movement like the camera swinging to portray the young Asian photographer (13:00), a jump cut where this character has suddenly disappeared, like a ghost (14:00) or a swift turn that reveals an intra-diegetic spectator watching Lydia Lunch's performance (20:20).

Altogether, both films rely heavily on fragmented aesthetics but in different ways. While the dispersion of storylines and the variety of characters keep the spectator busy putting everything together and open representation to reassessment in *Born in Flames*, in *Guerillere Talks* fragmentation directly concerns the female protagonists' bodies, which are cut into unexpected parts through framing. Eventually, reassessing and giving up our expectations about the feminine is one of the results of fragmentation in both these films.

Inventing a language and a world for women

In addition to reframing the spectator's gaze, both films give women a voice. Indeed, de Lauretis's analysis of Borden's film foregrounds the need for a new voice, with new categories, since 'the notion of gender, or "sexual difference", cannot be simply accommodated into the preexisting, ungendered (or male-gendered) categories by which the official discourses on race and class have been elaborated' (1987: 138–9). In *Guerillere Talks*, speaking is, obviously, at the core of the film, although speech is not present everywhere, as in the silent episodes mentioned above. Nevertheless, some episodes are very chatty, justifying the title of the film. For instance, in the third episode, a young woman (Beate Nilsen) talks about talking. She expresses a clear desire to exercise her power of speech; it almost appears to be a political obligation: 'I feel we have to do a whole lot of these films.' Putting together the 'I' who says 'I wanna talk' and the 'we' brings us close to the women's liberation rallying cry 'the personal is political'. Through its texture, both light and slightly raspy, as we can hear her inhale, the actor's voice creates a feeling of softness and intimacy, whereas what is said evokes the body and even its inner organs: 'I feel like my insides are coming out.' In this sequence, the gaze is not relevant; the performer's eyes are unseen since either her body is cut off at the chin, or she turns to look off-screen or the back light leaves her eye sockets completely in the dark. The microphone is at the centre of the frame and the recording makes the voice sound very close to us. The voice and the 'grain' of performance – what makes the actor's presence radically singular yet ordinary (Barthes, 1982: 236) – compete with the spoken 'I'. The emergence of the voice seems to be difficult as the actor repeats 'I want' several times before she can say 'I want to talk'. The wholeness of her being is at stake: she says 'my insides are coming out', which refers first to her body but also to her inner thoughts and emotions. In the same ambiguous way, she mentions that she wants to be 'thrown up against the wall' or 'exploded'. Body, voice and speech are taken apart and available for a free reconstruction of the self, which occurs outside traditional female roles.

The dialectic of voice and body is given a slightly erotic turn in the episode where Pat Place reads a letter she has received. Her thin body is feminine, yet free to move in unconventional postures. It is also both revealed and hidden by the woolly catsuit she wears. This unique physical appearance and the timbre of her voice appeal to our senses, making the words less relevant. These are, in effect, at odds with what we see, since she reads a letter, probably from her family, where all her suggestions are rejected. She neatly closes the letter and finishes the reading by speaking to herself and saying, 'Hmm, it is another world.' The world in the letter is the world of bourgeois conventions, where one should 'hold on' to records by the Beatles because 'they will be worth much more later', where one considers warnings from a figure of authority such as a doctor. In the world we can visually access, Pat Place's activities are unconventional and even idiosyncratic (she tries to nail something on the wall with a hammer and, failing to do so, attempts to nail it into her skull). She does not seem to depend on any figure of authority to decide what she does. The bareness of the apartment (which contains a telephone, a bed, a hammer, a plastic snake and a toy gun) hints at reduced means or total lack of interest in material possessions. Thus, this episode succeeds in depicting 'another world', more open to free self-expression that is not specifically female. In this other world, a female may express herself through clothing that is both tight yet unseductive – like children's or workers' winter underwear. She also may try to do some home improvement herself without enlisting male help, yet be totally ineffective. She can also engage in child's play with a toy gun, for example. In her 'other world', she may reject all that is linked to homemaking and seduction, hold a hammer (a reputedly masculine activity) and retain a childlike ability to play. Her subjective expression here seems unfettered by gendered or age categories. In this way she creates a new model for female spectator: 'something else to be' (de Lauretis, 1987: 138).

In a number of episodes, subjectivity is reinforced as the 'I' becomes an unstable place because of the self-reference game played by the actors who become 'self-dramatizing personalities' (Hoberman, 1982: 105). For example, Lydia Lunch uses her own name but speaks as if she were a bored teenager. At the time, she was already quite famous as the singer of the punk band Teenage Jesus and the Jerks, as well as of James Chance and the Contortions. The complex timbre of her singing voice, described by Vera Dika as 'an audible screech – delivered from the depths of subjugation to be sure – gnarled and choked, but nonetheless allowed its freedom' (2012: 58–9), can be heard in this episode when she speaks. Hence, the mutability between role, self and *persona* hardly qualifies her as a proper fictional female character. Dick remarks,

> I think the performers or 'characters' are usually very aware of the fact that they are playing a role as well as acknowledging that is who they are now. The self-referencing is part of that slipping between personas. This is a very female experience of being in the world, I think. We, who were never 'subject' in the philosophical scheme of things, are very at home here. (Dick and O'Brien, 2011: 58)

Born in Flames uses voice in a very different way – as the title suggests, it is more about coming into existence than about language or about the power of speech. At the age of eleven, the filmmaker changed her name from Linda to Lizzie (Lane, 2000: 127). Through this personal declaration of independence, she no longer bore the name her parents had given her, but the one of a nineteenth-century criminal suspected of having killed her stepmother and father as the rhyme goes:

> Lizzie Borden took an axe
> And gave her mother forty whacks.
> When she saw what she had done
> She gave her father forty-one. (Hughes, 2016)

As reflected by the filmmaker's change of names, *Born in Flames* oscillates between speech and violence. In this manner, it reflects on the possibility of understanding and getting involved in the world around us. First, within the fictional world, it depicts political action. The film screens the planning and execution of several terrorist acts, one of which aims at blowing up the media transmitter of the World Trade Center. Secondly, *Born in Flames* has a real-world political goal: it endeavours to convince spectators that a different world can exist, for better or for worse. By opening our imagination, this film accomplishes the task that Richard Rorty assigns to philosophy: 'anything that philosophy can do to free up our imagination a little is all to the political good, for the freer the imagination of the present, the likelier it is that future social practices will be different from past practices' (Rorty, 1991: 221).

The film foregrounds the importance of the media as well as mastery of language: when they deploy mobile radio stations and they plan to have even more media presence, one of the members of the Women's Army declares, 'For some time, we have control about the way we represent ourselves.' It is not about self-expression but about spreading a different language and an alternative ideology. The powerful Zella is able to suddenly interrupt the prime minister's speech on television, about to introduce 'wages for housework'. She unexpectedly appears on the screen to explain that this measure is a way to pacify women and to maintain traditional gender roles as well as to exclude women from other types of employment.

As the film unfolds and especially after the climax of Adelaide's murder, the voice becomes increasingly female, namely because the male FBI voice-over disappears and is replaced by a female voice-over, that of one of the *Youth Socialist Review* editors, who now supports the Women's Army. *Born in Flames*'s strategy is thus to put women at the head of the media and give them top jobs where they would have power, using their voices instead of male voices, whereas *Guerillere Talks* lets us hear voices that outline the way a female subject could be born. It shows us women becoming subjects 'in the philosophical scheme of things' (Dick and O'Brien, 2011: 58), who are able to have agency and expression, yet whose gender identification as female is quite mutable, which enables them to escape being assigned to strictly feminine norms.

Conclusion

Both films use fragmentation to portray a wide range of women who vary in race, age and social status. Their personalities, activities and opinions are also very diverse. This strategy destroys the binary opposition between men and women by reintroducing differences among women. Gender can no longer be seen as a category, a criterion, that overrides all others. It recedes to the benefit of other distinctions.

Yet these films have diverging methods. *Born in Flames* attempts to convince audiences of the possibility of another gender balance and of the importance of such a change. While it conveys ideology in a filmic style that remains relatively classical and intelligible for general audiences, its power comes from narrative content that denounces the wrongs done to women and exposes political proposals. Yet the consistency of its film style is still partly caught in a logic of heroes and causality inherited from patriarchal narratives. One may say that *Born in Flames* weakens its scope of action, since it relies only on spectators to change the world around them and does little to change cinema itself, falling short of Mulvey's call to break down cinematic codes and challenge the pleasure they provide (1975: 18). In other words, just watching *Born in Flame* is not enough for change; change would have to take place afterwards, outside of the theatres – a rather risky bet. *Guerillere Talks*, in turn, does not try to act on the world, nor does it create a new discourse. It does not denounce anything. It changes filmic conventions and is able to show a new, different woman. The mere act of watching here changes the spectator, even if minimally. We have to agree to change our viewing habits, otherwise we cannot watch the film. Like Wittig's guerilleres, Dick has managed to create a language for what was outside the masters' cinematic language, here the conventions of mainstream cinema. By doing so, she is able to represent 'what was in the cracks', and as we follow her we are transformed into a new spectator.

However, both films undo the wholeness of the fictional world built through the classical style of Hollywood cinema and especially the standardized system of shot-reverse-shot that sutures space, in order to give female protagonists an active gaze and the ability to speak and act. In both films, rejecting the state of to-be-looked-at-ness is a feat. It may involve direct action such as illegally broadcasting a speech on TV. Or it may involve a mirror game with one character hiding from the camera behind a camera, or even an erotic, ambivalent, tongue-in-cheek rewriting of another filmic game of to-be-looked-at ness: Warhol's *Screen Tests* (1964–8). Not all protagonists take the opportunity to speak. Some remain quiet or decide to lend their voice to another, for example, by reading a bourgeois letter, letting their image speak for them. Those who do talk do it differently in each film. Speech is unproblematic in *Born in Flames*, while in *Guerillere Talks* speech has to be extracted, sometimes painfully, from the depth of one's body and self. In both films, speech is valued and is never seen as desultory chatter or gossip. The way the films use sonic material and image in an interrelated yet relatively independent way gives the speakers' words a specific emphasis – all the more so that words compete with, or are emphasized by, the protagonists' bodily presence, which constantly garners significant attention. Thanks to many idiosyncratic activities that they deliberately perform without conforming to social expectations on feminine behaviour, apparel and opinions, the female characters and performers unmistakably appear as female subjects. They decide for themselves to play pinball, to work in construction, to organize a revolutionary movement, to wear woolly onesies or hard hats and to develop strategies and a philosophy of action to change wider institutions. Such freedom in showing and expressing subjectivity is not possible if women on-screen remain in mainstream feminine activities, and spectators remain locked in the traditional structures of the gaze, as can happen in less radical cinema.

Women on-screen are also filmic subjects since their construction and reception occurs through a filmic language that is specific and renewed. It rejects many of the mainstream conventions that convey patriarchal ideology. To call this language strictly female would probably be an exaggeration, and it would lend weight to the binary distinction that the films attempt to dismantle. But we can safely say that this language is not male-oriented, or male-dominated. Talking about lesbian art, Ruth Iskin and Arlene Raven (1977) say that lesbian artists replace 'the implicit heterosexual model of male (erotic) domination over woman/art/materials' by a 'harmonious relationship' and that they give up the model of 'the active creator and the passive model/art work which is acted upon' (quoted in Citron et al., 1978: 97). This is very reminiscent of the change that both Dick and Borden brought about. The reason why they are felt as female filmmakers is not a question of femininity, but it is positional and social – it has to do with how they stand regarding patriarchal power. Renewing the place of the gaze and structures of identification are the sign of the presence and of the agency of a female filmmaker. In *Guerillere Talks* and *Born in Flames*, Dick and Borden seek to bring change on three levels: introducing different and varied female characters, transforming the experience of the woman spectator and presenting a filmmaker's perspective that differs from that of the male active artist/creator. The female filmic subject is each of them and also the three of them interacting to foster change.

Notes

1 The term was later coined by Crenshaw (1989).

2 Combahee River Collective (1978: 271): 'The most general statement of our politics at the present time would be that we are actively committed to struggling against racial, sexual, heterosexual, and class oppression, and see as our particular task the development of integrated analysis and practice based upon the fact that the major systems of oppression are interlocking.'

3 Angell (2006: 14):

> [Warhol] created a set of diabolically challenging performance instructions for his sitters, who suddenly finding themselves up against the wall and face to face with the Warhol's Bolex, struggled to hold a pose while their brief moment of exposure was prolonged into a nearly unendurable three minutes. The subjects' emotional and physiological responses in this ordeal are often the most riveting aspect of *Screen Tests*.

4 Redescription is a concept by liberal philosopher Richard Rorty. It consists in sublating contradiction by creating new distinctions: 'As far as I could see, philosophical talent was largely a matter of proliferating as many distinctions as were needed to wriggle out of a dialectical corner.' It is an anti-essentialist tool whose validity depends on its efficacy: 'It is not that we think the world unintelligible, but rather that we view redescription of it as a tool for social or individual change, rather than as an attempt to grasp intrinsic features of the real' (Rorty, 2000: 10, 220).

5 By a musical analogy, we compare here some of the various channels of the cinema (non-diegetic music, diegetic sounds and image) to different melodic lines as handled in a musical counterpoint. These lines have a meaningful relationship and a measure of independence. The spectator is invited to follow these lines individually as they develop in time, and at the same time to pay attention on how at any given moment they interact. For example, one can pay attention to the film music and to image, but also one can reflect on how music and image interact.

6 The sequence is a direct quote from the depiction of the guerilla groups in *The Battle of Algiers* (Pontecorvo, 1966) (Nastasi, 2016).
7 Policing of both organized and street crime was decreased, resulting in increased muggings, burglary, drug trafficking and violent crime (Tabb, 1982: 30, 49).

Works cited

Angell, Callie (2006), *Andy Warhol Screen Tests: The Films of Andy Warhol*, New York: Harry N. Abrams.

Barthes, Roland (1982), *Le Plaisir du texte*, Paris: Éditions du Seuil.

Baudelaire, Charles (2010), *Le Peintre de la vie moderne*, Paris: Fayard/Mille et une nuits.

Bhabha, Homi K. (1992), 'Freedom's basis in the indeterminate', *October*, 61: 46–57.

Bordwell, David, Janet Staiger and Kristin Thompson (1988), *The Classical Hollywood Cinema*, London: Routledge.

Brody, Richard (2016), 'The political science fiction of "Born in Flames"', *New Yorker*, 19 February. Available online: https://www.newyorker.com/culture/richard-brody/the-political-science-fiction-of-born-in-flames (accessed 10 March 2021).

Burrough, Bryan (2016), 'The bombings of America that we forgot', *Time Magazine*, 20 September. *Available online:* https://time.com/4501670/bombings-of-america-burrough/ (accessed 29 March 2021).

Citron, Michelle, Julia Lesage, Judith Mayne, B. Ruby Rich and Anna Marie Taylor (1978), 'Women and film: A discussion of feminist aesthetics', *New German Critique*, 13: 82–107.

Connolly, Maeve (ed.) (2011), *Between Truth and Fiction: The Films of Vivienne Dick*, London: British Film Institute.

Crenshaw, Kimberlé (1989), 'Demarginalizing the intersection of race and sex: A black feminist critique of antidiscrimination doctrine, feminist theory, and antiracist politics', *University of Chicago Legal Forum*, 1989.8: 57–80. Available online: https://chicagounbound.uchicago.edu/uclf/vol1989/iss1/8 (accessed 10 April 2020).

De Lauretis, Teresa (1987), *Technologies of Gender: Essays on Theory, Film, and Fiction*, Bloomington: Indiana University Press.

Dick, Vivienne, and Scott MacDonald (1982), 'Interview with Vivienne Dick', *October*, 20: 83–101.

Dick, Vivienne, and Tessa O'Brien (2011), 'Guerillere filmmaker: An interview with Vivienne Dick', in Maeve Connolly (ed.), *Between Truth and Fiction: The Films of Vivienne Dick*, 56–68, London: British Film Institute.

Dika, Vera (2012), *The (Moving) Pictures Generation: The Cinematic Impulse in Downtown New York Art and Film*, 1st edn, New York: Palgrave Macmillan.

Elmer, Jonathan (1998), 'The archive, the Native American, and Jefferson's convulsions', *Diacritics*, 28.4: 5–24.

Foster, Gwendolyn Audrey (1995) *Women Film Directors: An International Bio-Critical Dictionary*, Westport, CT: Greenwood.

Grayson, Saisha (2020), 'Creating sparks: Five questions with Lizzie Borden', *Smithsonian American Art Museum*, 4 March. Available online: https://americanart.si.edu/blog/creating-sparks-five-questions-lizzie-borden (accessed 28 February 2021).

Heath, Stephen (1977), 'Notes on suture', *Screen*, 18.4: 48–76.

Hilderbrand, Lucas (2013), 'In the heat of the moment: Notes on the past, present, and future of *Born in Flames*', *Women & Performance: A Journal of Feminist Theory*, 23.1: 6–16.

Hoberman, Jim (1980), 'Notes on three films by Vivienne Dick', *Millennium Film Journal*, 6: 90–4.

Hoberman, Jim (1982), 'A context for Vivienne Dick', *October*, 20: 102–6.

Hollinger, Karen (1987), '"The look", narrativity, and the female spectator in vertigo', *Journal of Film and Video*, 39.4: 18–27.

Hughes, Sarah (2016), '"She gave her mother 40 whacks": The lasting fascination with Lizzie Borden', *The Guardian*, 4 December. *Available online:* http://www.theguardian.com/books/2016/dec/04/lizzie-borden-40-whacks-lasting-fascination (accessed 9 March 2021).

Jean, Raymond (1970), 'Les Guérillères de Monique Wittig', *Le Monde*, 13 June. Available online: https://www.lemonde.fr/archives/article/1970/06/13/les-guerilleres-de-monique-wittig_3118067_1819218.html (accessed 27 December 2021).

Lacan, Jacques (2005), *Le Séminaire: [1975-1976], Livre XXIII: Le Sinthome*, ed. Jacques-Alain Miller, Paris: Seuil.

Lane, Christina (2000), *Feminist Hollywood: From Born in Flames to Point Break*, Detroit: Wayne State University Press.

Levinas, Emmanuel (1990), *Totalité et infini: Essai sur l'extériorité*, Paris: Librairie générale française.

Marks, Laura U., and Dana Polan (2000), *The Skin of the Film: Intercultural Cinema, Embodiment, and the Senses*, Durham, NC: Duke University Press.

Mueller, Charles (2017), 'Seduction and subversion: The feminist strategies of Siouxsie and the Banshees', *College Music Symposium*, 57. Available online: https://symposium.music.org/index.php/57/item/11366-seduction-and-subversion-the-feminist-strategies-of-siouxsie-and-the-banshees (accessed 27 December 2021).

Mulvey, Laura (1975), 'Visual pleasure and narrative cinema', *Screen*, 16.3: 6–18.

Mulvey, Laura (1981), 'Afterthoughts on "visual pleasure and narrative cinema" inspired by "Duel in the Sun" (King Vidor, 1946)', *Framework: The Journal of Cinema and Media*, 15.17: 12–15.

Nastasi, Alison (2016), '"Choice is paramount to everything": Filmmaker Lizzie Borden on the radical feminism of "Born in Flames"', *Flavorwire*, 19 February. Available online: https://www.flavorwire.com/561757/choice-is-paramount-to-everything-filmmaker-lizzie-borden-on-the-radical-feminism-of-born-in-flames (accessed 3 March 2021).

Randolph, Sherie M. (2015), 'Not to rely completely on the courts: Florynce "Flo" Kennedy and black feminist leadership in the reproductive rights battle, 1969–1971', *Journal of Women's History*, 27.1: 136–60.

Raven, Arlene, and Ruth Iskin (1977), '"Through the peephole: Toward a lesbian sensibility in art', *Chrysalis*, 4: 19–31.

Reynolds, Simon (2010), *Totally Wired: Postpunk Interviews and Overviews*, New York: Soft Skull.

Rorty, Richard (1991), 'Feminism, ideology, and deconstruction: A pragmatist view', in Slavoj Zizek (ed.), *Mapping Ideology*, 227–34, New York: Verso Books.

Rorty, Richard (2000), *Philosophy and Social Hope*, London: Penguin.

Sussler, Betsy (1983), 'Lizzie Borden by Betsy Sussler', *BOMB Magazine*, 1 October. Available online: https://bombmagazine.org/articles/lizzie-borden/ (accessed 28 February 2021).

Tabb, William K. (1982), *The Long Default: New York City and the Urban Fiscal Crisis*, New York: Monthly Review.

Taubin, Amy (1979), 'The other cinema: Films of Vivienne Dick', *Soho Weekly News*, 12 July.

The Combahee River Collective (1978), 'A black feminist statement', *Women's Studies Quarterly*, 42.3–4 (Fall/Winter): 271–80.

The Red Krayola (1980), 'Born in flames', in *Born in Flames*, London: Rough Trade Records.

Trinh, Thi Minh-Ha (1992), *Framer Framed*, New York: Routledge.

Willse, Craig, and Dean Spade (2013), 'We are born in flames', *Women & Performance: A Journal of Feminist Theory*, 23.1: 1–5.

Wittig, Monique (1969), *Les Guérillères*, Paris: Minuit.

Wittig, Monique (1971), *Les Guerilleres*, trans. David Le Vay, New York: Viking.

Yokobosky, Matthew (2006), 'Not a part of any wave: No Wave cinema', in Marvin J. Taylor (ed.), *The Downtown Book: The New York Art Scene, 1974–84*, 17–128, Princeton, NJ: Princeton University Press.

2

Daughters behind the camera

Nicole Cloarec

The French critic Roger Odin, who pioneered the studying of home movies[1] and retrieved them from the 'garbage dump of film and cultural studies', to borrow Patricia Zimmerman's words (1995: xv), notes that the history of home movies has traditionally been constructed within the family institution characterized by a specifically patriarchal structure that regulated and defined the roles of each family member.

> In the first instance, there was the bourgeois patriarchal family that was prevalent from 1945–75, the great period of familiarism (cf Zimmerman 1995, 122–3). This structure can be described as a combination of constraints that regulate the actants in a given space. Within this structure, the father has a particular position; it is he who directs the formation of familial memory; it is he who oversees the building of the cemetery grave; he who orders the painted family portraits; who takes the photographs; and, obviously, it is he who shoots the films. (Odin, 2014: 16)

In this respect, home movies appear to be a perfect vehicle for reproducing the restrictive gendered roles and power relationships inscribed in this type of domestic image-making process, where, among records of family reunions and ceremonies, outings, holidays or national festivals, we can find overwhelmingly numerous pictures of mothers smiling at the camera, surrounded by equally grinning children. Filmmaker Michelle Citron herself stated, 'We are not naive. We know these images are staged. We've all been asked to pose in front of a famous landmark or file past the camera, waving as we look directly into the lens' (1999b: 11).

While a number of feminist filmmakers proceeded to interrogate and deconstruct prevailing representations of women in Hollywood fiction films or popular media, using domestic images produced by fathers or the filmmaker's family has been theorized as one key strategy in women's revisionist documentary practice. As film scholar Maureen Turim writes, 'images usually taken by fathers or found in someone else's home movies are one way filmmakers have found to explore the manner in which film gathers and transforms fragments of lived experience' (1986: 86).

As a significant example, Roger Odin cites Australian filmmaker Merilee Bennett who, in *A Song of Air* (1987),[2] appropriates the home movies produced by her father while adopting a diametrically opposed approach to filmmaking. Whereas her father was most unusual in his home movie production which he conceived according to all the rules of classical cinema, paying attention to balanced framing and image focus, respecting continuity editing and imposing pre-established scenarios, the daughter reappropriates the neat footage by reframing, recombining, speeding up or slowing down images. As the filmmaker herself explains in the voice-over, 'to find my own vision, I had to reject yours'.[3] Ironically, Merilee Bennett foregrounds the fact that the camera her father used was originally a present he had given to his wife, implying her father somehow hijacked her mother's means of expression; the film opens with a written statement that accounts for the origins of the film material that constitutes Merilee Bennett's film:

> My father, Arnold Lucas Bennett, bought a 16mm Bolex movie camera in 1956, as a gift for my mother, Nancy. He then used it himself, until his death in early 1983, to document family life, in and around Brisbane, Queensland, and to film the stories he wrote, directed and edited, and in which his family acted.

Roger Odin recalls that to fully fulfil their function, namely of building up a collective mythologized history and reinforcing the family unit, home movies must precisely eschew the rules of high production values and employ instead a number of features such as the absence of continuity in narrative and editing, approximate framings, jump cuts and other jerky matches, uncontrolled camera movements, out of focus and blurred visions.

> To work well, the home movie should be made like a random succession of scenes only offering snippets of family life from which each family member might be able to reconstruct the family history in his or her own way: … in other words, using the 'cinema film' as a comparison, the home movie works well when it is badly made. (Odin, 2014: 16)

These features of poor amateur aesthetics are precisely what Merilee Bennett strives to instil back into her father's footage but, ironically, the daughter's re-filming and re-editing ultimately reproduces the same authorial gesture as her father's: through her project of 'exhausting' the images produced by her father, she eventually imposes an equally personal vision onto what is supposed to be collective material.[4]

What I want to analyse in the present chapter are some examples of documentary and semi-documentary works produced by female filmmakers that precisely manage to eschew that type of closure while reclaiming their family's story and still finding a voice of their own. In Michelle Citron's *Daughter Rite* (1978), Su Friedrich's diptych about her parents, *The Ties that Bind* (1986) and *Sink or Swim* (1990), and Sarah Polley's *Stories We Tell* (2012), three daughters behind the camera try to come to grips with their lineages, exploring family relationships, investigating their parents' history while questioning gender roles and their identities as daughters.

Their common approach involves a twofold process. First, all four films display skilful appropriation of home movie footage – processed, recut, reframed and recontextualized – which act as some sort of 'radioactive fossils' as defined by Laura U. Marks after Gilles Deleuze,[5] to refer to images that bear an indexical relation to the past but exceed its mere historical dimension so as to refract upon the present, arousing other memories that had been forgotten (Marks, 1999: 227). Then they show great care at not imposing any new closed meaning upon these images but rather leave the gaps and scars open, building up a space for polyphony and multiple voices. To do so, they artfully use various audiovisual materials and filmic practices, intermingling found footage with re-enactment scenes and talking head interviews, thus highlighting the hybrid nature of their films and foregrounding discontinuity. Rather than 'gaining control of the word and the image, so that the voice of women may be heard' (Freiberg, 1987: 337), the filmmakers' discourse emerges from the artfully self-reflexive editing that accommodates a plurality of voices and perspectives as well as irrevocable absences.

Michelle Citron's *Daughter Rite* is now recognized as a major reference in both documentary and feminist cinema. At first sight, the film seems to fit perfectly E. Ann Kaplan's account of the 1970s women's movement when she described feminism as 'very much a movement of daughters', as part of a reaction to 'our mothers, who had tried to inculcate the patriarchal "feminine" in us, much to our anger'.[6] *Daughter Rite* opens with filmic documents shot by Citron's father (in Citron 1999a: 276) – home movies – which the filmmaker reframes, whose movement she slows down or reverses, creating visual loops as if to suggest some lasting painful memories and question the neat surfaces of these official family images.[7] Most of the pictures are fairly conventional, showing Citron's mother with her and her sister as children, while on holidays or at parties, or at home doing the dishes [Figure 2.1]. Commenting on these images, the voice-over tells of her difficult relationship with her mother whose role model she rejects while feeling most ambivalent towards a woman whom, she says, 'I am very much alike and not alike at all'. As the voice over recounts,

> I haven't seen her since she moved away – two years during which time I have been incredibly angry at her – for so totally controlling me as a child, for not giving me love the way I wanted it, for not being the woman I wanted her to be, for teaching me to be weak.

Figure 2.1 Home movie footage in *Daughter Rite* directed by Michelle Citron © Iris Films 1980.

This personal grievance against a mother who could not fulfil her daughter's expectations is further echoed by the insertion of talking head interviews of two sisters who both recall painful memories and blame their mother for being either too intrusive, prying into their diaries, for example, or, on the contrary, critically absent as when she feigned to ignore the rape of one of her daughters.

However, Citron's film proves far more complex than offering a heartfelt critique of a traditional maternal figure through the guise of retrieved found footage and *cinéma vérité* documentary. Rather than forging a straightforward incriminating discourse, the film multiplies the figures of discontinuity and decentring. First, the halting, broken-down movements given to the looping images of home movies, rather than denouncing the restrictive social roles epitomized by such a mode of domestic image-making,[8] reveal all the minute gestures that have been missed or left incomplete, as with the repeated image of the mother and daughter running towards each other but never embracing.

Most importantly, the film frustrates all predictable logical relationships between its different narrative threads and aesthetic categories. Thus, the narrative voice only partially comments upon the images but rather expatiates autonomously, recalling dreams and fantasies as well as memories. Whereas most voice-over narrations work as guidelines to impose meaning on the visuals, here, the voice has a disconnected, disembodied effect, which only reinforces the unrealistic quality created by the manipulation of the images.

Then, the interviews that seemingly bring about further authentic testimonies of the daughters' predicaments are revealed in the end credits to have actually been staged and enacted by actresses,[9] thus questioning the audience's assumption of documentary realism. As critics have since noted, the use of fiction disguised as *cinéma vérité* offered a critical examination of the prevailing aesthetics adopted by early feminist documentary filmmakers.[10] In this respect, Citron's film was the direct answer to Claire Johnston's influential 1973 essay 'Women's Cinema as Counter-Cinema' in which the critic took issue with this dominant form in women's documentaries and called for 'any revolutionary strategy [which] must challenge the depiction of reality'.[11]

Most specifically, by intermingling different film techniques and aesthetics and blurring the frontiers between reality and fiction, the filmmaker decentres the first-person narratives to create a 'floating free play of associations' (Feuer, 1980: 12) and a kaleidoscopic, pluralistic portrait. In using her father's home movie footage, the filmmaker does not merely denounce their fallacious idealized content; as the use of pseudo *cinéma vérité* sequences also testifies, no images or films can pretend to 'tell the truth'. If some truth can emerge, it can only be contradictory and plural, the result of multiple perspectives,[12] and this unresolved dialectic is conveyed through elaborate editing that foregrounds ruptures and discontinuity. Most tellingly, *Daughter Rite*'s last shot is a black screen, leaving the tensions unresolved as the voice-over speculates on her mother's viewpoint: 'I imagine my mother seeing this – feeling the pain, eroding the pleasure. "Why do you have to say all this?" she asks.' Throughout this composite portrait made up of various materials and voices, the figure of the mother appears to be present only obliquely, through the marks left by her absence and silence, which seems appropriate for a figure that appears to be a unifying as much as a dividing force.[13]

Significantly, the use of lengthy fades-to-black is one of the most striking features in Su Friedrich's filmic portrait of her mother which investigates her mother's own traumatic childhood in Germany during the 1930s and 1940s. Despite its psychologically meaningful title, *The Ties that Bind*, and although some narrative continuity is provided by the mother's story in voice-over, what prevails once again are figures of disruption through heterogeneous materials and a self-reflexive montage. In *The Ties that Bind*, Friedrich intertwines photographs and other family documents, historical archives, her recording of her own journey to Germany, *cinéma vérité*-style sequences with her mother, talking head interviews, titles and scenes in which a model of a house is being assembled, all punctuated by long silences and fade-outs as well as a few white screens. As Noël Burch noted about Stan Brakhage's *Reflections on Black* (1955), the recurring black screens no longer have a function of punctuation, simply marking the end of an image and the beginning of another, but acquire a value of their own, the interstice between two images being as important as representational images themselves, constituting what Deleuze called 'a so-called irrational cut which belongs neither to one nor the other, and sets out to be valid for itself'.[14]

In her doctoral dissertation 'Formes et manifestations de la subjectivité dans le cinéma documentaire personnel américain',[15] Marie Danniel-Grognier uses the opposite term of seamed editing – in French 'montage couturé' – as opposed to the seamless editing of classical cinema – to refer to a type of montage where the seams between heterogeneous materials and techniques remain apparent. She also underlines the propinquity of the term with the motif of the scar, so apt to suggest the traumatic memories of the past – be it the filmmakers' or their families' – that are probed into and unearthed in these films. In *The Ties that Bind*, Friedrich's presence appears through her handwritten titles,[16] which she inserts in a dialogue with her mother's voice. Her hands are also visible in scenes in which she assembles the 3D model house, evoking her mother's home in Germany that Friedrich went to visit, and more generally the memories she gathers and reconstructs to find her own place in the family history. Thus, these rather simple and austere shots provide a self-reflexive commentary on the object of the film which aims to convey the workings of memory as an editing process. However, after about two-thirds of the film, the filmmaker starts trampling on the now-completed house before finally setting it on fire. While illustrating the traumatic legacy of her mother's story, this destructive gesture comments upon the whole film for which any totalizing closure is denied.

In *Sink or Swim*, Friedrich adopts yet a different strategy. Here she appropriates her family's home movies, which she reprocesses in slow and stop motion, as occurs in Citron's *Daughter Rite*. The visual effect conveys the filmmaker's will to dissect her ambivalent relationships with a distant father, evoking painful memories as well as his cultural legacy. The film can be read as an open letter to this absent father, and significantly enough, the only synchronized sound heard reproduces the typewriting of a letter which the girl writes to her father in the aptly named chapter 'Ghost', which appears like a film negative. However, *Sink or Swim* displays a number of distancing effects which break down the traditional first-person mode of autobiography, allowing viewers to focus on formal relationships and associations rather than her personal story. The first, most obvious, distancing effect is the use of a third-person narrative referring to the 'girl' and 'her father'. As Friedrich explains in an interview with film scholar Scott MacDonald,

> I was using stories from my own life and began by writing them in the first person, but I got tired of that very quickly. It sounded too self-indulgent. Writing them over in the third person was quite liberating. The distance I got from speaking of a 'girl' and 'her father' gave me more courage, allowed me to say things I wouldn't dare say in the first

> person, and I think it also lets viewers' identify more with the material, because they don't have to be constantly thinking of me while listening to the stories.[17]

But most strikingly, *Sink or Swim* is organized along the structuring principle of twenty-six chapters which correspond to the twenty-six letters of the alphabet, recalling the formal strategies associated with 'structural film'.[18] While the reference to the minimal units of our symbol system for written language establishes a direct link with her father's profession as a linguist, it also playfully sets up a contradiction, as it reverses its conventional order. Thus, to evoke her birth, the film starts with the end – the letter Z for 'Zygote' – and it ends with the first letter by multiplying alternative founding myths with not one but three female figures from Greek mythology (Athena, Atalanta and Aphrodite) who all fuelled the little girl's imagination. Divergence thus governs both the deviously straightforward structuring of the film and the relationships between the image track and the voice over narration. From the onset, playful contradictions prevail: while the film opens with images from a science documentary showing the fertilization of an ovum and its subsequent meiosis, the narration has nothing to do with the biology of human procreation but instead relates the mythical birth of Athena, who 'sprang from [Zeus's] head fully grown and dressed for battle'.

Last but not least, the filmmaker adds a coda to further preclude her narrative from following the strict linear logic of the reverse alphabetic list. In this coda, the same image of a little girl aged around twelve (Friedrich herself) appears again and again while on the soundtrack an adult's voice recites the traditional children's 'Alphabet Song', but the voice multiplies to form a canon of polyphonic voices before ending with the single voice again which says, 'Now I've said my A-B-Cs, tell me what you think of me.' The first and only time the I-person is used not only appears as part of a discordant polyphonic round but also ends on an open question which might still be construed as a child's plea for her father's recognition though finally addressed to us, the film's viewers.[19]

Sarah Polley's more recent feature *Stories We Tell* offers another remarkable example of autobiographical film based on a polyphonic structure. At first sight, Polley's film seems to follow a more traditional use of home movies which consists in questioning the official images of the past to uncover hidden truths and exhume its traumatic secrets. The movie starts ostensibly as a quest to know more about her late mother, who died when Sarah was eleven years old. And the film does constitute a moving portrait of a mother, an actress who enjoyed performing in life as well as on stage, but found herself trapped in her social roles of wife and mother.[20] But this presumed agenda becomes increasingly complex, contradictory and inconclusive. Recurring images are thus probed over and over, adding new layers of meanings with fresh revelations and perspectives, as with the opening shot which shows a snowy landscape from a train window and whose symbolic abstract meaning (the track of life) acquires a disturbing significance when it recurs to illustrate Diana's journey to an abortion clinic before she changes her mind.[21]

As the story progresses to reveal a number of surprising narrative twists, *Stories We Tell* displays an elaborate self-reflexivity in both *mise en scène* and editing. Like the other aforementioned films, Polley's movie deploys a wide variety of audiovisual materials and filmic practices, blurring the frontier between fact and fiction as it interweaves home movies with re-enactments of key events which she films with the same jerky cranked-up rhythm as the other home footage – but then, how could one believe so many key events had been so conveniently recorded? As this footage alternates with numerous talking head interviews, it further questions the putative 'immediacy' of documentary film by revealing the 'making-of' of the film within the film, all the cogs and wheels that are supposed to remain behind the scenes. When Sarah's siblings are first introduced, sound booms and microphones are visible in the frame; then Sarah herself appears on-camera and guides her father to a sound studio where she sets him up and makes him repeat his lines. These self-reflexive devices culminate at the end when Sarah appears on-screen, pointing the camera at her cameraman and ultimately at the audience (Figure 2.2).

Figure 2.2 Self-reflexivity in *Stories We Tell* directed by Sarah Polley © National Film Board of Canada 2012.

Turning a personal quest for identity into the documenting of its own filmmaking now represents a fairly common trope in contemporary autobiographical documentaries, thanks to the pioneering works of, for example, Ed Pincus in *Diaries, 1971–76* (1981).[22] What is far more original in Polley's film is that, unlike most other personal filmic accounts, these self-reflexive devices are not used to place the filmmaker's subjectivity at centre stage, where all the mirror effects and echoes ultimately deflect into a self-portrait. Far from using herself as focal point, Polley redirects self-expression about her own quest for identity to question the adequacy of so-called realist techniques of representation and more specifically the potential deceits that come with all filmmaking and editorial process.

Near the end, her father Michael points out the responsibility Polley will have in selecting scenes from more than 'six hours of stuff' and editing them.

> You realize, when you've finished all this, you'll have about six hours of stuff, and you'll decide what you want out of it. It'll be exactly like the story. ... If any one of us were trying to edit it and decide what we wanted to keep, it would be the same farcical kind of theatrical exercise

> that we're all involved in. ... That's an enormously different thing from simply doing an interview straight and never doing any editing of it whatsoever, but letting it run as it is. That would have been at least as close to truth as you can get, whereas your editing of this will turn this into something completely different.

While the edited film remains undoubtedly the director's responsibility, the outcome of her choices through which her narrative voice resonates, the film, however, persistently decentres her narrative and filmic authority. The film emerges as a truly collaborative process, multi-faceted and confrontational, a 'multi-narrator cinematic personal essay,' according to film critic Nick McCarthy (2013). Not only does she ask all the people to 'tell the whole story from the beginning until now *in [their] your own words*', but most tellingly, most of the voice-over comes from the narration that her father Michael wrote, in which he refers to himself as a character in the third person. The filmmaker's subjectivity refracts through these dialogical relationships and again, even when Sarah's narration appears in voice over, it refers to her correspondence with her biological father Harry.

In *Slant Magazine*, McCarthy compares *Stories We Tell* to 'adapting a family photo album into a humane *Rashomon*-esque documentary' (ibid.), and, true enough, it conveys a genuine polyphony so as to accommodate the different perspectives of all the people involved.[23] Rather than imposing her own personal story that would end all 'official' family stories, Polley's project is made explicit when she explains to Harry, 'What if the main focuses in the documentary are the *discrepancies* in the stories?' (my emphasis). Interestingly enough, the only person who objects to this multi-voiced, inconclusive project and instead claims there is only *one* possible truth, which of course he owns, seeking to wrest control upon the narrative, is Harry, Sarah's biological father.[24] But then, he was not there to shoot the home movies.

Through reclaiming the highly gender-defined genre of home movies, Michelle Citron, Su Friedrich and Sarah Polley not only investigate their relationships with their parents and their identities as daughters but also question the ability of any image-making processes to tell the truth, deconstructing the so-called realistic documentary filmmaking techniques while eschewing the narcissistic indulgence of subjective self-scrutiny. Instead, they all foreground a self-reflexive mode of editing that is structured on discontinuity, exposing the heterogeneous variety of their audiovisual materials as well as their gaps and absences, interweaving different filmic practices, highlighting the ruptures of linear logic and ultimately decentring the first-person narration to create polyphonic narratives that preclude any definite closure. Although one must be wary of any attempt at essentializing what could constitute a 'feminine' style of filmmaking,[25] these three women filmmakers' claim to accommodate plurality through skillful formal innovation and elaborate montage is precisely what defines their points of view, expanding discourses about their subjectivities while allowing them to find voices of their own.

Notes

1 Here I follow Roger Odin's definition: 'My definition of a home movie is a film (or video) that is made by a family member about characters, events or objects that are somewhat related to the history of this family and mainly destined for the private use of this family' (Odin, 1995: 27; my translation).

2 About Merilee Bennett's film, see ibid. and Danks (2002).

3 Bennet (1988: n.p.):

> Almost every Sunday evening after tea we'd watch movies. We saw ourselves growing up, laughing at fashion changes and private jokes, and above all, had Dad's image of family life re-enforced. To find my own vision, I had to reject yours, and test myself to find out what I was made of. Out of love you tried to prevent my pain, but your safety is like suffocation.

4 Adrian Danks aptly remarks, 'The irony of this encounter between home photography and the experimental film is that often it is this second gesture – let us call it the avant-garde one – which, ultimately, tends to fix the meanings and the form of these materials.' However, one should note

that Bennett's whole project 'to exhaust the images produced by and of the father' may be qualified by the very last shot of the film which shows her father swimming, now displaced from behind the camera, the object of someone else's home movie. Commenting upon the new tension it brings to the whole film, Danks sums up:

> The final sequence of *A Song of Air* is indicative of the complex motivations of the entire film. In some respects, the purpose of the film seems to be to exhaust the images produced by and of the father. In other respects, the final shots of the film are a kind of gift, a setting free of the image of the father and a recognition that any attempt to read these images must recognise gaps and excesses that are never accessible to a single film, spectator or ideological perspective. (Danks, 2002)

5 'On dirait que le passé surgit en lui-même, mais sous forme de personnalités indépendantes, aliénées, déséquilibrées, larvaires en quelque sorte, fossiles étrangement actifs, radio-actifs, inexplicables dans le présent où ils surgissent, d'autant plus nocifs et autonomes' (Deleuze, 1985: 148) / 'It is as if the past surfaces in itself but in the shape of personalities which are independent, alienated, off-balance, in some embryonic, strangely active fossils, radio-active, inexplicable in the present where they surface, and all the more harmful and autonomous' (Deleuze, 1989: 112–13).

6 'Feminism was very much a movement of daughters. The very attractiveness of feminism was that it provided an arena for separation from oppressive closeness with the Mother; feminism was in part a reaction to our mothers, who had tried to inculcate the patriarchal 'feminine' in us, much to our anger' (Kaplan, 1983a: 81).

7 'In my family, home movies were powerful and necessary fictions that allowed us to see and explore truths that could only be looked at obliquely' (Citron, 1999b: 6).

8 This criticism is, however, still present as Kaplan (1983b: 182) notes:

> The home-movie footage is seen as 'deconstructing' a familiar 'realist' film mode. … [I]t is also seen as demonstrating male domination in filmmaking practice in that the mother and daughters are constantly 'objects' of the father's camera, performing

for his (voyeuristic) camera eye; they look out to the camera, aware of its presence and of the need to present the 'ideal family look' for that camera.

9 Citron explained she used some unstaged interviews she did with thirty-five women and transformed them into material that is scripted and acted into fictional scenes by two actresses, but then Citron also added she staged some entirely fictional scenes. Cf. Citron (1999a: 276–7).

10 As Julia Lesage (1978: 3) writes, 'Many of the first feminist documentaries used a simple format to present to the audience (presumably composed primarily of women) a picture of the ordinary details of women's life, their thoughts – told directly by the protagonists to the camera.' The scenes in *Daughter Rite* adopt all the characteristics of this form of filmmaking, namely, handheld camera, synchronous sound with no additional commentary or musical accompaniment, long takes with no cuts, tight framings of the people who testify and who are filmed evolving in their environment either in private conversations with others or in talking head interviews.

11 Johnston (1973: 214–15):

> Much of the emerging women's cinema has taken its aesthetics from television and *cinéma vérité* techniques … these films largely depict images of women talking to camera about their experiences, with little or no intervention by the film-maker. … Clearly, if we accept that cinema involves the production of signs, the idea of non-intervention is pure mystification … women's cinema cannot afford such idealism; the 'truth' of our oppression cannot be 'captured' on celluloid with the 'innocence' of the camera: it has to be constructed/manufactured. New meanings have to be created by disrupting the fabric of the male bourgeois cinema within the text of the film. … Any revolutionary strategy must challenge the depiction of reality; it is not enough to discuss the oppression of women within the text of the film; the language of the cinema/the depiction of reality must also be interrogated, so that break between ideology and text is effected.

12 'In my films my motivation for mixing modes involved a strategy for examining the issues. As far as I am concerned there is not one truth,

no single perspective that will give you the truth. And I think that the only way you can even approximate or approach it is by having multiple perspectives' (Citron, 1999b: 75).

13 In Feuer's (1980: 12) terms, 'both sets of sisters both hate and love the mother. In both, the mother is painted as devouring and yet nurturing. In both each sister in turn reveal a "good" and "bad" relationship to the mother.'

14 Deleuze (1985: 260):

> Cette nouvelle valeur de l'écran noir ou blanc nous semble correspondre aux caractères analysés précédemment: d'une part, ce qui compte n'est plus l'association des images, la manière dont elles s'associent, mais l'interstice entre deux images; d'autres part, la coupure dans une suite d'images n'est plus une coupure rationnelle qui marque la fin de l'une ou le début d'une autre, mais une coupure dite irrationnelle qui n'appartient ni à l'une ni à l'autre, et se met à valoir pour elle-même.

For the English translation:

> This new value of the black or white screen seems to us to correspond to the characteristics analysed earlier: on the one hand, what is important is no longer the association of images, the way in which they associate, but the interstice between two images; one the other hand, the cut in a sequence of images is not now a rational cut which marks the end of one or the beginning of another, but a so-called irrational cut which belongs neither to one nor the other, and sets out to be valid for itself. (Deleuze, 1989: 206)

15 PhD presented and obtained on 15 November 2008 at the University of Poitiers (supervisor Gilles Menegaldo).

16 The same device appears in Merilee Bennett's *A Song of Air* in which all titles and dedications seem handwritten.

17 Su Friedrich interviewed in MacDonald (1992: 308).

18 Stuart Klawans (1991) about Su Friedrich's works: 'The films demonstrate Friedrich's considerable technical talents and formal creativity as well as her canny historical sense in reappropriating the formal strategies generally associated with the "structural film".'

19 William C. Wees (2005: 35) has commented upon the way 'Friedrich breaks down the usual first-person, one-to-one relationship between an autobiographical subject and the form and content of an autobiographical film. The "I" is dispersed among cultural references, recollected personal experiences, and the open, multilayered structure of the work itself.'

20 Diana Polly is first introduced married to a husband – Sarah's father – who had radically different tastes and lifestyles, as 'Diana loved parties and Michael loved solitude', and who admits he was not able to fulfill her expectations. We then learn about a possible affair Diana would have had while acting in Montreal, after which little Sarah was born. As she grows up among unseemly family jokes about her physical dissemblance with her father, Sarah decides to investigate the matter. It turns out the man everyone surmised was her father was not but she eventually finds her biological father. Meanwhile, we learn that Diana was married before she met Michael, had two children from this first marriage but eventually lost custody of the children. Her case was then widely publicized as it was apparently the first time in Canada that a father won a case over custody – Diana being deemed too loose a woman for being a mother. The film ends with a last interview after a long fade to black, as if it were an afterthought, that reveals a final twist which sheds yet new light and casts some last doubts on what we have just learnt. As the elder sister testifies when she learns of her mother's affair, 'a truth like that that opens up kind of begets other truths and when you discover truths like that, how you think about truths within that are concealed'.

21 One constantly recurring image shows Diana crying while on the phone as she is filmed behind a half-closed door.

22 To name but a few outstanding examples: Ross McElwee's *Sherman's March* (1985) and Alan Berliner's *A Family Album* (1986).

23 Polley makes the film's project explicit in a number of emails that the filmmaker writes to Harry and which she reads:

> I'm just extremely uncomfortable at being involved in the telling of this story unless it includes the whole picture, which is to say my experience of it, your experience of it, as well as my family's. ... I've been thinking about your desire to tell the story

and my own desire to document this experience through film. As I begin this process, I don't know what form my project will take; I don't know if it's a personal record for myself or something to be made into a piece for others to see at some point; I don't know how it would take or how it would ever get finished and I would not ever pretend at this point that I know how to tell it beyond beginning to explore it through interviews and everyone involved so that everyone's point of view, no matter how contradictory, is included.

24 Harry's sister declares that 'when he considers this documentary, being Harry, being a producer', her brother will not like it 'because he doesn't have control of everything'. When Sarah asks him about 'the concept of me making a documentary where we're sort of giving equal weight to everyone's version of the story', Harry answers bluntly that he does not like it and concludes, 'The reality is essentially the story with Diana, I'm sorry to say, is only mine to tell; I think that's a fact.'

25 All the more so since gendered identity cannot be separated from other variables like class, nationality and sexuality.

Works cited

Bennett, Merilee (1988), *A Song of Air Press Kit*, Darlinghurst: Australian Film Institute.

Citron, Michelle (1999a), 'Fleeing from documentary: Autobiographical film/video and the "ethics of responsibility"', in Diane Waldman and Janet Walker (eds), *Feminism and Documentary, 271–86*, Minneapolis: University of Minnesota Press.

Citron, Michelle (1999b), *Home Movies and Other Necessary Fiction*, Minneapolis: University of Minnesota Press.

Danks, Adrian (2002), 'Photographs in haunted rooms: The found home experimental film and Merilee Bennett's *A Song of Air*', *Sense of Cinema*, 23, 12 December. Available online: https://www.sensesofcinema.com/2002/feature-articles/haunted/ (accessed 29 December 2021).

Danniel-Grognier, Marie (2008), 'Formes et manifestations de la subjectivité dans le cinéma documentaire personnel américain', PhD presented and obtained on 15 November 2008 at the University of Poitiers (supervisor Gilles Menegaldo).

Deleuze, Gilles (1985), *Cinéma 2. L'Image-temps,* Paris: Editions de Minuit. For the English translation: Deleuze, Gilles (1989), *Cinema 2: The Time Image*, Minneapolis: University of Minnesota Press.

Feuer, Jane (1980), '*Daughter Rite*: Living with our pain, and love', *Jump Cut,* 23, October. Available online: https://www.ejumpcut.org/archive/onlinessays/JC23folder/DaughterRite.html (accessed 29 December 2021).

Freiberg, Freda (1987), 'Time's relentless melt: Corinne Cantrill's *In This Life's Body*', in Annette Blonski, Barbara Creed and Freda Freiberg (eds), *Don't Shoot Darling! Women's Independent Filmmaking in Australia*, 334–42, Richmond, Australia: Greenhouse.

Johnston, Claire (1973), 'Women's cinema as counter-cinema', in Claire Johnston (ed.), *Notes on Women's Cinema*, *24–31,* London: Society for Education in Film and Television.

Kaplan, E. Ann (1983a), 'The case for the missing mother: Maternal issues in Vidor's *Stella Dallas*', *Heresies*, 16: 81–5.

Kaplan, E. Ann (1983b), *Women & Film: Both Sides of the Camera*, London: Routledge.

Klawans, Stuart (1991), 'The year in film', *The Nation*, 30 December.

Lesage, Julia (1978), 'The political aesthetics of the feminist documentary film', *Quarterly Review of Film Studies*, 3.4: 507–23.

Macdonald, Scott (1992), *A Critical Cinema 2: Interviews with Independent Filmmakers*, Berkeley: University of California Press.

Marks, Laura U. (1999), 'Fetishes and fossils: Notes on documentary and materiality', in Diane Waldman and Janet Walker (eds), *Feminism and Documentary*, 224–43, Minneapolis: University of Minnesota Press.

McCarthy, Nick (2013), 'Review: *Stories We Tell*', *Slant Magazine*, 18 March. Available online: http://www.slantmagazine.com/film/review/stories-we-tell (accessed 25 July 2015).

Odin, Roger (1995), 'Le film de famille dans l'institution familiale', in Roger Odin (dir.), *Le Film de famille: Usage privé, usage public*, 27–41, Paris: Méridiens Klincksieck.

Odin, Roger (2014), 'The home movie and space of communication', trans. Barry Monhahn, in Lara Rascaroli and Gwenda Young (eds), *Amateur Filmmaking: The Home Movie, the Archive*, 15–26, London: Bloomsbury Academic.

Turim, Maureen (1986), 'Childhood memories and household events in the feminist avant-garde', *Journal of Film and Video*, 38.3–4 (Summer–Fall): 86–92.

Wees, William C. (2005), 'No more giants', in Jean Petrolle and Virginia Wright Wexman (eds), *Women & and Experimental Filmmaking*, 22–44, Urbana: University of Illinois Press.

Zimmerman, Patricia R. (1995), *Reel Families: A Social History of Amateur Film*, Bloomington: Indiana University Press.

3

Molly Haskell's take on feminist film theory: The place of feminist film criticism outside academia

Anne Hurault-Paupe

It is unusual to associate Molly Haskell and feminist film theory. Indeed, Haskell's work is *not* theoretical; to the contrary, she has repeatedly criticized feminist film theory, especially in her two books which deal explicitly with feminism and film: *From Reverence to Rape: The Treatment of Women in the Movies* and *Holding My Own in No Man's Land: Women and Men and Film and Feminists*.[1] This should hardly be surprising, as Haskell officially defines herself as a film critic, not as a film scholar: 'Molly Haskell is a film critic and author who has written and lectured widely on film and the roles of women.'[2] The author presentation on the jacket of *Holding My Own in No Man's Land* explains that 'she has been the staff critic of the *Village Voice*, *New York Magazine*, and *Vogue*. Her work has also appeared in *The New York Times*, *The Nation*, *The New York Review of Books*, *Psychology Today*, and *Ms.*, among other places' (Haskell, 1997). Nevertheless, although her writing is not theory-oriented, Haskell has frequently been mentioned as a key representative of the first wave of feminist film analysis.[3] In this context, it is useful to adopt David Bordwell's classification of 'interpretive institutions' (1989: 20) into three distinct categories: journalistic criticism (published in 'newspapers and popular weeklies' or broadcast in 'television and radio programs'), essayistic criticism (published in 'specialised or intellectual monthlies or quarterlies') and academic criticism (published in 'scholarly journals');

Haskell's work has alternately belonged to journalistic and essayistic criticism, while being oft quoted in works of academic criticism, so that she can be considered as a key intermediary between three different sorts of readerships.

The purpose of this chapter is to study Haskell's position within the evolution of film criticism and reviewing from the 1970s to the 1990s. As a consequence, Haskell's works will be studied not only for their explicit content but also for what they reveal about three issues: first, the degree of interplay between journalistic, essayistic and academic discourses on film; second, the evolution of discourses about film feminism or feminist film criticism in mainstream to cinephiliac publications; and third, the constantly ongoing redefinition of film criticism as a profession. To do so, the first part provides an overview of the place of *From Reverence to Rape* within film studies. It aims at showing that, despite the book's theoretical limitations, its pages on the woman's film, on women directors and on stars were fraught with insights which contributed to audiences' awareness of feminist film criticism. The second part discusses Haskell's stance on feminist film theory, showing that her criticism of the psychoanalytically oriented theory of the gaze was part of an anti-elitist discourse which belonged to a long tradition in the history of film criticism, and that it enabled her to develop a successful career as an outsider to academic film criticism. Finally, the third part uses enunciative discourse analysis to show the linguistic and stylistic strategies developed by Haskell in order to create a feminist writing persona. It shows how she establishes her own legitimacy, differentiates herself from other film critics, engages a female implied reader and speaks as an intermediary between spectators and an imagined establishment.

Haskell's place in film studies

From Reverence to Rape is mostly remembered by scholars as one of the pivotal works in what later came to be known as the 'image of women on film' approach. It belonged to the first wave of feminist film criticism along with Marjorie Rosen's 1972 *Popcorn Venus* and Joan Mellen's 1973 *Women and Their Sexuality*. Its methodology uses plot and character analysis and focuses on sex stereotypes.

Haskell focuses on female film characters as reflections of images of real women, as evidenced by the following quote:

> Far more than men, women were the vessels of men's and women's fantasies and the barometers of changing fashion. Like two-way mirrors linking the immediate past with the immediate future, women in the movies reflected, perpetuated, and in some respects offered innovations on the roles of women in society. (1987: 12)

The reference to 'two-way mirrors' and the use of verbs such as 'perpetuated' and 'offered innovations on' insist on the idea of a reciprocal exchange of influence between films and cultural stereotypes. This suggests that such a process is straightforward. Haskell also implies that women's films are somehow more accurate representations of society than other images, even when they were 'unconscious reflections':

> Women's films, particularly those of the thirties, have a stronger sense of social reality than their glossy-magazine or vacuum-sealed television equivalents. Aside from the portrait of American society they give as a matter of course, there are unconscious reflections of misery 'in passing', like the image of a drunk or a prostitute reflected on the shiny surface of a parked limousine. (Ibid., 174)

Haskell's focus on films and society can be seen as part of a line of thought exemplified by Siegfried Kracauer, who claimed in his 1960 *Theory of Film* that 'in its preoccupation with the small the cinema is comparable to science. Like science it breaks down material phenomena into tiny particles' (50).

Haskell's book was published at a time when film studies were emerging as an academic research field, which developed very rapidly in the United States in the 1970s.[4] The differences between scholarly and cinephiliac magazines only gradually appeared. This was even more complex in the case of *feminist* film studies, the development of which was part of an emerging trans-Atlantic dialogue of diverging theories. In this context, Haskell's book was criticized in Great Britain, where continental theories of the human psyche were being reworked into psychoanalytic and semiological theories of the gaze based on the concepts of voyeurism, fetishism and scopophilia, a key example of which was Laura Mulvey's 1975 'Visual Pleasure and Narrative Cinema'.[5] At the same time, Haskell's defence of the woman's film directly clashed with Claire Johnston's article on 'Women's Cinema as Counter-Cinema', which had been published in 1973, and in which Johnston argued that

> in rejecting a sociological analysis of woman in the cinema we reject any view in terms of realism, for this would involve an acceptance of the apparent natural denotation of the sign and would involve a denial of the reality of myth in operation. (1973: 27)

While they mostly did not mention Haskell's book, the proponents of Lacanian feminist film theory in the 1970s and 1980s fundamentally rejected it when they demonstrated the complexity of identification. By the mid-1980s, when they themselves faced criticism by the likes of Jane Gaines (1986: 59–79) and bell hooks (1996), it did not mean that Haskell's book came back into favour, as both Gaines and hooks criticized all previous feminist theories for their lack of attention to factors such as race and class in film reception.

However, it would be erroneous to dismiss Haskell's work as obsolete, as her contribution to the study of the woman's film demonstrates. In her chapter on the woman's film in *From Reverence to Rape*, Haskell offered a typology of the genre which influenced future academic work: she differentiated between four types of woman's films, that is, those which were based on a woman's sacrifice, those which focused on affliction (a woman is struck by an affliction which she keeps secret), those which centred on choice (a woman has to choose between suitors) and those which hinged around competition (between the female protagonist and a rival). Two decades later, in *The Desire to Desire* (1987), Mary Ann Doane used a similar division of the genre into four types, though she changed the names of the categories. While Haskell's typology was based on plot characteristics, Doane's was more heterogeneous, as it focused on types of discourse (seeing the affliction-based woman's films as films based on medical discourse), on character types (replacing the sacrifice-based woman's film with the maternal melodrama) or on cultural categories (the choice-based woman film became the love story, while the competition-based woman's film became the gothic melodrama). As Linda Williams stressed in a review of Doane's book, the 'real value of this organization is that it frequently dovetails with excessive psychic states, masochism, narcissism and paranoia, for example' (1987: 44). Therefore, Doane gave a more psychoanalytic angle to what was essentially Haskell's typology.

Additionally, Haskell was among the first authors who defended the woman's film and claimed that it should not be considered inferior to other genres.[6] She praised specific directors of woman's films, writing that 'the woman's film reaches its apotheosis under Ophüls and Douglas Sirk in the late forties and fifties, at a time when the genre was losing its mass audience to television soap opera' (Haskell, 1987: 187). Haskell, who had studied at the Sorbonne and been a frequent cinemagoer to the repertory movie theatres of Paris, may be considered as one of the key figures who introduced European taste to American audiences, as Ophüls and Sirk were revered by European cinephiles and mostly ignored by American audiences. She can also be seen as an important figure in the transition towards a new canon, which emerged as 1980s film studies scholars focused on the woman's film and the melodrama (Doane, Mellenkamp and Williams, 1983: 67–82; Modleski, 1984: 19–30). As opposed to Thomas Elsaesser, her contemporary, whose 'Tales of Sound and Fury' addressed the specialized cinephiliac audience of *Monogram* magazine, she was a more mainstream advocate of the woman's film. Consequently, she can be seen as typical of the critic as mediator between a canon and 'the uneducated mass public' (Frey, 2015: 51).

Other aspects of Haskell's work have also shown potential, namely her focus on women directors such as Dorothy Arzner[7] and on 'woman's directors' such as Max Ophüls, Douglas Sirk, Otto Preminger, Ernst Lubitsch, George Cukor or Ingmar Bergman (Haskell, 1987: 159). Last but not least, Haskell's merit lies in her focus not only on actresses such as Clara Bow, Joan Crawford and Bette Davis[8] but also on more conservative stars such as John Wayne (Haskell, 1997: 147–60). Similarly, her pages on Doris Day have been used as references by star studies scholars.[9] Her ability to focus on 'intellectual' actresses such as Meryl Streep shows that her interests go beyond the mainstream. A comparison of *From Reverence to Rape* and *Holding My Own* shows how Haskell developed a one-sentence portrait of Streep in the 1987 book – 'a composite of striking roles and a symbol of Artistic Integrity, … an actress who is typecast as an actress who is not typecast' (1987: 373) – into a full-blown portrait in the 1997 book, in which she qualified her previous assessment, showing how Streep was actively controlling her career as 'an actress who has delighted in playing unconventional, even unpleasant women, and who has made a fetish out of not giving the public what it wants and expects from a star' (1997: 44). While neither theorizing nor becoming involved in star studies, Haskell may be considered as one of its harbingers.

In sum, Haskell's career as a film essayist and reviewer has run on a parallel track with the development of film studies: on the one hand, Haskell's focus on the assumption that films reflected social norms was eclipsed by the academic success of psychoanalytic film theory. On the other hand, her wide-ranging knowledge of the cinema and her intuitions on directors or actors have kept being used as reference by scholars. In a way, while academics may have deemed her to be totally 'wrong' in 1974, they had started considering her as partly 'right' by 1990.

Haskell's dual position

Haskell's approach is best analysed within the more long-term framework of film history. Indeed, as Mattias Frey has pointed out, the original function of film criticism which emerged in the 1920s was that 'film criticism has always been a service sector, but, rather than consumers, the original task was to guide the industry' (2015: 43). Since it aimed at denouncing misogynistic trends in recent films, *From Reverence to Rape* may be seen as a return to this historical role of criticism. However, while 'a major theme in the earliest film criticism was the advisory mode of guiding the cinema's aesthetic progress' (ibid.), Haskell's goal was to prompt the industry in the direction of ideological progress, as she explained in a 1981 interview:

> I had become interested in the women's movement and feminism … and, at the same time, I was struck by the fact that, at a time when women were doing so many things, making great advances …, they were disappearing from the movies. So, very naturally, this became my theme. (Crowdus and Wallace, 1981: 3)

Ideological progress was also the objective of the academic film critics who wrote in feminist film journals, when they analysed the underlying implications of film images; yet, their prime objective was to make theoretical advances on the nature of cinema, not to change moviegoers' attitudes and viewpoints. Mulvey's statement that 'it is the place of the look that defines cinema, the possibility of varying it and exposing it. … Going far beyond highlighting a woman's to-be-looked-at-ness, cinema builds the way she is to be looked at into the spectacle itself' is a case in point (1975: 17). As Janet Bergstrom and Mary Ann Doane have underlined, 'in "Visual Pleasure," there is no trace of the female spectator' (1989: 7). Conversely, Haskell's *From Reverence to Rape* was written for and about the female spectator.

As a consequence, there never was an alliance between Haskell and the proponents of psychoanalytic theory. To the contrary, in the same 1981 interview, Haskell insisted that she never read *Camera Obscura* (Crowdus and Wallace, 1981: 3), pointing out that their attitude to films was at odds with her own:

> The problem with the structuralists in general is that they have no passion, no feeling, for film. You somehow don't recognize in their

> articles the same film that you have seen. They're always talking about texts. The language that they use is so completely removed from the film viewing experience. (Ibid., 4)

With these words, Haskell asserts her own passionate approach to cinema as the main ground for her distaste for 'the structuralists'. By thus grouping together several separate strands of film theory into one single (bluntly inaccurate) category, Haskell prompts her readers to side with her in her detestation of theory. The quote implies that, to her, the point of film reviewing is to produce a textual account which will enable its readers to be immersed in 'the film viewing experience' again. In other words, Haskell proudly displays her cinephilia, with its key elements of love of movies, fond reminiscences and focus on film-going as an experience. This is the polar opposite of the scholarly approach, which by definition needs to make it clear that it separates itself from its object of study and views it in a dispassionate way, in order, as Bordwell has pointed out, to garner professional credibility and justify research grant applications (1989: 22–3).

The difference between Haskell's position and that of psychoanalytic theory can be further exemplified by her comments on psychoanalytic interpretations of Howard Hawks's *Gentlemen Prefer Blondes* (1953):

> But [psychoanalytic film theory] fails to capture both the spirit of the film and the camaraderie of the women [i.e. the female characters in the film] and, in disavowing its female parentage, becomes party to the patriarchal usurpation it criticizes! We're engaged in a process of identification, admiration, and amusement, send-up and celebration, not in the alienation effect.[10] (1997: 10–11)

In this quote, Haskell suggests that it is worthwhile to focus on the film's energy and on the diegetic interactions between characters. To her, these elements are directly linked to the richness of female spectators' immediate reaction to Hawks's film. Although her criticism of the 'alienation effect' is a reductive view of the theory of the gaze, it simultaneously enables her to portray herself as both informed about and superior to theory.

While it may have been true that Haskell did not read *Camera Obscura*, she nevertheless demonstrated some awareness of the key ideas of psychoanalytic feminist film theory, for instance, when she criticized these ideas in the 1987 re-edition of *From Reverence to Rape*:

> In leaning so heavily on the unilateral notion of male oppression, a good many feminists ignored the other half of the equation, the active role of women in permitting, encouraging, and controlling scenarios of dominance and submission. As habitual (and not unwilling) exhibitionists, we're entitled – and compelled – to acknowledge a certain complicity in the shadowy delights of male voyeurism. In denying this complicity, in insisting on the thesis of victimization, feminists not only deprived women of a collaborative autonomy in the imagining of love stories, but of a secret pleasure in the dark side of sex, those delirious (and politically 'incorrect') fantasies of dominance and submission which it was the function of sexual liberation to allow us to express. (382)

In a way, one can read into Haskell's stance something quite similar to the reflection on hegemony, oppression and resistance which was then developing in British cultural studies.

Furthermore, Haskell confirmed her familiarity with recent developments in feminist film theory when she wrote that

> Mulvey and Johnston neglected the context in which the films they studied were made and seen, that tremendous audience diversity. … For example, what about female audiences? Are men the only ones who 'gaze' …? (Ibid., 283)

As recent scholarly work had been based on similar criticism and had developed more historically oriented studies of the female spectator, Haskell can be seen as a mainstream echo of these developments: it is quite likely that she expressed views shared by non-scholarly feminists who were more familiar with the latest developments in feminist film theory.

The question of Haskell's relationship to theory remains a key point in her introduction to *Holding My Own* in 1997, where she turns her pretended ignorance of theory into an advantage in order to elaborate on her persona as an astute outsider to academic film criticism. She waxes ironical about accidentally discovering a discussion of *From Reverence to Rape* in 'a quarterly on feminist film theory':

> It was treated as a sort of prehistoric text, once important but – now that theory had come to save the day – obsolete. The writer noted that for all my strengths and weaknesses, everyone had missed my one fatal defect: I was 'an uncritical celebrator of heterosexual romance'. (1997: 4)

She uses a similar strategy of dismissing theory as insufficient to account for moviegoers' experience, when claiming, 'I'm obliged, *faute de mieux*, to give my students reading lists of essays with titles like "The Inscription of Femininity as Absence". … Of course, there's some truth, as there always is, in what is basically Marxism in feminist drag' (ibid., 11).

Simultaneously, Haskell presents herself as attuned to the experience of mass audiences, stressing that she has met 'this large number of people who don't see many films' (Crowdus and Wallace, 1981: 5) when teaching at colleges and universities. By thus affirming an anti-elitist position, Haskell placed herself in the tradition of Louis Delluc, Gilbert Seldes, James Agee and Pauline Kael.[11] Haskell's distaste of theory is also akin to that of the earlier French cinephiles, who also were influenced by their school education (as shown by their idealizing an encyclopaedic knowledge of film and by their taste for writing) and distrusted university researchers (de Baecque and Frémaux, 1995: 139).

Haskell's attitude is thus dual in that it both engages with psychoanalytic film theory and rejects it. This is precisely what enables her to generate a credible feminist writing persona for herself, establishing her own legitimacy and specialty as a mediator between common women and feminist academics.

Haskell's feminism as a way of speaking of/to female spectators

As film critics are busy establishing cultural hierarchies, their discourses are centred on canon-building, prestige and gatekeeping. In turn, this means that they have to first establish their own legitimacy, which they seek to do by focusing on professionalism. In that regard, Haskell's dual position, in between academic feminists and female spectators at large, makes her an interesting object of study. In the following lines, I draw from the theoretical framework of enunciative discourse analysis and especially the concepts and methodology created by Dominique Maingueneau,[12] who defines discourse as both a linguistic and a social phenomenon shaping our perception of reality. Discourse is produced by an enunciator with a specific purpose; it implicitly involves a co-enunciator which it prompts to act by using, for instance, verbs such as 'suggest', 'ask', or 'claim'. This co-enunciator will be designated as the implied reader.

As Annette Kuhn has stated, 'in the early 1970s in the USA, Molly Haskell was one of three women critics to found a career on being a feminist film critic (the other two were journalist Marjorie Rosen and academic Joan Mellen)' (Kuhn and Radstone, 1990: 190) This career choice meant that Haskell's writing belongs to the field of critical journalistic discourse and that she has adapted to many different formats throughout her career, as her work is composed of reviews, features, interviews, portraits, non-academic monographs, exhibition introductions and lectures. This also means that she has complied with the requirements of different writing outlets, from popular magazines through film magazines to book publishers.

Throughout this varied corpus of texts, Haskell has kept positioning herself as a feminist film critic. In the preface of the second edition of *From Reverence to Rape*, published in 1987, she explicitly acknowledged that this had been part of a strategy which aimed at making her name familiar to the public:

> When *From Reverence to Rape* came out in 1974, I gave myself a tag line that was both convenient and comprehensible to the most illiterate talk show host that would have me: I was a film critic first and a feminist second. … I'll still hold to that designation. (ix)

One can extrapolate from this quote that Haskell wanted to be recognized first and foremost as a film critic because the profession enjoyed 'national celebrity' status in the United States in the mid-1970s (Taylor, 1976: 180–2), and that she used her feminism as a second characteristic in order to establish a distinctive persona for herself. When she wrote the preface to the second edition of *From Reverence to Rape* in 1987, Haskell still defined her authority as that of a critic, when she wrote that 'if a poet or novelist is bigoted or narrow-minded or unfair, critics have the right and obligation to say so' (ibid.). Her claim to cultural legitimacy was further enhanced by her reference to literary critics, as this profession has accrued added legitimacy thanks to its judgements on an established art-form.

In her 1974 book *From Reverence to Rape*, Haskell established her feminist voice within film criticism by berating her male counterparts from the UK and the United States:

> Among the Anglo-American critical brotherhood (and a few of their sisters as well), the term 'woman's film' is used disparagingly to conjure up the image of the pinched-up virgin or little-old-lady writer, spilling out her secret longing in wish fulfilment or glorious martyrdom, and transmitting these fantasies to the frustrated housewife. (154)

Because Haskell included 'a few' female British and American critics in her attack, her feminism was tinged with the defence of European tastes. This enabled her to differentiate herself from more populist female critics, such as Judith Crist:

> Women critics have hardly been in the vanguard of the effort to dignify the lot of the female. Judith Crist, an astute woman with more national power than any other film critic, male or female, gravitates instinctively to men and male material, frequently dismissing certain

> stories as 'soap opera' or 'women's films', and often complaining that this or that actress is too old or overripe for a part. (Ibid., 13–14)

Haskell was not just trying to achieve recognition as a feminist critic but also implying that she was culturally superior to Crist, who had appeared in the *Today* show from 1963 to 1973 and had been published in *TV Guide* since 1965 (Martin, 2012).

Haskell's position was thus in-between in more ways than one: this was first a consequence of her being a film reviewer turned book author, as she acknowledged it, stating, 'I've tried to bridge the two worlds, the popular and the scholarly, not always to either side's full satisfaction' (1987: 9). This may account for the fact that *From Reverence to Rape* is neither fully an academic book (as there is no notes section or bibliography) nor a collection of texts (since it is not adapted from previously published reviews and includes an index).

Second, Haskell's position as a film critic is also avowedly dual, as evidenced by the title of her 1997 book, *Holding My Own in No Man's Land*. Indeed, Haskell explains in her introduction,

> I had begun to think of myself as stranded in No-Man's-Land, like a soldier caught in that exposed area between Allied and German trenches in the First World War. Or a tennis player, caught in the one position on the court where you have no purchase on the ball – too far from the net to volley, too close to try for a ground stroke. (6)

In this quote, Haskell utilizes comparisons based on situations of conflict, whether they are lethal or playful ones, showing how feeling torn between her beliefs as a feminist and her tastes as a cinephile felt unbearable.

One can argue that this complexity led Haskell to devise solutions in order to overcome her in-between position. Indeed, Haskell acknowledges in *Holding My Own* that her work was subject to 'certain rhetorical simplifications – using the pronoun "we," for example, to embrace blithely and without fear of contradiction one-half of the human race' (ibid., 7). However, I would claim that Haskell's strategy is quite effective, because her use of the pronoun 'we' is unstable throughout her work. Indeed, in *From Reverence to Rape*, she uses it in four distinct ways; first, to refer to the audience in general:

> There are two cinemas: the films we have actually seen and the memories we have of them. The gap between the two widens over the years, and nowhere is this more apparent than in the chasm that separates us from the twenties – a time from which most of us have seen so little and 'remember' so much. (1987: 42)

In this case, Haskell's 'we' encompasses both genders and seems to refer to cinephiles at large. However, in other passages, she uses 'we' to refer specifically to women of her generation:

> She 'puts out' or she doesn't. She balls or she doesn't. Will she or won't she becomes the unspoken question when boys discuss girls, will you or won't you the underlying question of heterosexual dialogue. My generation fell into the trap, internalizing the either/or as we thought of ourselves as 'hot' or 'cold' and falling victim, once again, to the terms by which our sex had been conveniently divided for so many years. (Ibid., xiv)

Here Haskell's 'we' includes both 'hot' and 'cold' women of her generation. Yet, two pages later in the same text, she uses the pronoun 'we' to designate feminists:

> It is only recently that we have begun to examine the whole complex alliance of love and need and its primacy for women. … We are asking, in the books and movies by women who most honestly confront the subject, whether it is possible to disentangle the neurotic and imprisoning aspects of love from its positive and liberating ones. (Ibid., xvi)

In this case, it would be possible to extend Haskell's 'we' to include feminist men. Nevertheless, in the final chapter she added for the second edition in 1987, she used 'we' to refer to all 1987 women, except 'the theoreticians':

> in the messy here-and-now, with audiences (and feminists) divided over both films [*Dressed to Kill* and *Blue Velvet*], there is – mercifully – no

> consensus, no last word as to what is a correct, what a demeaning portrait of woman, and certainly no one has given the theoreticians a mandate to speak for all of us. (Ibid., 384)

Haskell diverges from academic writers, who use the pronoun 'we' to refer to themselves when they have been working in a team, and who tend to only use the pronoun 'I' when they belong to the humanities, where research is carried out alone. As a consequence, it may appear to academics that Haskell lacks credibility because her writerly persona is versatile and refers to a shifting range of implied readers. However, it is quite possible that she draws some authority with readers from her ability to speak for many different types of spectators.

Besides, Haskell's rhetoric is also based on engaging readers on an emotional level. As Bordwell has shown, most reviewers use 'ethical proofs' when they imply that they are virtuous, in order to warrant their opinions (1989: 36). Haskell is typical of this when she starts her 1974 introduction to *From Reverence to Rape* with a childhood memory: 'My first idol was Margaret O'Brien, not for any role in particular but for the twin privileges she claimed as a movie star and a tomboy' (1987: xi). She goes on to describe 'one of [her] most vivid childhood memories' as trying to talk her father into buying a magazine about O'Brien's 'offscreen activities' (x). Thus, despite being an established film critic, she begins her book by portraying herself as a young fan, that is, as the antithesis of a professional. This enables her to claim common ground with other fans and, therefore, to be accepted as one of their peers.

She uses a similar strategy in *Holding My Own*, when she rewrites several pieces from the 1970s into a chapter on John Wayne. Using the present tense, she thus describes the beginning of an interview with the actor: 'I discover I am awestruck and tongue-tied at the mere sight of him. In his presence, I feel like I am twelve years old' (1997: 150). By thus acknowledging her emotions and once again referring to childhood, Haskell generates a persona as a woman who has kept in touch with the simplicity and innocence of youth.

Bordwell suggested that reviewers present themselves as 'a solicitous consumer guide' (for instance, Gene Siskel and Roger Ebert), as 'the passionate advocate for the bizarre or overlooked film' (citing J. Hoberman as an example), as 'the vulgar but righteous film fan' (Pauline Kael) or the cultural pundits with stringent standards (John Simon)' (1989: 35–6). In line with this typology, I would suggest that Haskell has chosen to appear as an expert ventriloquist, in that she shows a great ability to use different voices in order to speak in the name of women who are not there.

Conclusion

This overview of Molly Haskell's take on feminist film theory has shown the rhetorical, methodological and axiological differences between her position and that of an academic: first, Haskell tends to act the part of an outsider to the academy, whereas scholars ground their expertise on their knowledge of past research and hence position themselves as insiders to the world of knowledge. Second, academics rely on rationality, while Haskell uses subjectivity to engage readers. However, the references to psychoanalytic film theory in her work tend to indicate that Haskell is knowledgeable about it, thus suggesting that her choice of a distinctive feminist persona within mainstream culture was mostly a career choice.

Besides, Haskell's work shows how her career has run a parallel course to the development of research on film. *From Reverence to Rape* was a cinephile's book based on the writer's film-going experience and culture, which meant that Haskell did not develop what her brand of feminism entailed in great detail. Yet, the book was structured chronologically, not around individual reviews, and its ambition rivalled with that of contemporary works by academics, such as Stuart M. Kaminsky's *American Film Genres* (1974). Haskell's 1987 additions to the book suggest that she was fully aware that feminist film theory had prospered in the academic world since 1974. *Holding My Own*, published in 1997, was a collection based on rewritten articles and therefore more in line with typical reviewers' book such as Kael's works. While it acknowledged the existence of and criticized scholarly film feminism (in its introduction mostly), the latter book remained distinctively outside the scope of academic work.

This study of Haskell's work also gives insight into how she constructed her persona as a film critic, simultaneously pitting her authority against that of academics and creating a versatile voice which seemed to be able to speak for a wide range of implied readers. This suggests that, despite the many changes to film reviewing, the film reviewer's role as a key intermediary between films and spectators – which had emerged in the 1920s – remained central in the mid-1990s.

Notes

1 Haskell's *Steven Spielberg: A Life in Films* (2017), is her most recent book.

2 Guggenheim Memorial Foundation, *Molly Haskell*. Available online: http://www.gf.org/fellows/all-fellows/molly-haskell/ (accessed 30 June 2017). A similar biography can be found on the jacket of Haskell's recent books and on the list of the winners of awards from the Athena Film Festival (http://athenafilmfestival.com/award-winners/2013-athena-award-winners/ (accessed 30 June 2017)).

3 For example, B. Ruby Rich includes *From Reverence to Rape* in the 'major events of the 70's in North America and Great Britain' (1985: 343). Judith Mayne (1985: 84, note 5) mentions Haskell's book among 'the first and most influential studies of images of women in film'. Janet Bergstrom and Mary Ann Doane include Haskell's book in an overview of feminist film criticism in 'The Female Spectator: Contexts and Directions' (1989: 6).

4 See Grieveson and Wasson (2008).

5 For an anthology, see Doane, Mellencamp and Williams (1983).

6 She was preceded by Thomas Elsaesser (1973).

7 Arzner's work was also studied by the proponents of psychoanalytic film theory, cf. Johnston (1975).

8 On Clara Bow, see Haskell (1974: 79–80); on Joan Crawford, see ibid., 175–81; on Bette Davis, see ibid., 215–21.

9 Haskell (1987: 262–7) and Haskell (1997: 21–34). Jeremy G. Butler (1990: 55–6) and Dennis Bingham (2006: 6) refer to Haskell's book.

10 Although Haskell does not provide the exact reference of the work she is criticizing, the quote she provides makes it possible to infer that it is probably Maureen Turim's 'Gentlemen Consume Blondes', in Nichols (1985: 369–78).

11 On Delluc and Seldes as anti-elitist critics, cf. Frey (2015: 53–5). On Kael and Agee's anti-elistism, cf. Charney (1996: 113–26).

12 As Marie-Anne Paveau and Laurence Rosier have shown, there are six main approaches within the wide and varied field of discourse analysis: discursive semantics (Michel Pêcheux (1969)), traditional discourse analysis (Zellig Harris (1991)), interactive discourse analysis (Catherine Kerbrat-Orecchioni (2005)), critical discourse analysis (Teun Van Dijk (2007) and Norman Fairclough (1995)), enunciative discourse analysis (Dominique Maingueneau (1996)) and communicational discourse analysis (Patrick Charaudeau (2011)).

Works cited

de Baecque, A., and T. Frémaux, (1995), 'La cinéphilie ou l'invention d'une culture', *Vingtième siècle, revue d'histoire*, 46 (Avril–Juin): 133–42.

Bergstrom, Janet, and Mary Ann Doane (1989), 'The female spectator: Contexts and directions', *Camera Obscura*, 20–1 (May–September): 5–27.

Bingham, Dennis (2006), '"Before she was a virgin …": Doris Day and the decline of female film comedy in the 1950s and 1960s', *Cinema Journal*, 3 (Spring 2006): 3–31.

Bordwell, David (1989), *Making Meaning: Inference and Rhetoric in the Interpretation of Cinema*, Cambridge, MA: Harvard University Press.

Butler, Jeremy G. (1990), 'College course file: Star images, star performances', *Journal of Film and Video*, 42.4 (Winter): 49–66.

Charaudeau, Patrick (2011), *Les Médias et l'information: L'impossible transparence du discours*, Brussels: De Boeck-Ina.

Charney, Leo (1996), '"Common people with common feelings": Pauline Kael, James Agee, and the public sphere of popular film criticism', *Cinémas*, 6.2–3 (Spring): 113–26.

Crowdus, G., and M. Wallace (1981), 'Film criticism and feminism: An interview with Molly Haskell', *Cineaste*, 7.3: 2–11 and 41.

Doane, Mary Ann (1987), *The Desire to Desire: The Woman's Film of the 1940s*, Bloomington: Indiana University Press.

Doane, Mary Ann, Patricia Mellencamp and Linda Williams (eds) (1983), *Re-Vision: Essays in Feminist Film Criticism*, Frederick: University Publications.

Elsaesser, Thomas (1973), 'Tales of sound and fury: Observations on the family melodrama', *Monogram*, 4: 2–15.

Fairclough, Norman (1995), *Critical Discourse Analysis: The Critical Study of Language*, London: Longman.

Frey, Mattias (2015), *The Permanent Crisis of Film Criticism: The Anxiety of Authority*, Amsterdam: Amsterdam University Press.

Gaines, Jane (1986), 'White privilege and looking relations: Race and gender in feminist film theory', *Cultural Critique*, 4 (Autumn): 59–79.

Grieveson, Lee, and Haidee Wasson (eds) (2008), *Inventing Film Studies*, Durham, NC: Duke University Press.

Harris, Zellig (1991), *A Theory of Language and Information: A Mathematical Approach*, Oxford: Clarendon Press.

Haskell, Molly (1974), *From Reverence to Rape: The Treatment of Women in the Movies*, New York: Rinehart and Winston.

Haskell, Molly (1987), *From Reverence to Rape: The Treatment of Women in the Movies*, 2nd edn, Chicago: University of Chicago Press.

Haskell, Molly (1997), *Holding My Own in No Man's Land: Women and Men and Film and Feminists*, New York: Oxford University Press.

Haskell, Molly (2017), *Steven Spielberg: A Life in Films*, New Haven, CT: Yale University Press.

hooks, bell (1996), *Reel to Real: Race, Sex and Class at the Movies*, New York: Routledge.

Johnston, Claire (1973), 'Women's cinema as counter-cinema', in Claire Johnston (ed.), *Notes on Women's Cinema, 24–31,* London: Society for Education in Film and Television.

Johnston, Claire (ed.) (1975), *The Work of Dorothy Arzner: Towards a Feminist Cinema*, London: British Film Institute.

Kaminsky, Stuart M. (1974), *American Film Genres: Approaches to a Critical Theory of Popular Film*, New York: Dell.

Kerbrat-Orecchioni, Catherine (2005), *Le Discours en interaction*, Paris: Armand Colin.

Kracauer, Siegfried (1960), *Theory of Film*, Princeton, NJ: Princeton University Press.

Kuhn, A. and Radstone, S. (eds) (1990), *The Women's Companion to International Film*, Berkeley, Los Angeles: University of California Press.

Maingueneau, Dominique (1996), *Les termes clés de l'analyse du discours*, Paris: Seuil.

Martin, Douglas (2012), 'Judith Crist, a blunt and influential critic, dies at 90', *New York Times*, 7 August. Available online: https://www.nytimes.com/2012/08/08/movies/judith-crist-film-critic-dies-at-90.html (accessed 30 December 2021).

Mayne, Judith (1985), 'Feminist film theory and criticism', *Signs*, 11.1 (Autumn): 81–100.

Mellen, Joan (1973), *Women and Their Sexuality in the New Film*, New York: Horizon Press.

Modleski, T. (1984), 'Time and desire in the woman's film', *Cinema Journal*, 23.3 (Spring): 19–30.

Mulvey, Laura (1975), 'Visual pleasure and narrative cinema', *Screen*, 16.3: 6–18.

Nichols, Bill (ed.) (1985), *Movies and Methods: An Anthology*, vol. 2, Berkeley: University of California Press.

Pêcheux, Michel (1969), *Analyse automatique du discours*, Paris: Dunod.

Rich, B. Ruby (1985), 'In the name of feminist film criticism,' in Bill Nichols (ed.), *Movies and Methods: An Anthology*, vol. 2, 340–58, Berkeley: University of California Press.

Rosen, Marjorie (1972), *Popcorn Venus*, New York: Coward, McCann & Geoghegan.

Taylor, J. Russell (1976), 'The critic as superstar', *Sight and Sound*, 3 (Summer): 180–2.

Van Dijk, Teun (2007), *Discourse Studies*, London: Sage.

Part Two

Women in semi-independent cinema

4

Racial bodies in Kathryn Bigelow's *Strange Days* (1995)

Hélène Charlery

Directed by Kathryn Bigelow and co-written by James Cameron and Jack Cocks, *Strange Days* (1995) is set in a chaotic Los Angeles two days before the end of the millennium. Lenny Nero (Ralph Fiennes), a former LAPD officer, lives off smuggling an illegal device, originally created for police technological surveillance, known as SQUID (Superconducting Quantum Interference Device). The device records experiences that are lived by characters. The tapes are then sold, allowing its users to 'live' those recorded memories on playback from a first-person point of view (POV) to feel the thrill of the experiences as the device operates on the users' cortex. This is epitomized in the film's opening sequence that displays the images of the playback clip of a corner shop robbery. Lenny Nero has become a leading figure in this illegal market and also uses the technology so as to 'relive' moments of his past loving relationship with his ex-girlfriend, Faith (Juliette Lewis), who, in the diegetic present, is now partnered with music producer Philo Gant.

The film's convoluted plot includes racial tensions as Black rap singer and political icon Jeriko One (Glenn Plummer), one of Gant's artists, is killed by two white LAPD officers, an echo to the 1992 Rodney King beating and to its video (Hultkrans, 2013: 100). Iris, a prostitute and Faith's former friend (Brigitte Biko), records the murder through the SQUID technology and gives the tape to Lenny before she is brutally raped and killed. Her rape and murder are seen through a POV shot as Iris's murderer is wearing the wiring technology when committing the crimes, an echo to Michael Powell's 1960 *Peeping Tom* (Shapiro, 2003: 170). The fact that the film's crimes occur through the SQUID technology shows how Bigelow examines the spectatorship of racial and sexual violence. As the filmmaker put it herself in 1995, 'the film is about watching, the consequences of watching, the political consequences of experiencing someone else's life vicariously' (Horeck, 2004: 106). The film also interrogates the male gaze as Lenny reveals very early in the film that men are the device's main customer base. This chapter discusses the different ways in which Bigelow's *Strange Days* examines male gazes over female bodies, whether Black or white, and attempts at building those bodies as sites of resistance to their construction as visual objects. As pointed out by Deborah Jermyn and Sean Redmond, 'the rape sequence where Lenny, and by extension the cinematic spectator, experiences the attack from the position of both female victim and male rapist ... led to horrified condemnations of [Bigelow's] voyeurism' (Jermyn and Redmond, 2003: 10; Horeck, 2004: 107). This voyeuristic construction is associated to a white female victimization that depicts the white female character as a 'hysterical figure who needs to be rescued or protected [and is] either raped or killed, or both, in order to provide a motivation for the hero's revenge' (Tasker, 1993: 16). However, as I shall demonstrate in the first part of this chapter, rather than endorsing it, Bigelow actually interrogates this voyeurism by emphasizing the artificiality and fragility of the cinematic white male gaze.[1]

The criticisms leveled against Bigelow's construction of womanhood in *Strange Days* also tend to elude the role and function of Lornette Mason (played by Angela Bassett), known as 'Mace', the film's Black female character. Mace is Lenny's long-time friend and supports him in his quest to solve Iris's murder and to protect Faith. As Lenny mentions it, Mace is 'a security specialist trained in defensive combat'. The slender bodies of the two victimized white female characters, graciously moving in front of the camera, contrast with the muscular gestures deployed by Mace. Although Mace's body is at first glance estranged from the filmmaker's deconstruction of the white male gaze, the analysis of Lenny's gaze over the Black female body when portrayed with male and female signifiers – 'a tight black dress and a gun holstered in between her upper thighs' (Lane, 2003: 190) – at the end of the film reveals Bigelow's 'ambitious vision of the action-adventure heroine', even more so than in *Blue Steel* (1990) (ibid., 189). According to Christina Lane, Mace 'represents one of Bigelow's toughest "bad-ass" heroines to date, although she is not *Strange Days*' protagonist nor does she receive many of the film's points of view shots' (ibid.). In the second part of this chapter, I will examine Bigelow's visual techniques to '[ground] spectators within an action heroine's subjectivity' (ibid.). This chapter indeed discusses the way Bigelow relies on Laura Mulvey's deconstruction of scopophilia which consists in 'taking other people as objects, subjecting them to a controlling and curious gaze' (Mulvey, 1975: 835), and uses her camera to film white and Black female bodies and build female characters as subjects, independent from the film's male objectifying gazes. The chapter underlines the two different ways in which Bigelow films the white and the Black female subjects.

Beauty, desirability and the white body in *Strange Days*

Strange Days and its final screenplay are based on Cameron's original scriptment (Lane, 2003: 191). Faith's depiction in the film does not differ from Cameron's original scriptment:

> The woman is FAITH JUSTIN, but lately she just goes by FAITH [.] Lenny is desperately in love with her. It's not hard to see why. She is beautiful, in an alive, dynamic way. Her hair is a wild dark mane, and her eyes are spectacular … intense. She moves with a lithe, sinuous grace. She is dressed in shorts and a halter top, showing lots of her ivory skin.

In the scriptment, much attention is paid to the character's physical beauty, the nakedness of the female body and its ideal whiteness ('showing lots of her ivory skin'). Later in the document, Cameron further elaborates on Faith's exposed beauty and whiteness, similarly referring to her 'creamy skin' or to her 'milk-white skin'. The character's description echoes the traditional construction of white womanhood and nudity in Western art. Amelia Jones writes that 'in the history of Western art and the most prominent part of aesthetic judgment, the naked white female body has long been staged as the most consistent ... trope of aesthetic beauty' (2012: 65). Bigelow's visual construction of Cameron's scripted description of Faith similarly articulates the nudity of her white body and its aesthetic beauty. Faith first visually intervenes in a playback sequence, one of the film's few sequences shot in daylight and its second POV sequence. Sitting in his dark bedroom, Lenny is 'wire-tripping' on his past relationship with Faith. The female character appears rollerblading on the Venice boardwalk. The audiences discover Faith, through a first-person shot sequence, dressed in a pair of black panties and a halter-top, thus 'showing lots of ivory skin'. The POV shot allows the audience to discover the progressive exposure and display, front and back, of the white female character's semi-naked, and then naked, body. The alternation of shots between Lenny's dark bedroom and the lighting and setting of the playback images visibly intensifies the progressive exposition of the white female body. Both Cameron and Bigelow orchestrate the construction of the Faith character as a visual object.

However, Bigelow adds visual elements that illustrate the fact that the character's appearance in the narrative is not a mere visual reproduction of Cameron's description. In the original scriptment,

> [Lenny] fishes around in a shoebox among a bunch of tapes, squinting at the hand-written dates and descriptions. We can't read much of his scrawl, but what all the tapes in the box seem to have in common is the word FAITH, printed on them clearly.

Bigelow adds a close-up of the tape Lenny chooses, on which eyes are sketched, building a visual invitation to the audience to watch the spectacle that Lenny is about to indulge in. Bigelow here underlines the complicit role of cinematic audiences in the visual objectification of the white female body. Through editing, Bigelow reproduces the back-and-forth movement of the scriptment from the lighter images of the playback clip and those of Lenny's dark room, where his reaction to the clip 'emotionalizes the piece' for the film's viewers, as it would later on with Iris's rape and murder (Horeck, 2004: 108). The screen composition of some of the shots in the dimly lit room brings together the white male character and his reflection in a mirror, further inviting the audiences to share his pleasure at watching the white female body.

The shift from the boardwalk to Faith's apartment, from a public to a private space does not interrupt the camera's visual obsession with the white female body. Reproducing Lenny's obsession with that body, the camera movements of the playback clip follow the white female body's movements wherever it goes and whatever it does: rollerblading, drinking cold water or being penetrated. Throughout the entire scene, the camera follows Lenny's fastened gaze over Faith's body, displaying it in part or as a whole, as the character rollerblades on the boardwalk or strips in front of the camera in the apartment. The camera movements, originating from Faith's performance in front of the camera, suggest a striptease which *Strange Days*'s audiences are invited to watch. The camera becomes static when Lenny grabs Faith and both characters find themselves in front of the apartment's looking glass. The screen composition frames the two characters solely within the mirror in front of which they stand, turning the upcoming lovemaking scene into a spectacle and Faith as its object. Faith's actional invitation to Lenny ('You want to watch or you gonna do') – not part of Cameron's original scriptment – bears a twofold meaning as the POV sequence and the SQUID technology allow Lenny to do *and* watch, and the film's audiences to watch as if they were doing. Lenny's answer ('Watch and see') articulates what is being seen on screen – Faith's available body – and its characterization as a spectacle. In the scene introducing Faith, Bigelow recreates Mulvey's analysis of the construction of the cinematic male gaze whereby the white female body is built as a spectacle made by and for male visual pleasure. In this playback clip, Faith's white body is thus made the passive object of individual (Lenny's) and collective gazes (the audiences'). While the opening playback clip picturing a shop robbery through a first-person POV illustrated the active position of male users in the SQUID technology, Faith's introducing playback clip visually constructs female passivity under a cinematic white male gaze.

According to Susanne Wegener, the scene lighting participates in the construction of the 'gleaming whiteness of Faith's beautiful, seductively moving body' (2014: 107). The clip's light would thus suggest that Bigelow also articulates whiteness, the naked body and aesthetic beauty. However, as Wegener adds, the clip's lighting and its setting emphasize the 'staged artificiality of Faith's behavior', supported by her 'encouraging pep-talk', commenting on Lenny's grotesque attempt at roller skating ('You're doing good Sweety'). According to Wegener, the first clip with Faith is 'the production of a simulacrum of erotic love, a celebration of scopophilic fetishization' (ibid., 108). Framed into a voyeuristic introduction, Faith's white femininity and nudity are performative as theorized by Judith Butler. Her gender identity is literally built through 'the constituted effect of repeated poses, gestures, behaviors, positioning and articulations' (Barton, 2002: 312). The filmmaker thus recreates the white female body, its nakedness and beauty as a visual fabrication born out of the artificiality of the coded cinematic male gaze.

The film challenges the reliability of this early construction of the white male gaze at the end of the film, when Lenny watches a tape through the SQUID device and is convinced of watching Faith being raped when in fact she is not. In the tape, Faith similarly looks at the camera and, while being penetrated by Lenny's best friend, says, 'I love you Max,' which echoes her line in the original playback clip: 'I love your eyes Lenny. I love the way they see.' In the first playback clip, Faith's use of 'see' participates in the construction of the white female body as an object of white male pleasure. However, the repetition of Faith's line at the end of the film ('I love you Max') challenges Lenny's nostalgic memories of his past relationship with Faith and reinforces the unreliability of the early voyeuristic cinematic gaze.

The contrast between Lenny's dark room in the diegetic present and the broad daylight of the playback clip also underlines that the scene belongs to Lenny's past. This is reinforced by the fact that in the film's diegetic present, having access to Faith and to her body requires much more effort from Lenny than simply sitting on his bed and watching a clip. Indeed, Faith has become a lead singer for music producer Philo Gant. To touch Faith's body, Lenny can no longer orchestrate his visual pleasure in the confinement of his bedroom. He now has to watch Faith's performance on stage at a distance and to share Faith's body with the rest of her intra-diegetic audiences, as illustrated by the larger shots of Faith on the stage of the club in which she performs a song.

Although in the original scriptment Faith calls Lenny after he was thrown out of the club where she had performed, in the film's final version, Lenny creeps in through the window of the same nightclub and follows her backstage. In a room filled with other characters, Faith moves back and forth between two looking glasses hanging on opposite sides of the room, the camera following her movements just like in the original playback clip. The scene thus repeats the same gestures, facial expressions and movements of the female character's body: the character is indeed refreshing with water and moisturizing her body parts. However, Bigelow insists here on the fabrication of the white female body as an object of male obsession through the collision of cameras. The subjective camera which follows Lenny's gaze over Faith's body depicts parts of it erotically, such as the close-up of her legs or of her eroticized smile. The objective camera, however, portrays the same gestures and body positions independently from the white male character's visual pleasure (Figure 4.1). While Lenny is absent from the scene's subjective shots, he – along with other intra-diegetic characters – is brought into the objective ones. Yet, in the objective shots, the angles chosen by the filmmaker make it impossible to articulate the gaze of the white male character with the visual sight of Faith's body at the same time. When it does occur and the camera reproduces the same situation as in the opening playback clip, whereby Lenny stands behind Faith in front of the looking glass, the male character is suddenly

Figure 4.1 Countering the intra-diegetic and extra-diegetic male gazes in *Strange Days* directed by Kathryn Bigelow © Lightstorm Entertainment 1995.

embarrassed over Faith's public, yet unnoticed, nakedness, leading him to progressively leave the shot, though the conversation between the two characters goes on. Faith is left alone, moisturizing her naked bust, unnoticed by the characters that are framed in the looking glass. The mirror in the original playback clip was given a symbolic dimension, that of framing the spectacle of white naked beauty. In the club's backstage scene, the mirror loses that symbolic dimension. Her white nakedness is no longer staged as a performance for the male gaze. Bigelow engages here in a dichotomy between Faith's nudity in the original playback clip and her nakedness in the backstage room. In 1956, in *The Naked and the Nude*, Kenneth Clark claimed that

> the word [nude] was forced into our vocabulary by critics of the early eighteenth century. … To be naked is to be deprived of our clothes, and the word implies some of the embarrassment most of us feel in that condition. The word 'nude', on the other hand, carries, in educated usage, no uncomfortable overtone. (2002: 121)

In *Ways of Seeing*, John Berger further elaborated on Clark's distinction pointing at the objectification behind the construction of nudity: 'To be naked is to be oneself. To be nude is to be seen naked by others and yet not recognised for oneself. A naked body has to be seen as an object in order to become a nude' (Berger, 2015: 296). Thus, while in the original playback clip Lenny's and the audiences' objectifying gazes build Faith's nudity, in the backstage room scene, her body is turned naked. Very interestingly, when Faith yells to Lenny that 'it's over', the screen composition articulates the female character – on the right – and the reflection of her back in the mirror behind her – on the left – putting an end to the passive female object/male active subject dichotomy and reinforcing the character's nakedness in opposition to its formerly built nudity.

The comparison between the two scenes points at how, in spite of the impression of voyeurism, the filmmaker indeed draws on the male cinematic gaze, its identification with the audiences' and its construction of the eroticized white female nude body, but then upsets it, by pointing at its artificiality and fragility. Bigelow frames the white female body within visual techniques that reveal the female character as subject rather than object. Her treatment of the film's action heroine, Mace, employs challenging visual techniques similar to those showing how Faith's body has escaped from Lenny's controlling gaze. If Bigelow uses Faith's character so as to bring the demise of the white male gaze and the construction of white aesthetic female beauty, she uses Mace's to interrogate the phallic symbolism and erotic spectacle of action heroines.

The action heroine and the Black female body in *Strange Days*

It is noteworthy that *Strange Days* is one of the few action movies of the 1990s to portray a Black action heroine (Sims, 2006: 179). In the character's description, Cameron's original scriptment makes a single reference to the character's skin colour ('a black woman') and diverts her Blackness onto the character's strength and attire, her clothes and the car she drives.

> CUT TO a hand pulling a little digital cellular out of a black jacket. Follow the hand and phone to the face of a black woman. LORNETTE

> 'MACE' MASON. Late twenties. Striking features. Hair pulled back tight to her skull. She is driving, but we don't see the car, or anything but her face and some moving lights outside. ... OUTSIDE A BLACK LIMO pulls into the lot. It is a Continental armored stretch, downsized from today's standards. The door opens and Mace gets out. She is compactly built, dressed in black slacks and a conservative black jacket. Heavy rubber-soled shoes, like cop shoes. She glances around as she heads for the Coral Lounge entrance, the unconscious sweeping gaze of a security professional.

The comparison between Faith's and Mace's descriptions in the scriptment illustrates the passive construction of the white female character contrary to the action-oriented portrayal of Mace. The descriptions and their emphasis on attire distinguish the exposition of Faith's skin and Mace's covered body. Faith's 'lithe, sinuous grace' contrasts with the description of Mace, framed within details of her car and her outfit as a security driver.

Mace is estranged from *Strange Days*'s discourse on beauty, gaze or the naked body. The distinction drawn between Faith's 'ivory skin' and Mace's Black womanhood reveals the dichotomy between the 'reality' that Mace is supposed to represent, on the one hand, and the fantasy that Faith is to embody, on the other (Tasker, 1998: 88). Throughout the film, contrary to Faith whose skin is constantly revealed, Mace's masculine attire indeed includes a tuxedo, a leather jacket, pants and heavy boots that all underline her 'compactly built' body. Mace's body illustrates Yvonne Tasker's concept of 'musculinity' (ibid., 3), whereby 'a developed musculature [and signifiers of strength are] not limited to the male body within representation' (ibid., 149). Although depicted as an action heroine, the 'muscular' woman '[is] still marked as [a woman]' (ibid.). However, in the scriptment, Mace is only characterized as 'a black woman', contrary to Faith's characterization, in which her beauty is built on traditional assumptions of femininity. African American feminist and film theorist Mia Mask questions *Strange Days*'s construction of the beauty and desirability of the Black female character:

> Precisely because Mace is in love with Lenny, the continual fixation on white womanhood and negation of black womanhood underscores the desirability of white femininity and implies the unrecognizability of black womanhood as desirable. It is not only a question of seeing Bassett objectified. It is a matter of not seeing her beauty acknowledged within the narrative. (2012: 184)

According to Mask, the film's obsession with the white heterosexual male gaze for the white female body reproduces (ibid.) and re-enacts a 'phallocentric spectatorship where the woman to be looked at and desired is "white"', as bell hooks put it in her essay 'The Oppositional Gaze' (1992: 119). Using Manthia Diawara's conceptualization of 'resisting spectatorship', Mask thus rephrases hooks's analysis as follows:

> Even if they find Lewis attractive, most African American spectators cannot help but notice and resist the racial and gendered hierarchy of *Strange Days* and the way this film positions Bassett's Mace as the abject object, while privileging Lewis as the desired object of the male gaze. (2012: 183)

By framing the film's abjection and desirability of the female characters according to the white male leading protagonist, Mask's analysis validates the white male gaze. However, Mace's narrative femininity and desirability are indeed problematic when confronted with Faith's. Lane argues that the characterization of Mace as a hard-bodied woman is the result of the film's two 'problematic moments of female victimization' (2003: 190), the real rape and murder of Iris and the fake sexual assault on Faith. Lane adds, 'To have featured a less developed, less tough character in Mace alongside the troubling rape sequences would have been to disengage feminism alongside entirely' (ibid.). Thus, as Lane puts it, Mace's hard-bodied characterization aims at compensating for the victimization of the film's white female characters. Mace's characterization as a supporting character is determined according to the film's discourses on white femininity, Faith and Iris, and white masculinity. Throughout the film, in spite of the 'male/female variant' in the biracial buddy formula (Tasker, 1998: 85), Mace's physical abilities also counterbalance Lenny's physical weakness and vulnerability. Until Lenny and Mace split at the New Year's Eve party at the Bonaventure Hotel, Lenny is recurrently beaten up and Mace comes to his rescue, just as he tries to rescue Faith, which supports Mask's analysis of the film's 'racial and gendered hierarchy'.

However, the script did not mean to focus on the character's Blackness (Brady, 1995: 33). In Cameron's original scriptment, Mace's physical counterpart, Cindy 'Vita' Minh, one of Gant's bodyguards, is a member of a Vietnamese street gang. In the scriptment, she is described as 'slit-eyed' and 'stone fox, very tough'. In the film's final version, the name 'Vita' was given to another character imagined by Cameron, Constance, 'a massively built bodybuilder, who contrasts her hulking frame with a low-cut dress and pearls. Like a woman imitating a drag-queen, but definitely female … and somehow sexy and terrifying at the same time.' Bigelow's elimination of the original Asian female character de-racializes the film's tough action heroines and allows the filmmaker to concentrate the film's discourse on gender. Vita's physical attire includes garter belts over naked legs and corsets or tops that purposefully reveal the muscled arms of the Canadian dancer Louise Lecavalier, pointing at her musculinity. Bigelow interestingly chose to introduce Mace's visual femininity outside the white male gaze and influence, but rather through her function as an action heroine.

Mace's characterization is similar to Rikke Schubart's description of the contemporary action heroine: 'The female hero's body becomes a paradoxical object: female, yet not a sexual spectacle, fit for fight, yet not aggressive' (2007: 159). Although bearing a gun, throughout most of her action sequences Mace does not shoot at characters but threatens them to protect herself or Lenny. The only time she fires a shot is to open the trunk of the car she had driven into the river to escape the two police officers that had killed Jeriko One. Mace's gun is therefore not used aggressively but as a defensive mechanism. In spite of this, the gun is a central element of Mace's attire, particularly in her confrontation with Vita.

If the action heroine's hard body is not a sexual spectacle, as Schubart put it, its eroticization or erotic attractiveness had become quite common at the end of the 1990s (Smelik, 2007: 179). Vita's exposed skin may suggest that 'the narrative is ... twisted to legitimise' the action heroine's hard body, eroticizing it by 'showing as much skin as possible' (Schubart, 2007: 159). But such exposition of Vita's skin is offset by Mace's covered body. As Mask rightfully noticed, Bigelow uses high-angle shots in the rape and lovemaking scenes involving the two white female characters, Iris and Faith (2012: 184). But when depicting the combat scene between Vita and Mace, the filmmaker uses eye-level angles. Through the clothing and the shooting of the combat scenes of the film's two hard-bodied female characters, Bigelow mixes different gender signifiers. Most particularly, in the shot in which Vita – in the back of the shot – is running to attack Mace from the back, the latter stands in front of the camera, holding the gun in front of her chest, pointing at its defensive symbolism. The shot interestingly mixes traditionally identified masculine signifiers (Mace's suit and the phallic symbol of the gun) with feminine and sexualized ones (Vita's black garter and corset) which are deployed over the bodies of the two female characters. Thus, Bigelow uses the bodies of the film's action heroines so as to blur action films' traditional reading of masculine 'phallic weaponry' and 'hypermasculine physicality'.[2]

Later in the film, the filmmaker further develops such blurring through a skilful use of editing techniques. During the New Year's Eve party, Mace's attire changes from the leather outfit to a short tight black dress. Both in Cameron's original scriptment and in the film's final version, Lenny casts an objectifying gaze over Mace's 'feminised' body, or, as Tasker puts it, Lenny 'sees' Mace's body as feminine (Tasker, 1998: 83). That gaze is associated in both documents with Mace sliding her gun into the holster strapped to her thigh. In the written text, Mace puts the gun before Lenny realizes that she 'is a girl' and before he 'is caught by a sudden realisation of her woman-ness' so that the two actions occur separately:

> Mace is wearing a short black cocktail dress, very sheer. It's cut low at the top and high at the bottom, showing plenty of her muscular legs. The high heels are doing good things for her calves. Mace's braided

> hair is loose and full, around her shoulders, like the mane of a lion. She is even wearing lipstick and eye-makeup. She looks hot. Mace unselfconsciously hikes up the dress and adjusts the Velcro on the elastic-holster strapped to her right thigh. She is all business as she slips her 380 auto into the holster and pulls the dress down. You can't see the gun, hidden between her upper thighs, just above the hemline. In fact, it looks like she couldn't be concealing a quarter anywhere on her body. Lenny glances at Mace and does a double take. She is a girl.

The script is written so that it is Lenny's gaze that identifies her as a girl. In other words, the white male gaze determines femininity and its desirability, as Mask put it. However, in the film's final version, Bigelow alters the chronology of the scriptment's actions and brings together Mace's gesture and Lenny's realization. Unable to drive forward through the crowd, Mace and Lenny decide to walk to the Bonaventure Hotel. The camera follows Lenny as he steps out of the car. As he starts to 'see' Mace's femininity and the camera shows how his gaze is moving along Mace's body, the camera cuts from a shot of Lenny gazing to a close-up shot of what he is gazing at, Mace's bottom. The cut logically reproduces the camera angles of the male-coded cinematic gaze. The camera indeed turns to Lenny as he calls Mace and says, 'Hey, Mace, you look sexy in that dress.' However, in the short-reverse-shot structure of the scene, the camera cuts back to Mace as she turns to look at Lenny and *simultaneously* straps the gun in the holster on her inner thigh. The visual access to Mace's crotch, shot in a high-angle close-up, is barred by her two hands that put the gun in the holster, making it impossible for the Black female body to continue being gazed at and thus defeating the eroticization of her body [Figure 4.2]. It is not possible to see Mace's crotch the way Iris's and Faith's had been openly viewed and objectified earlier in the film. In the close-ups of Mace's crotch, the gun has come to fill that feminine space that was marked as empty for Faith and Iris. The gun and its protective symbolism act as visual block to Lenny's gaze building Mace's desirable femininity. In other words, Bigelow's construction of feminine 'phallic weaponry' is more 'functional' (Brown, 2011: 25) than erotic.

Figure 4.2 Blocking Mace's objectification by the male gaze in *Strange Days* directed by Kathryn Bigelow © Lightstorm Entertainment 1995.

The shift in the chronology from script to film also separates the actions as they unfold for the two characters in the rest of the film. Indeed, so far, Lenny had been the centre and subject of the film's narrative and action. When Mace and Lenny part during the New Year Eve's party, each character handles the separate actions of the film's plot: Lenny runs to Faith's rescue and Mace, who had been able to deliver the tape of Jeriko One's murder to the Deputy Police Commissioner, makes her way through the crowd to run away from the two guilty white police officers. Mace's physical strength is also no longer only displayed to protect the film's white male character in his quest to save the main white female character. Bigelow uses visual techniques to frame Mace's body as the central weapon of the second plot's action. If Faith and Iris run away from their pursuers, their chase is shot so that their victimization starts from the moment they are under the gaze of their attackers. Bigelow interrupts Mace's chase and victimization when the female character decides to stop running from the two police officers. She pulls the gun out of the holster to confront them. The gesture of Mace pulling the gun out of the holster is again singled out in an inserted close-up shot of Mace's crotch, at eye level. Later in the scene, in her physical confrontation with the police officers, the short tight dress she wears reveals the character's crotch very often. Yet, Bigelow organizes the screen composition of the close-up shots so that the crotch is systematically protected from the two male attackers and from the visual gaze.

It is interesting, then, that it is once she has handcuffed the two murderers and dropped the gun as summoned by the police to do so that Mace is beaten up, which reinforces the protective symbolism of the gun. The film then starts its 'revisionist' (Hobson, 2012: 105) rewriting of the Rodney King beating which puts an end to the film's discourse on women and their bodies as subjects rather than objects. As the plots develops, the murder of Jeriko One loses its political and racial dimension as it is no longer tied to a structural form of racism within the LAPD but the sole and isolated act of the two white police officers. The film moves from a discourse on systemic racism to individual corruption. In the final re-dramatization of the Rodney King beating through Mace's character, the film portrays an interracial and multicultural crowd that rises up against police brutality, thereby removing the racial discourse of the real-life beating. Most importantly, shots combining the brutalized Mace on one side of the screen and the rioting crowd on the other isolate a lit-up prostrated Black female body from a crowd essentially composed of men. Having visually defeated the power of the white male gaze and its objectification of the white female body, and celebrated her (Black) action heroine, Bigelow eventually sacrifices her powerfully strong phallic female character at the end of the film.

The film's conclusion provides a more conservative reading of gender. As Barry Keith Grant puts it,

> strangely – or perhaps not strangely, since this is, after all, a Hollywood movie – *Strange Days* builds to a climax that denies what has come previously, that seems to recuperate its own ideological critique. … Finally, the honest white male commissioner, brandishing the evidence in his raised hand, parts the suddenly compliant crowd like the archetypal patriarch … and calls for the arrest of the two rogue cops. Power, ultimately, is retained in the (literal) hands of the white male, who now supersedes the once-capable and independent woman. (2011: 189)

Janell Hobson also argues that Bigelow unravels the cinematic discourse on gender that was developed in the film through the depiction of its different female characters (2012: 105). Lenny's sudden and narratively unprepared desire for Mace almost one minute before the film's ending title credit leads the Black action heroine to shift from the protection of the white Deputy Police Commissioner to Lenny's and thus to be 'rescued [and] protected' (Tasker, 1993: 16) by the white men she was formerly confronting or protecting. Although the white female character has left the narrative, the shift from the chaos of the riots to the street celebration of the New Year and the social order on which the film concludes also rehabilitate the racial and gender hierarchy that it has challenged through its visual construction of subjective white and Black female characters' bodies. The film concludes conventionally on the couple's final kiss. In Tasker's words, 'if Mace represents "reality" ... against Faith as illusion (as image), the use of fantasy/cliché images of romance to suggest [Mace and Lenny's] new relationship seems ironic. Their partnership-cum-romance, then, both covers over and reveals the fault lines in the narrative' (1998: 88).

Conclusion

In their introduction to the collection of essays on Kathryn Bigelow's films, Jermyn and Redmond and the collection's authors

> locate Bigelow as a film-making artist who is able to transcend the collective, industrial and commercial constraints of Hollywood cinema machine to *individually author* her films in innovative and transgressive ways [pushing] cinematic boundaries [notably in] the representation of gender. All Bigelow's films are marked by a play with genre, and by ideological practices that question and undermine the formation of masculine and feminine identity. (2003: 2)

As I demonstrated in this chapter, up to *Strange Days*'s final beating, Bigelow's visual techniques indeed challenge traditional cinematic constructions of femininity and the visual representations of female bodies. By moving away from the film's original script and its vision of white and Black femininity, Bigelow indeed astutely uses Mulvey's gaze theory to challenge the objectifying power of the male gaze, mainly by pointing at how its mechanisms can easily be defeated through film aesthetics and plot twists. Although Mulvey's landmark article has rightfully been challenged since 1975, Bigelow's *Strange Days* uses Mulvey's statement that 'the unconscious of patriarchal society has structured film form' and that 'the unconscious (formed by the dominant order) [had structured] ways of seeing and pleasure in looking' (1975: 383–4). Framing white and Black female bodies in front of her camera, Bigelow therefore plays with the film's male characters' and the audiences' 'voyeuristic fantasy' (Mulvey, 1975: 836), turning female characters from objects into subjects and the female body's objectification into the female character's subjectivity. Bearing in mind that Mulvey's gaze theory dealt with classical Hollywood films, the fact that Bigelow applies Mulvey's political tool to a contemporary action film shows how she considers that Hollywood still structures its films to satisfy the voyeuristic male gaze.

It is interesting that, through the filming of Faith's and Mace's bodies, Bigelow treats the white and Black female bodies differently when building their claims to be subjects. Through Faith, Bigelow deconstructs the historically built fragile white femininity, bringing back the character at the end of the film to show that she controls her body to serve her malevolent interests; through Mace, Bigelow engages with discourses on the action heroine, whose violence is meant to protect the body. Bigelow dissociates the moments when Mace rejects Lenny's male objectifying and sexualising gaze (Mace as woman), and when she is powerless as a Black person facing police brutality (Mace as Black). This might reveal the limits of the 'innovative and transgressive ways' Bigelow pushes the 'cinematic boundaries' in 'the representation of gender'. Bigelow uses the Black female character to build her cinematic discourse on action heroines, not on a Black action heroine, pointing at the limit of her feminist discourse on intersectionality.

Notes

1 For an analysis of Iris's rape and murder, see Horeck and her examination of Bigelow's 'interrogation of the violence and sexual voyeurism of cinema' (2004: 108).

2 See Robinson (2014: 153–71).

Works cited

Barton, Sabrina (2002), 'Your self storage: Female investigation and male performativity in the woman's psychothriller', in Graeme Turner (ed.), *The Film Cultures Reader*, 311–30, Oxon: Routledge.

Berger, John (2015), 'Chapter 3 of *Ways of Seeing* [1972]', in Hilary Robinson (ed.), *Feminist-Art-History: An Anthology, 1968–2014*, 293–9, Malden, MA: John Wiley and Sons.

Brady, James (1995), 'In step with Angela Bassett', *The Item*, 24 September: 33.

Brown, Jeffrey (2011), *Dangerous Curves: Action Heroines, Gender, Fetishism and Popular Culture*, Jackson: University Press of Mississippi.

Clark, Kenneth (2002), 'The naked and the nude [1956]', in John McEnroe and Deborah Frances Pokinski (eds), *Critical Perspectives on Art History*, 121–6, Upper Saddle River, NJ: Prentice Hall.

Grant, Barry Keith (2011), *Shadows of Doubt: Negotiations of Masculinity in American Genre Films*, Detroit: Wayne State University Press.

Hobson, Janell (2012), *Body as Evidence: Mediating Race, Globalizing Gender*, Albany: State University of New York Press.

hooks, bell (1992), 'The oppositional gaze', in *Black Looks: Race and Representation*, 115–31, Boston: South End Press.

Horeck, Tanya (2004), *Public Rape: Representing Violation in Fiction and Film*, London: Routledge.

Hultkrans, Andrew (2013), 'Reality bytes', in Peter Keough (ed.), *Kathryn Bigelow Interviews*, 95–102, Jackson: University Press of Mississippi.

Jermyn, Deborah, and Sean Redmond (2003), 'Introduction. *Hollywood Transgressor: The Cinema of Kathryn Bigelow*', in Deborah Jermyn and Sean Redmond (eds), *The Cinema of Kathryn Bigelow: Hollywood Transgressor*, 1–19, London: Wallflower Press.

Jones, Amelia (2012), *Seeing Differently: A History and Theory of Identification and the Visual Arts*, London: Routledge.

Lane, Christina (2003), 'The strange days of Kathryn Bigelow and James Cameron', in Deborah Jermyn and Sean Redmond (eds), *The Cinema of Kathryn Bigelow: Hollywood Transgressor*, 178–97, London: Wallflower Press.

Mask, Mia (2012), 'Angela Bassett and Halle Berry: African American leading ladies', in Anna Everett (ed.), *Pretty People: Movie Stars of the 1990s*, 166–88, New Brunswick, NJ: Rutgers University Press.

Mulvey, Laura ([1975] 1999), 'Visual pleasure and narrative cinema', in Leo Braudy and Marshall Cohen (eds), *Film Theory and Criticism: Introductory Readings*, 833–44, New York: Oxford University Press.

Robinson, Janet S. (2014), 'The gendered geometry of war in Kathryn Bigelow's *The Hurt Locker* (2008)', in Karen A. Ritzenhoff and Jakub Kazecki (eds), *Heroism and Gender in War Films*, 153–71, New York: Palgrave Macmillan.

Schubart, Rikke (2007), *Super Bitches and Action Babes: The Female Hero in Popular Cinema, 1970–2006*, Jefferson, NC: McFarland.

Shapiro, Steven (2003), 'Straight from the cerebral cortex: Vision and affect in *Strange Days*', in Deborah Jermyn and Sean Redmond (eds), *The Cinema of Kathryn Bigelow: Hollywood Transgressor*, 159–77, London: Wallflower Press.

Sims, Yvonne (2006), *Women of Blaxploitation: How the Black Action Heroine Changed American Popular Culture*, Jefferson, NC: McFarland.

Smelik, Anneke (2007), 'Lara Croft, *Kill Bill*, and the battle for theory in feminist film studies', in Rosemarie Bulkema and Iris van der Tuin (eds), *Doing Gender in Media, Art and Culture*, 178–92, London: Routledge.

Tasker, Yvonne (1993), *Spectacular Bodies: Gender, Race and the Action Cinema*, London: Routledge.

Tasker, Yvonne (1998), *Working Girls: Gender and Sexuality in Popular Cinema*, London: Rutledge.

Wegener, Susanne (2014), *Restless Subjects in Rigid Systems: Risk and Speculation in Millennial Fictions of the North American Pacific Rim*, Bielefeld: Transcript.

5

'She's a whole lotta woman': Pam Grier's star image in *Jackie Brown* (1997)

David Roche

The fact that Quentin Tarantino's third feature film is the only one with a title that is 100 percent eponymous is a clear indication of the central role of the lead character played by Pam Grier. The film is intricately bound to her star image. A star image, Richard Dyer argues, embodies a 'finite multiplicity of meanings and affects' (1998: 3) that originate from various media, including films, posters, interviews, tie-ins and basically everything that audiences perceive of a star's life, so that the stars and the industry can only control these images up to a certain point. In 1997, Grier's star image was still largely based on the 1970s Blaxploitation films she starred in (Dunn, 2008: 107), including *Coffy* (1973), *Foxy Brown* (1974), *Sheba, Baby* (Girdler, 1975) and *Bucktown* (Marks, 1975); *Coffy* and *Foxy Brown*, both written and directed by Jack Hill and produced by AIP, were not only successful when they came out but also have to this day enjoyed cult status. Grier's image was that of a strong, sassy woman or, as Samuel L. Jackson put it, 'almost the ultimate girl. You didn't quite want a girl that was that tough. But you did want a girl that was that tall, that had a big fro. You didn't want a girlfriend that could actually be able to kick your ass.'[1] Her dating basketball player Kareem Abdul-Jabbar, and provocateur comedians Freddie Prinze and Richard Pryor, no doubt, reinforced that image. A brief overview of the parts she played in the 1980s and early 1990s confirms the impression that the Blaxploitation image stuck. With the exception of the drama *On the Edge* (Nilsson, 1986), a box office flop, Grier was mainly employed in secondary roles in action movies like *Tough Enough* (Fleischer, 1983), *The Vindicator* (Lord, 1986) and *The Package* (Davis, 1989),[2] and crime dramas like *Miami Vice* (NBC, 1985–90) and *Crime Story* (NBC, 1986–8). Significantly, though, most of these fictions are centred on a white male character, with the tough Black woman often reduced to acting as a mere foil. In 1996 both Tim Burton and John Carpenter employed her in secondary roles in *Mars Attacks!* and *Escape from L.A.* as a nod to Blaxploitation. Grier's first major part since *On the Edge* was in the Blaxploitation homage *Original Gangstas* (Cohen and Williamson, 1996), but the film was also a box office flop, as were the comedy *Fakin' Da Funk* (Chey, 1997) and the crime film *Strip Search* (Hewitt, 1997).

So Tarantino was by no means the first to tap into Grier's Blaxploitation image: everyone was doing it. The difference between *Jackie Brown* and the other films lies elsewhere: Tarantino not only gave Grier another chance, but he made the film *about* her, or rather, he made it a metafictional study of a star image via Grier's own, something he'd problematized less extensively but to similar effect in *Pulp Fiction* (1994) with John Travolta's own star image and the Jack Rabbit Slim scene (Roche, 2018: 254–5). Grier's cinematic past is directly invoked by citing *Foxy Brown* via the protagonist's last name and the title of the film. Thus recontextualized, the two-syllable first name ending in /iː/, which is the same as in *Rum Punch* (1992), the Elmore Leonard novel Tarantino's film is based on, reinforces the reference to the 1974 film. The usage of a first name introducing agency in place of a nickname that directly evokes the figure of a sexy Black woman the 1974 movie exploited is a declaration of intent: *Jackie Brown* is not merely going to pay homage to Blaxploitation through Grier; it is going to be about the reinvention of her image through the heroine's reinvention of her self. Of course, both the title and the name are also indications of how Tarantino is going to adapt Leonard's novel. Changing the female protagonist's last name (Burke in the novel) to Brown foregrounds the racial change, while keeping the first name indicates that there will also be elements of continuity. The combination of the two thus draws attention to the intersection of race and gender that Grier's persona involves and that Tarantino's film is going to spotlight.

This chapter thus considers *Jackie Brown* as a metafictional work that is about its lead actress's star image and, more generally, about African American women in American cinema and culture. By explicitly referencing one of Grier's most famous roles in the title and inviting us to reconsider *Coffy* and *Foxy Brown* as hypotexts, the film points to the extent to which an African American actress's career was determined by a cultural history of representations, in which racial stereotyping complicates the boundaries of femininity and masculinity. But above all, the film is a celebration of the actress's capacity to negotiate such roles as best she could through a narrative in which the heroine rejects subjection to patriarchy and asserts her agency.

About a third of the way into *Foxy Brown*, the heroine's brother Link's white girlfriend, who has just witnessed Foxy scold Link, trash his apartment and banish him from New York City, asks him, 'Who does she think she is?' Link offers by way of explanation: 'That's my sister, baby. And she's a whole lotta woman' (33:38–36:47). This sentence, which comes as a punch line of sorts at the end of the scene, is more ambiguous than first seems. Foxy is undeniably portrayed as a very 'feminine' woman: she wears a colourful shirt displaying her belly button, a matching turban and tight-fitting jeans, and she clearly represents a mother figure to her childish brother cowering in the corner, invoking their mother's name as the reason why she doesn't kill him for causing the death of her lover. In this respect, Foxy conflates characteristics associated with two stereotypes of Black femininity common in Hollywood films and American culture: the non-sexualized 'Mamma' and the sexualized tragic mulatto[3] – pointedly, her name is Brown, not Black. However, her aggressive behaviour and her brother's comment that only a 'big man' could deal with the villains also associate her with 'masculine' characteristics, and her 'masculinity' is further established at the expense of her brother's when she tells him the villains have got 'a stick of dynamite up his ass'. This scene suggests that the hypersexual phallic Black woman[4] of Blaxploitation is, in a sense, the female avatar of the Black Buck, which films like *Slaughter* (Starrett, 1972) and even *Sweet Sweetback's Baadasssss Song* (Van Peebles, 1971) were thought to perpetuate and/or exploit by African American activists of the time.[5] Thus, Grier's characters in the movies *Jackie Brown* refers to – *Foxy Brown*, as we have seen, but also *Coffy* via the music of Roy Ayers, and the women-in-prison films via actor Sid Haig's cameo and the song 'Long-time Woman' from Hill's *The Big Doll House* (Hill, 1971) – conflate features drawn from racialized stereotypes that are both 'feminine' and 'masculine'. This is epitomized in the opening credits of *Foxy Brown* that parody those of the James Bond franchise, with the heroine embodying both the martial-art-expert spy and his three sexy girls and closing the sequence by firing a gun at the audience (0:18–2:40).

In *Jackie Brown*, the characterization of the eponymous heroine is based on a play between similarities and contrasts with the characters Grier is famous for. Like Coffy and Foxy, Jackie is an attractive and intelligent woman but, like Leonard's character, she is middle-aged. Like Coffy and Foxy, Jackie is concerned about her looks[6] and often changes clothes between scenes, but the switch is always motivated by the narrative – tellingly, she relies on the male cops' belief that a woman could actually be enough of a fashion freak to buy a suit in such a critical situation to effect the exchange with Melanie in the fitting room (97:40). Like Coffy and Foxy, Jackie has a love interest (Max Cherry), but he is white and their relationship remains fairly chaste, whereas positive interracial relationships between Black women and white men are conspicuously absent from Blaxploitation films. All in all, Tarantino's movie defuses both the hypersexuality and the action heroine traits associated with Grier's persona. Jackie is never shown nude, and her clothing does not exploit her cleavage – she sports a very ordinary bathrobe when Max visits her in the morning (Figure 5.1, 53:34). Unlike Coffy and Foxy, she doesn't need to resort to sex to get what she wants but relies exclusively on her intelligence and talents of seduction. There are no lengthy fight scenes, and the audience is denied one of the staple scenes of AIP productions: the women's fight scene. On

Figure 5.1 Jackie in her bathrobe in *Jackie Brown* directed by Quentin Tarantino © Miramax Films 1997.

the contrary, Jackie is rather kind towards Ordell's girlfriends: she looks at Sheronda with sympathy and gives Melanie some cash, whispering conspiratorially, 'What the fuck did Ordell ever do for us, huh?' (106:17). This potential interracial sisterhood, like her relationship with Max, could be mere manipulation on Jackie's part, but her expression, never gloating, always benign, suggests otherwise.

The only scenes that recall Grier's action scenes are the two violent confrontations with Ordell Robbie. In the first, the gangster pays her a night-time visit to silence her once and for all, until Jackie's pointing a gun at his private parts leads him to have a sudden change of heart; there follows an exchange in which Jackie dictates her terms to her employer (47:20–53:14). In many ways, this scene recalls the scene between Foxy and her brother from *Foxy Brown*, insofar as Jackie reveals herself to be 'a whole lotta woman'. There is, however, a substantial difference. The fact that Jackie never talks this way throughout the film, either in tone or language (this is the only time she uses the n-word), suggests that she is acting the part of the stereotypical Black male gangster. In so doing, she displays her ability to perform a type of 'Black masculinity' Ordell adheres to and Jackson was already famous for portraying in

Pulp Fiction. Her exaggeratedly contemptuous tone and snarling demeanour draw attention to the artificiality of this masculinity, clashing with the cool confidence Ordell has in it – and which, the film suggests and the novel explicates, is actually a show suggesting an inner weakness.[7] The scene also foregrounds the symmetry that structures both the narrative and their relationship, even more so than in the novel where Jackie Burke's being white makes it an asymmetrical relationship in terms of gender and race.

For on a metafictional level, this scene initially appears as a face-off between the Black female and male protagonists of Blaxploitation. Ordell's get-up recalls the 1970s representation of the pimp[8] – he speaks of his three girlfriends as 'the bitches [he] got set up' (76:18) – more than 1990s gangsta rap fashion. Ordell is even more concerned with his appearance and clothes than Jackie, for, unlike her, his changing clothes is never justified by the narrative; the first shot of him reveals how 'feminine' the male viewer/critic/gun expert actually is: legs crossed, dressed in trendy white shirt and shorts (4:21).[9] Yet the character of Jackie Brown is, in effect, at the intersection of several intertexts that associate her with genre characters that are both male and female. The film cannot be reduced to a mere equation such as femme fatale versus male gangster, or Coffy versus Super Fly. Indeed, *Super Fly* (Parks Jr., 1972) serves as a hypotext to both Ordell's and Jackie's arcs in that order. Like the 1972 drug dealer, Ordell wants to get $1 million to bail out of town, but Jackie is the one who effects a money exchange (in a changing room instead of an elevator) and is filmed driving around in lateral close-up (102:24). The *Super Fly* hypotext thus foregrounds the shift from male to female protagonist and suggests that Jackie's female masculinity holds a mirror up to Ordell's male femininity. The face-off is central in that it reveals the constructedness of a certain 'Black masculinity' which is endowed with a 'feminine' quality it seeks to deny.

The second confrontation promises to be a repetition of the first – with Ordell again entering a dark room and acting all innocent even though he's carrying a gun – only to be immediately shot by Ray Nicolette (Michael Keaton) when Jackie shouts he has a gun. Expectations of

Grier delivering an accusatory tirade like her Blaxploitation heroines have thus been thwarted. Jackie is not a righteous female vigilante out to avenge male characters (brother or friend): she is entirely her own agent out to make a profit for herself. Naming the film after the Black female protagonist – instead of after a cocktail, as is the case of the novel – is a promise that the film is going to be about empowerment and agency.[10]

This is confirmed by the narrative structure. The film can be divided into four acts: (1) Ordell's handling of a business crisis (3:52–27:32); (2) the preliminary stages of Jackie's plan (27:33–84:14); (3) its rehearsal and enactment (84:15–119:43); and (4) the resolution of the conflict opposing Jackie and Ordell (119:44–144:26). The first act mainly follows Ordell whose criminal activities set events in motion: he employs a bail bondsman (Max) to get his employees (Beaumont, then Jackie) out of jail, offs the first and tries to off the second. The confrontation between Jackie and Ordell in her home is the film's turning point, which may explain the impression that the film only gets started once Jackie gets out of jail. Jackie goes from being an employee, and thus another one of the Black patriarch's submissive women (in the novel, Ordell would clearly like to possess her sexually as well), to dictating her terms and becoming his 'agent' or 'manager' (72:36). She goes from being someone whose actions are determined by men, whether it be Ordell for whom she makes deliveries or the law that puts her in jail, to orchestrating the actions of others. In the process, she not only prevents Ordell's plan to murder his employee from repeating itself, but also becomes the director who makes others go through the motions, first in a rehearsal, then for the actual show.

At first glance, focalization seems to be spectatorial, giving viewers a cognitive advantage over the characters[11] and enabling them to witness the shift from Jackie's being just another one of Ordell's subjects to a subjecting agent. If it initially serves to depict Ordell's command of the crisis he is facing, and thus the trap closing in on Jackie, it subsequently shows all the other characters acting as consenting or unknowing cogs in her plot. In some scenes, focalization even verges on external, as the viewer is not in on certain aspects of Jackie's plan. More so even than Tarantino's first movie *Reservoir Dogs* (1992), *Jackie Brown* invites comparisons with Stanley Kubrick's *The Killing* (1956). Tarantino thus reprises Kubrick's multiplication of points of view on the actual heist without the voice-over: we go through the scene first with Jackie (103:25–109:30), then with Louis and Melanie (109:31–114:03), and finally with Max (114:04–119:43). At the end of the first take on the scene, Jackie plays her part so well that a degree of uncertainty remains as to whether her plot went according to plan. The viewer is further alarmed in the second take when Louis notices Max, leading Jackie's accomplice to walk away. It is only in the third take when Max comes out with the money that the viewer is reassured that all went according to plan. So the multiple points of views in *Jackie Brown* serve to show just the opposite of *The Killing*: it relates a heist gone right and the mastermind protagonist retaining control of the narrative if not of the narration. Tension is a purely aesthetic effect created not by Jackie and Max's failure but by our lack of knowledge. Of course, a degree of contingency is introduced by Louis murdering Melanie[12] and Ordell subsequently murdering Louis (125:10). The fourth act then depicts Ordell's struggle to regain control of the narrative and failure to do so. Again, the viewer is not let in on Jackie's plan for her final confrontation with Ordell, as we are led to believe she is alone in Max's office. Although the film invites us to place our 'allegiance' with Jackie and Max, we are, in many ways, 'aligned' with Ordell, to use Murray Smith's terminology.[13]

By the end of the film, Jackie has acquired a greater degree of control over her life, as the contrast between the opening credits and the final shot indicates. The use of the same song invites the viewer to reflect on the distance she has come (149:00). The song 'Across 110th Street', from the 1972 crime film directed by Barry Shear, designates the racial boundary between Harlem and Central Park, and evokes a deterministic world where one of the usual modes of survival for a poor Black woman is prostitution. Initially, the lyrics are not at all in tune with the context presented in *Jackie Brown*: the film is set in Los Angeles, and the Black woman we see is an attractive, confident-looking airline stewardess. As the credits progress, however, Jackie starts walking faster and looking more anxious, suggesting that life, for a lower-middle-class African American woman, is still the daily struggle to 'make ends meet' described in the song, even if it turns out that she is merely late to work. In the light of Western iconography, her moving from right to left further confirms that she is by no means making any progress, a predicament that will be confirmed when one of the detectives, Mark Dargus, untactfully lists the companies she has worked for and concludes that she 'didn't exactly set the world on fire' (30:06). The final frontal close-up of Jackie driving confirms that she has gained some control over her life, while the repetition of the song underlines that Jackie did not have to go the 'feminine' route of prostitution to make it but succeeded in the more 'masculine' (according to the song) path of hustling, a transformation that is parent in her clothing – the stereotypical sex fantasy of the nurse has given way to a 'badass' (as the saleswoman puts it) business woman in a suit (105:11). However, the sad look that creeps over her face introduces a tragic note. For all their obvious differences, both the opening credits and the final shot describe a shift from Jackie having control over her life to her lack of it. The repetition of the song emphasizes that, emotionally at least, Jackie has gone full circle. The end of the film thus abides by the conventions of noir and melodrama by denying the criminal woman who is, in the case of Jackie, denied the love of Max Cherry.

Indeed, in spite of a higher degree of agency, Jackie cannot control *everything*, notably contingency, which the film equates to time and the body. For what the usage of parallel montage during the heist scene also evidences are the little details that do not run like clockwork: Melanie and Louis being late, Louis noticing Max, and finally, the death of Melanie that metonymically stands for the destruction of the female body. In the end, like another figure of the director, Joe Cabot in *Reservoir Dogs*, Jackie does not control her performers 100 per cent, even though she, unlike Cabot, succeeds in her enterprise. We have seen that Jackie is herself a great performer; she confronts the police with poise, reprising the body language of 1940s femme fatales:[14] head held high, elbow cocked and cigarette in the air, lips at times set in a contemptuous snarl (30:07). Yet her motivation for devising this plot, for trying to master time and other people's bodies, lies in her awareness of her lack of control over time. She confesses to Max that she is worried about growing old, not just because her 'ass' is 'bigger', but because she 'always feel[s] like [she's] starting over' (59:03). What the opening credits and final shot both confirm is that, although 'her walk, between strut and swagger, her *look*, exudes an absolute self-assurance and self-possession' (Miklitsch, 2004: 291), Jackie cannot beat time, and that you never know whether you might not be starting over just to start over.

The final close-up is also the moment when the film most clearly establishes the fact that it is about Pam Grier: when Grier steps out of her role to lip-sync 'Across 110th Street', which had been previously identified as non-diegetic music (Figure 5.2).[15] *Jackie Brown* ends on a tragic note for what it says about the actress's career and her star image: not, obviously, that she is not as young and hardbodied as she was in the 1970s – pointedly, the part of her body ('ass') Jackie mentions to Max is one that the exploitation films of the 1970s fetishized – but

Figure 5.2 Last shot of Jackie in *Jackie Brown* directed by Quentin Tarantino © Miramax Films 1997.

that it has taken us all this time to recognize her talent as an actress. By calling on the actress's star image to put the spotlight on everything it has obscured, *Jackie Brown* does with Grier what *Pulp Fiction* does with Travolta: it shows that she is an incredibly talented actress not because of the physical assets that were exploited in the sex and action scenes, but because of her wit; and by drawing attention to her age, it points at all the years during which Grier's talent had been wasted. Her talent has since been recognized, as she was nominated in the category Best Actress both for the Golden Globes and the Screen Actors Guild Award and went on to have a major role in the successful Showtime series *The L-Word* (2004–9). Yet perhaps the greatest disappointment of *Jackie Brown* is that, in spite of Grier's stellar performance, it did not renew her career as much as *Pulp Fiction* renewed Travolta's, which can, no doubt, be put down to the fact that she is a Black woman. The imperfect happing ending even seems to regretfully anticipate this likely outcome: Jackie, unlike Vincent, has successfully carried out what she views as her last performance, significantly effected in a changing room, only to leave the film on a melancholy note in the final close-up, and even Max's sad look after she leaves can be seen as Forster's tearful farewell to his collaboration with the Black actress (148:20). Given the place of women and minorities in Hollywood, which, to this day, is far from being equal to that of white men – in 2015 the highest paid actress, Jennifer Lawrence, was still not making as much money as male superstars, and in 2016 Scarlett Johansson became the first actress to top all salaries independently of gender[16] – the effect, I feel, is far more poignant than in the case of Travolta.

Notes

1 In the documentary *BaadAsssss Cinema*.

2 She also starred in *Stand Alone* (Carlson, 1985), *Nico* (Davis, 1988) and *Class of 1999* (Lester, 1989). Even her small part as Sergeant McLeesh in the teen comedy *The Allnighter* (Hoffs, 1987) emphasizes her image as a phallic woman.

3 Yvonne D. Sims says that 'these macho goddesses answered a multitude of needs and were a hybrid of stereotypes, part Buck, part Mammy, part Mulatto' (2006: 68).

4 Stephane Dunn argues that *Coffy* and *Foxy Brown* perpetuate the racist 'mythology of sexually wild black female slaves' and the figure of the 'jezebel' but exaggerates the fetishizing potential of specific shots in *Foxy Brown* that actually keep Foxy's breasts, for instance, in the shadows (2008: 111–15). Dunn rightly points to 'the connection between black male disempowerment and black female agency' (124) and describes Foxy as a phallic castrator (130).

5 See *BaddAsssss Cinema.*

6 Jackie asks Max to take her to some place dark 'because it looks like [she] just got out of jail' (43:39).

7 Adilifu Nama insists on the film's complex portrayal of Ordell as a 'self-loathing' Black man with a 'pathological adoration of whiteness' (58).

8 Samuel L. Jackson said he wanted his character to look like the 1972 Super Fly and that Tarantino was initially reluctant: http://www.thedailybeast.com/galleries/2013/11/28/ranking-samuel-l-jacksons-craziest-onscreen-hairdos-from-pulp-fiction-to-oldboy-photos.html (accessed 9 May 2017).

9 Ordell is also obsessed with cleanliness, scolding Max on his second visit: 'Uh, uh, uh. I didn't hear you wash your hands' (35:46).

10 Significantly, Tarantino's three eponymous titles (*Jackie Brown*, *Kill Bill* and *Django Unchained*) all involve protagonists striving to free themselves from their social chains.

11 For François Jost, 'spectatorial focalization' occurs when the narration enables the viewers to know more than the characters, 'external focalization' when the viewers are made to know less (Gaudreault and Jost, 1990: 138–41).

12 The murder of Melanie is less expected in the film than in the novel, which devotes more time to the character of Louis, who, along with Jackie, differs most from the source text.

13 For Smith, alignment 'concerns the way a film gives us access to the actions, thoughts, and feelings of characters', and allegiance 'the way a film attempts to marshal our sympathies for or against the characters in the world of the fiction' (1995: 6).

14 Dunn also compares Coffy and Foxy to femmes fatales (2008: 114).
15 K. Silem Mohammad has also noted this effect (2007: 116).
16 See Robehmed (2015 and 2016).

Works cited

BaadAsssss Cinema (2002), [Documentary] Dir. Isaac Julien, Independent Film Channel / Minerva Pictures.

Dunn, Stephane (2008), *'Baad Bitches' & Sassy Supermamas: Black Power Action Films*, Urbana: University of Illinois Press.

Dyer, Richard ([1979] 1998), *Stars*, London: BFI.

Foxy Brown (1974), [Film] Written and directed by Jack Hill. With Pam Grier (Foxy Brown), Antonio Fargas (Link Brown), Peter Brown (Steve Elias) and Karthyn Loder (Katherine Wall), American International Pictures, DVD. MGM / United Artists, 2004.

Gaudreault, André, and François Jost (1990), *Le Récit filmique: Cinéma et récit II*, Paris: Nathan.

Jackie Brown (1997), [Film] Written and directed by Quentin Tarantino, based on Elmore Leonard's novel *Rum Punch*. With Pam Grier (Jackie Brown), Samuel L. Jackson (Ordell Robbie), Robert Forster (Max Cherry), Bridget Fonda (Melanie Ralston), Michael Keaton (Ray Nicolette), Robert De Niro (Louis Gara), Michael Bowen (Mark Dargus) and Chris Tucker (Beaumont Livingston), Miramax / A Band Apart / Lawrence Bender Productions / Mighty Mighty Afrodite Productions, DVD. TF1 Vidéo, 2004.

Miklitsch, Robert (2004), 'Audiophilia: Audiovisual pleasure and narrative cinema in Jackie Brown', *Screen*, 45.4 (Winter): 287–304.

Mohammad, K. Silem (2007), 'I didn't know you liked the Delfonics: Knowledge and pragmatism in *Jackie Brown*', in Richard Greene and K. Silem Mohammad (eds), *Quentin Tarantino and Philosophy*, 111–22, Chicago: Open Court.

Nama, Adilifu (2015), *Race on the QT: Blackness and the Film of Quentin Tarantino*, Austin: University of Texas Press.

Peary, Gerald (2013), *Quentin Tarantino: Interviews*, Jackson: University Press of Mississippi.

Robehmed, Natalie (2015), 'The world's highest-paid actresses 2015: Lawrence leads with $52 million', *Forbes.com*, 20 August. Available online: https://www.forbes.com/sites/natalierobehmed/2015/08/20/the-worlds-highest-paid-actresses-2015-jennifer-lawrence-leads-with-52-million/#4063d8d64c0a (accessed 17 May 2017).

Robehmed, Natalie (2016), 'Scarlett Johansson is the top-grossing actor of 2016', *Forbes.com*, 7 December. Available online: https://www.forbes.com/sites/natalierobehmed/2016/12/27/scarlett-johansson-is-the-top-grossing-actor-of-2016/#db687ed14330 (accessed 17 May 2017).

Roche, David (2018), *Quentin Tarantino: Poetics and Politics of Cinematic Metafiction*, Jackson: University Press of Mississippi.

Sims, Yvonne D. (2006), *Women of Blaxploitation: How the Black Action Film Heroine Changed American Popular Culture*, Jefferson, NC: McFarland.

Smith, Murray (1995), *Engaging Characters: Fiction, Emotion, and the Cinema*, Oxford: Oxford University Press.

6

Women on the border: A cosmopolitan approach to the representation of contemporary femininity in *It's a Free World*... (2007)

Celestino Deleyto

It is a paradox of early-twenty-first-century experience that while both feminist and cosmopolitan sensibilities are on the rise, the cosmopolitan subject continues to be imagined, overwhelmingly, as a male subject. Cosmopolitan theory remains, for the most part, blind to the gender dynamics of globalization. Borders, as will be argued below, are the central site of the cosmopolitan experience and are crossed by millions of men and women every day. Yet the border crosser, with significant exceptions at the lower end of the social scale, tends to be, in cultural representations, a male crosser. In a brief account of the gender hierarchies of the cosmopolitan, Gillian Youngs argues that cosmopolitanism may be seen as part of a gendered power dynamics that continues to identify man/woman as subject/object. For instance, both a global business magnate and a trafficked sex worker may experience global mobility, but the constraints are much greater for those crossing borders as objects (the female sex worker) than as subjects (the male magnate). The complex ways in which their respective agencies are expressed must – but generally do not – take into account their gender identity (Youngs, 2009: 147).

Following their greater centrality in contemporary experience, borders have continued to proliferate in filmic narratives, while becoming more central and complex in cinematic production and distribution practices. Whether we describe the process as a genre, a cycle, a trend or a thematic cluster, geopolitical borders, urban borders and borderlands have become a major concern in twenty-first-century cinema, from early films like *The Terminal* (Spielberg, 2004), *The Three Burials of Melquiades Estrada* (Jones, 2005) and *Babel* (Iñárritu, 2006) to more recent ones like *Prendre le large* (Noel, 2017), *Gräns/Border* (Abbasi, 2018) and *The Farewell* (Wang, 2019). Like these, many movies in the last two decades construct their plots around borders, border crossers and people affected by the border in various ways.

Some of these and other recent border films may be gender-blind, but many others tell stories with female protagonists or co-protagonists and often reflect the problems of representation that underscore women's position in a global world. All of these call for an understanding of the gendered realities of both the real experience and cultural representations of global processes as they impact on people. Their analysis requires cosmopolitan perspectives and border theory that are alert to gender politics. In this chapter, I offer a cosmopolitan reading of *It's a Free World…* (Loach, 2007), a film that attempts to tackle the complications arising when the protagonist of the story is a woman (and a single mother). This is a film that deals directly with the consequences of globalization, notably the spread of a neoliberal logic in labour relations, and the position of women in this scenario. After offering a brief account of the potential of cosmopolitan theory for contemporary film analysis, and arguing for the centrality of border consciousness and the border as both a material reality and a cultural trope, I frame the movie within Loach's oeuvre and its depiction of gender relationships and transnational issues. Finally, I use these frameworks to tease out the meanings constructed around the film's protagonist, Angie (Kierston Wareing), as a border woman.

Cosmopolitanism and its discontents

Writing about the media in general, Alexa Robertson explains that contemporary mediascapes can no longer be contained by national settings and are very much part of the global flows that characterize twenty-first-century societies. Quoting Ulrich Beck, she contends that globalization is making people cosmopolitans by 'default' (2012: 178). As part of such mediascapes, contemporary cinema bears, in its industrial practices, its production of cultural meanings, its diversified distribution platforms and its reception, the imprint of a society that in many ways exceeds the national. For this reason, cosmopolitan theories have much to offer to the understanding of current cinema practices and the analysis of films. As with people, cosmopolitanism may also be seen as the new default identity in the cinema of globalization. Robertson differentiates between political cosmopolitanism ('cosmopolitanism with a worried face') and cultural cosmopolitanism, concerned with discourse and everyday practices. Cinematic representations would belong in this second group, but even political cosmopolitanism, the defence of citizenship and human rights, has to do with images, visuality and meaning. In general, cosmopolitan practices demand 'a transformation of vision' (ibid., 181). In this context, a cosmopolitan approach to cinema is not about arguing that films are more cosmopolitan than they used to be (exactly what 'being cosmopolitan' means continues to be the subject of much debate among theorists), or that the aim of one's analysis is to decide whether films are more or less cosmopolitan. Rather, many contemporary films (and many that are not so contemporary) attempt to make sense of the surrounding world in the context of globalization and its economic, social and cultural consequences, and as such may be approached from a cosmopolitan perspective. In the cinema, as much as in the social sciences, cosmopolitanism is, as Gerard Delanty suggests, a framework of interpretation (2012: 3).

Ulrich Beck has argued for the need to replace what he calls methodological nationalism by methodological cosmopolitanism, that is, to abandon the nation as the centre of our intellectual enquiry, or 'the logic of exclusive oppositions' – that is, me against the Other – in favour of what he calls the 'this-as-well-as-that principle' (2002: 18–19). Like Beck, other social theorists have attempted to distil the essence of the cosmopolitan in various ways. For Delanty, for instance, that essence can be found at the 'cosmopolitan moment', a moment of openness to the other that brings about reflexive transformation (2006: 27–8), and in the 'global public', a discursive sphere that contextualizes political communication in a globalized world, and frames transformations in the local and the national in a global context (2009: 69). More modestly, for Robert Fine, the cosmopolitan project consists in the creation of a human rights culture (2009: 20). Nikos Papastergiadis describes the cosmopolitan imagination in terms of openness, a global sense of interconnectedness and an alternative sense of being in the world (2012: 229). For Ian Woodward and Zlatko Skrbiš, cosmopolitanism is a repertoire of cultural practices and outlooks that are performed selectively for purposes dealing with cultural diversity, hybridity and otherness, and a discourse, a way of managing meaning, that articulates an ideology of openness, thinking globally and resisting methodological nationalism (2012: 129–33). For Jacques Derrida, cosmopolitanism is about hospitality as defined in the Stoic, the Pauline, the Hebraic and the Kantian traditions, and the handling of refugees and asylum seekers (2001: 15–22).

The border, border spaces and borderlands occupy an important place at the centre of the cosmopolitan imagination. Beck and Natan Sznaider argue that methodological cosmopolitanism enables the empirical investigation of border crossings, which for them encapsulate the global experience (2006: 1). Anthony Cooper and Chris Rumford see borders as sites that connect individuals to the world, and as 'quilting points', where Delanty's 'moments of world openness' may take place (2011: 262). For them, borders are everywhere in today's society; they are mobile and in the process of being constantly transformed, not only by states but also by a multitude of non-state actors, including migrants. They call this daily transformation of borders 'borderwork', the activity of ordinary people making, shifting or dismantling borders, an activity that allows them to have cosmopolitan experiences (ibid., 262–4). Borderwork, or what they later call 'bordering processes', turn people into agents of cosmopolitanism. Derrida, in his habitual metaphorical idiom, talks about the threshold of cities of refuge, where a new order of law and democracy might be put to the test, based on the principle of hospitality, that would bring about a new cosmopolitanism (2001: 23). Given the centrality of borders within a cosmopolitan perspective, in a later article, Rumford expands on the idea of borderwork and suggests that we should 'look from the border' and 'see like a border' (as opposed to seeing like a state) (2012: 249). This comes close to Walter Mignolo's border thinking, his solution to surmount imperial and colonial differences (2012: 92, 97). Whereas for Cooper and Rumford both the observer and the agent of cosmopolitanism place themselves at the border – whether a line or a territory – for Mignolo, the only way to redress the logic of colonialism is to look and act from the other side of the border, from the position of the subaltern. Sandro Mezzadra and Brett Nielson foreground the symbolic dimension of borders and their centrality as cognitive processes – the border as a method, not a research object but an epistemological viewpoint that provides insights into how borders are constituted and reconstituted (2013: 14–19). In general, looking at films from the border allows us not only to be aware of bordering processes in their narratives but also to understand the extent to which borders structure contemporary fictional constructions of the world.

Borders are, as Cooper and Rumford argue, not disappearing but proliferating, and also becoming border zones, regions or whole countries, as Étienne Balibar also pointed out (1998: 220). This is what Gloria Anzaldúa had called 'borderlands' (1999), what Mezzadra and Nielsen call 'borderscapes' (2013: 12–13), and what Cooper and Rumford mean when they say that borders are 'spatial' (2011: 267). They are also diffused throughout society (Rumford, 2012: 246), not only in the vicinity of boundaries between states but also, for instance, in cities and other areas, as in Mike Davis's concept of the 'third border' (2000: 71). Even as they proliferate, borders retain their double meaning as, on the one hand, lines of exclusion and sites of exploitation, oppression and violence, and, on the other, as Rumford describes them, 'connective tissue' (2012: 248). They bring people together and foster moments of openness while at the same time controlling mobility (ibid., 247) and discriminating against certain people and groups of people. In general, borders have become, to return to Mezzadra and Nielsen, epistemological concepts that explain better than any other notion the dynamics of globalization.

Looking from the border in film studies means to be alert to the ways in which the industry follows a bordering dynamic in its production, distribution and exhibition practices within the logic of globalization, mobility and communication. It also means highlighting the ways in which individual filmic narratives are structured around borders and borderlands, as well as the ways in which borders, material and metaphorical, are visualized. Like individuals and political and cultural institutions, movies and other cultural texts are agents of borderwork.

The borderwork performed by people, individuals and cultural texts is inevitably gendered, as are mobilities, neoliberal global practices and cosmopolitan experiences. Questions of social class and elitist practices are at the centre of the cosmopolitan debate. For Craig Calhoun, for instance, 'cosmopolitanism is not free-floating, not equally available to everyone, not equally empowering for everyone' (2008: 217). Peter Nyers coins the term 'abject cosmopolitanism' to account for those that are regularly left out of the cosmopolitan radar yet perform cosmopolitan practices and borderwork in their everyday lives: asylum seekers, non-status residents, undocumented workers and other 'illegals' (2003: 1070). However, gender continues to be sidelined in the theoretical conversation. Within this background, Niamh Reilly offers a quick outline of what a cosmopolitan feminism would look like. For her, among the constitutive elements of cosmopolitan feminism are a global feminist consciousness that challenges oppressive patriarchal, capitalist and racist power relations, and recognition of the diversity of women's identities and experiences (2011: 371). Appreciation of the differences among women within patriarchal societies was one of the basic demands of postcolonial feminist critics, who complained about the homogenizing tendencies of the second-wave feminism of the 1970s. Likewise, consideration of the special forms of existing in a global world and, specifically, on the border, as well as of the specificities of borderwork carried out by women is central for an understanding of the intricacies of contemporary societies under globalization and, therefore, crucial for a cosmopolitan/bordering perspective on films. It is worth exploring, for instance, how Cooper and Rumford's look from the border is compromised when the looker is a woman, how gender impacts on mobilities and how openness to the other in Delanty's cosmopolitan moments is inflected by gender inequalities. *It's a Free World…* places a woman at the centre of a world of urban borders and transborder injustices that follows the logic of wild globalization practices in which the limitations of a gender-blind cosmopolitan perspective come to the fore and is thus a good space for the exploration of the interface between cosmopolitan and gender-based perspectives.

The road to cosmopolitanism in Ken Loach's films

Ken Loach's oeuvre, from the very specificity of its political concerns and the apparently narrow focus of the ideological discourses that it puts into play, offers a telling illustration of the epochal social changes undergone by our societies in the last five decades or so. Combining the tradition of British realistic cinema with an explicit left-wing sensibility to the injustices of the social class system in the UK, his is a cinema of class warfare that gives a voice to those that are left behind by the excesses of capitalism in its successive reincarnations. Starting with his work for the BBC in the Wednesday Play in the 1960s, his first feature films *Poor Cow* (1967) and *Kes* (1969) and the later miniseries *Days of Hope* (1975), Loach combined a celebration of the resilience and courage of the British working man with a Marxism-influenced analysis of the unbearable pressures of the capitalist system on the working class. His career experienced a considerable revitalization in the 1990s when the effects of Margaret Thatcher's right-wing policies – her clampdown on the welfare state and workers' rights – became consolidated in the country. Loach became internationally known through the films of this period, including *Riff-Raff* (1991), *Raining Stones* (1993), *Ladybird, Ladybird* (1994), *My Name Is Joe* (1998) and *The Navigators* (2001), among others. These were all what could be described as 'state or England' stories, which corresponded to the methodological nationalism paradigm described by Beck, coming out at the moment when that paradigm was changing and globalization, particularly economic globalization but also the revolution in communications, was beginning to gain a hold in people's lives and imaginations around the world. For Loach's early films, social injustice and political activism remained strictly within national bounds and, as his reputation crossed borders, his concerns remained almost exclusively national. In the course of the 1990s, however, national borders started to appear in his films, too, and border crossers became increasingly frequent. *Land and Freedom* (1995) and *Carla's Song* (1997) brought the British director outside the borders of the UK for the first time. *Land and Freedom* narrates, through a long flashback starting at the moment of his death many years later, the participation of its protagonist, David Carr (Ian Hart), in the Spanish Civil War as one of the thousands of foreigners that joined the struggle against fascism. This is still a story of workers' solidarity and one that signals the historical moment in which, from the director's perspective, the communist ideals suffered a definitive blow. *Carla's Song* is a contemporary story of asylum seekers. Glaswegian bus driver George Lennox (Robert Carlyle) meets and falls in love with Carla (Oyanka Cabezas), a Nicaraguan exile, suffering post-traumatic stress as a consequence of the horrors she experienced in her country under the Somoza regime. He accompanies her to Nicaragua to help her get over the ghosts of her past. A few years later, *Bread and Roses* (2000) saw Loach cross the ocean again, this time to tell a story of underpaid janitors in Los Angeles, in which Jewish union activist Sam Shapiro (Adrien Brody) encourages the workers, notably undocumented Mexican migrant Maya (Pilar Padilla), to fight for their rights. This brief description of the plots reveals, on the one hand, the irruption of borders, transnational experiences and the growing impact on the imagination of a fast-shrinking world, and, on the other, the difficulties of the films to engage with the representation of women in a way that might call attention to the social gains of the second wave of feminism but also the subsequent backlash against it. *Land and Freedom*, *Carla's Song* and *Bread and Roses* tell very different stories but have a structural similarity: they all feature male protagonists who become heroes, gain redemption or construct their openly left-wing political identities on the basis of the apparently selfless way in which they help, or attempt to help, a less-than-powerful woman in stories that are directly concerned with borders and border crossings. At the heart of *Land and Freedom* is David's love affair with Blanca (Rosana Pastor), the Spanish woman he meets at the front. At the end of the film, his moral stature is definitively sealed by his granddaughter's gesture as she lays the red scarf that belonged to Blanca and contains Spanish soil in his coffin. Blanca herself died during the war and becomes, through a dissolve of their two coffins across decades, a function of David's moral integrity and courage in a hostile and forgetful world. *Carla's Song* may feature the female protagonist in its title but Carla's centrality is more apparent than real. She is presented as a mental wreck that learns to cope with the horrors of her past through George's loving care. George persuades her to go back to Nicaragua to confront her ghosts and travels with her but, when he cannot stand the radical otherness of the Latin American country, he and the narrative literally drop Carla and return to Scotland, with George a transformed man, no more the foolish and unpredictable character of the beginning but a mature and complex individual. In *Bread and Roses*, Maya is the closest to a true protagonist in the three movies, yet her triumph and that of the other janitors in Los Angeles is facilitated by union organizer Sam, without whose help the protagonist and the other janitors would be helpless.

In all three films, the bias is not only one of gender but, consistently, a national one: the three men are either British or Americans; the three women are foreign, all from Spanish-speaking countries and all constructed as inferior. While in these films Loach follows the sign of the times in bringing his stories closer to the border and to Cooper and Rumford's advice to look from the border, he fails to cross the line and engage in a sustained way with the perspective of those on the other side. That in the film narratives those others are women is significant but also consistent with the director's earlier and many of his later films. Movies like *Riff-Raff*, *My Name Is Joe* and, more recently, *I, Daniel Blake* (2016) share a similar structure in which the main function of the various female characters is to prop up the moral prominence and wholesomeness of the male protagonists. Two earlier Loach films – *Poor Cow* and *Ladybird, Ladybird*– feature female protagonists but both Joy (Carol White) in the former and Maggie (Crissy Rock) in the latter appear in their narratives exclusively as victims of an oppressive social system, without the strength to fight the status quo displayed by the male protagonists of the other films. *Ladybird, Ladybird*, a film from the same period as the three border movies discussed above, also contains a border story: Maggie's sentimental partner is Paraguayan expatriate Jorge (Vladimir Vega), like Carla, escaping from a repressive Latin American regime, but this time, the man's love and patience do not lead to the strength of character necessary to revert the situation.

It can, therefore, be said that the central project of the majority of Loach's movies is to romanticize the British working-class male hero while, in the context of this analysis, gradually coming closer to the border consciousness of a globalized world but, simultaneously, failing to incorporate in his narratives the changes in gender relationships and politics that have taken place during his professional career. There are, however, important exceptions. *Ae Fond Kiss…* (2004) uses the structure of romantic comedy to allow for a certain balance in the construction of the heterosexual relationship between Irish schoolteacher Roisin (Eva Birthistle) and British Pakistani Casim (Atta Yakub) in a story set again in Glasgow, imagined here as a border city in more explicit terms than in *Carla's Song*. The intersection between gender, class, religion and national identity is depicted with a complexity found wanting in the examples mentioned above, while Roisin is given a degree of agency that was lacking in all of them. The 'love conquers all' paradigm may have come as an unwelcome surprise for Loach fans but it serves the film well to explore the intricacies of interracial and inter-religious heterosexual relationships in early-twenty-first-century UK. The narrative encapsulates in Tahara (Shabana Akhtar Bakhsh), Casim's teenage sister, the difficulties but also the strengths of contemporary multiple identities, even if the resolution of her narrative arc may seem like wishful thinking on the part of the filmmakers. She and Roisin become predecessors of Angie, the protagonist of *It's a Free World…*, as complex female characters whose lives in a global world are impacted by their femininity.

A woman in the world city

World City is the title of Doreen Massey's book about twenty-first-century London (2007). *It's a Free World…* can be seen as Loach's take on the global city. In the film, London is imagined as a border city – a city crossed by borders and constantly reshaped by borderwork. Massey starts her book with a chapter entitled 'Capital Delights', in which she describes the guilty pleasures of taking a walk around the much maligned Canary Wharf, Westminster, the London Eye, the South Bank, Tate Modern, St Paul's and the City. London has reinvented itself as a global city and a centre of world finance, attracting a new class of elite professionals that embody the worst excesses of financial capitalism (ibid., 30–5). Those parts of London that tourists visit provide an attractive face to the activity of the finance houses and multinational corporations that have turned the city into a hub of global capitalism. In an earlier essay, Massey had vividly described another part of London, Kilburn, the neighbourhood where she lived, one that illustrated her idea of place as a constellation of social relations meeting and weaving together at a particular location (1991: 27). This constellation is marked by an outstanding heterogeneity and diversity that is inseparable from Britain's colonial history, the history of class relations in the UK and a global economy that often forces people to migrate to places like London even if they do not particularly want to. Hanif Kureishi offers an updated version of this tension. The great energy of multiculturalism apparent everywhere in contemporary London has created, in local perceptions, something unique, free and tolerant. Yet the city's prosperity is more unevenly distributed than it has been for a long time and the poor are dispersed and disenfranchised (2017: 45). Similarly, for Massey, a strong element of the identity of London for many of its citizens is the recognition, even the celebration, of internal diversity, mixture and hybridity (2005: 191), yet this celebration, often used to shore up the image of global London, cannot be separated from its various histories of oppression, injustice and inequality, nor from its current gaping inequalities. Not unlike other global cities, London offers itself in discourse as a shining light that erases contradictions, traumatic histories and ongoing injustices.

Like many of Loach's features, *It's a Free World…* followed in its production and distribution strategies the logic of the transnational: more or less a British film, it was co-produced by a variety of companies from all over Europe, including Italy, Germany, Spain, Poland, France and Switzerland. But, like some of the films discussed above and *Ae Fond Kiss…* in particular, it also tells a transnational story, one that attempts to tackle the impact of globalization on people. Set in London, it evokes some of the histories, past and present, which have underpinned the rise of the British capital first as a colonial and then as a global metropolis. The London it offers for our gaze is not the official London of Massey's guilty pleasures but one that is more closely connected with the impact of globalization on individuals and the proliferation of borders in the global city. It continues a pattern of representation of places in Loach's movies that is closely connected with the Lefebvrian notion that social relations are spatially inscribed. As in his other films, whether their action is set in the urban spaces of Glasgow, in Manchester, Newcastle or in the hostile war zones of Aragón in the Spanish Civil War, Loach offers here a vivid sense of place, but these places are seen primarily as the location of social and political struggles. In *It's a Free World…*, the urban spaces of globalization are empty warehouses recycled as the hidden abodes of migrants, sweatshops that operate outside legality, invisible employment agencies run out of a pub backyard,

Figure 6.1 Urban refugee camps or the mezzanine spaces of sovereignty in *It's a Free World...* directed by Ken Loach © Sixteen Films 2007.

makeshift refugee camps (Figure 6.1), construction sites where workers are constantly cheated out of their wages, car parks and back streets where undocumented workers hang around in the hope of precarious employment, and motorways that, along with mobile phones and computers, link all of the former places under the logic of the free flows of global monetary and human capital.

The film visualizes the material anchor of global processes described by Saskia Sassen. Sassen argues that global processes do not only happen in virtual space but are, rather, very much place-centred. They are defined not only by top-level transnational managers and professionals but also by their secretaries and the janitors who clean the buildings where the new professional class works. They are also the world of immigrants that become the nannies, domestic cleaners and dog walkers of those top professionals, as well the assistants of the boutique shops where they buy their food in their exclusive neighbourhoods, and the drivers of the cabs that make their mobility possible (2006: 2). These 'place-bound' people are also the unwitting agents of the informal economy that thrives on deregulation. Angie, the protagonist of *It's a Free World...*, is not one of Nyers's 'abject cosmopolitans', the refugee and immigrant groups trying to resist their own exclusion (2003: 1072–3). Yet, from her position as one of the lower links between these abject groups and the higher managerial echelons, she is intensely place-bound while entertaining a fantasy of mobility, encapsulated in her motorbike, as she navigates the geography of the capital and provides a structure of meaning to the complex relations fostered by the new economy.

Levels of engagement

There is a certain correlation between this dynamic of aspiration against limitation of mobility and the film's circular structure: the story begins and ends in an Eastern European country – Poland at the beginning, Ukraine at the end – with Angie recruiting people for an agency that offers work in the UK, as if to suggest that nothing has changed in the course of the narrative and Angie remains caught in the net of global capitalism. In a different sense, however, the apparent return to the beginning is there mostly to emphasize the differences: at the beginning, the protagonist is an employee in an agency that offers legal work to the migrants. At the end, she is working for herself – 'Angie's Recruitment', with a rainbow and a woman on a motorbike for a logo – and offering illegal work. The events of the story have sunk her in what is apparently an untenable moral position. Her mobility across borders has turned her into an agent of borderwork but, as such, she appears to be more interested in exploiting and taking advantage of rather than reaching out to the other. Yet the spectator's response is complex. Her narrative trajectory, as defined by her aspiration and limited mobility, is linked to her social class and her femininity. Her family background, her accent and even Wareing's previous role in *EastEnders* unequivocally confirm her solid working-class origins. But her wish to strike out on her own and find a place in the new economy and even certain inflections in her accent represent recent developments in the British class system that are one of the film's main objects of analysis. At the same time, notions of femininity, even though impossible to disentangle from those of class and ethnicity, are constantly foregrounded. The film's perspective on cosmopolitan openness is highly contradictory, yet as the protagonist becomes forced to look from the border, she offers glimpses of the position of women in our brave new global world. As will be argued below, the realities of this position are most forcefully conveyed by the film through the patterns of engagement with the narrative that it knits for the spectators.

Unlike her father, who has had a steady job for thirty years, Angie has had a succession of unstable, poorly paid jobs and is getting nowhere. Globalization and deregulation open a world of possibilities, and she is willing to make many sacrifices, particularly moral ones, for her portion of the pie. Sassen explains how migrant women constitute a disempowered class of workers, but their access to pay, even if very low, as well as the feminization of the labour market brought about by the informal economy, give them opportunities that they had not had before (2006: 182). Angie is not one of these women, but her position in the complex labour structure of the global deregulated economy is close enough to exhibit certain parallels with Sassen's women: given her very low prospects in the traditional labour market, the informalization of the economy, here represented by the use of migrant labour, offers her possibilities that she, as a woman, has not had before. As we have seen, she starts the movie as a recruiting agent for a company taking Polish workers to the UK. Her own job, however, is so unstable that she is summarily sacked when she publicly accuses one of her bosses of sexual harassment. Jobless and with a son whose custody has been temporarily given to her parents, she goes into business with her friend Rose (Juliet Ellis), setting up their own recruiting agency, with a pitch that combines her previous experience with their femininity. In one of the few comic interludes afforded by this rather dark story, Andy (Raymond Mearns), one of Loach's usual salt-of-the-earth working men (and one of his frequent Scottish characters), marvels at the way women, smarter and better-looking than men, are taking over the world. Soon enough, with cloning, men will become redundant. Although the spectator's position vis-à-vis Angie will become increasingly complicated by her decisions, we do tend to sympathize with Andy's comic awe at the energy and savvy of the two women. Yet at the same time, we are aware that it is still very much a man's world. As another Scottish character, foreman Derek (Frank Gilhooley), warns her, by trying to carve herself a place in the informal structure, she is getting out of her depth.

Angie is the moral centre of the movie, not in the usual sense that she provides a clear moral standpoint for the spectator to identify with and one from which to understand the behaviour of the other characters, but because her own moral contradictions encapsulate the impact on the individual of economic globalization. Murray Smith provides a useful model to analyse Angie's impact as a textual and cultural construction in a world in which the nation has lost part of its currency to encompass social relations and the proliferation of borders has questioned the validity of the type of political theory that the Loach fan had been familiar with. Smith's theory is a response to what for him are the inaccuracies and the determinism of psychoanalysis-based identification theories. For him, rather than spectators becoming sutured to certain positions constructed by the text, texts 'produce or deny the conditions conducive for various levels of engagement' (1995: 82). In other words, films offer us a degree of freedom in our relation with what Smith calls their structures of sympathy instead of tying us to fixed identifications. He finds three levels of engagement: recognition, alignment and allegiance. At the level of recognition, we understand characters through psychological and cultural familiarity with the traits they display, from physical appearance to behaviour. Through alignment we gain access to the characters' actions, what they know and feel. Finally, our allegiance relates to our moral evaluation of characters: the extent to which we agree or not with the opinions and decisions that go into their narrative trajectory (ibid., 82–5). With this three-tier system, Smith rejects identification: by experiencing recognition, alignment and allegiance we may develop various degrees of sympathy for a character but we never 'replicate the traits, or experience the thoughts or emotions of a character' (ibid., 85), that is, we never become them, which is, for him, what theories of cinematic identification suggest.

We may or may not agree with Smith's preference for sympathy over identification as the best way to explain spectators' relationship with characters. For him, films and other fictions invite us rather than suture us – they offer us scenarios that we are invited to experience from a variety of perspectives (ibid., 81). But the further value of his theory lies in the multiplicity of levels of engagement. A character like Angie (but many other characters as well) seems to demand this multiplicity. Not only is she presented as a relatively strong, active heroine, who drives the plot forward, but she is also constructed melodramatically as a victim of society struggling to find her place in a ruthless world. She is present in most scenes and we are invited to perceive the film's spaces, the other characters and the events that make up the plot through her perspective. Yet, our allegiance to her is more problematic. At the beginning, she is contributing, as part of the company for which she works, to the exploitation of migrants, but when she decides to go into business for herself, she becomes more openly complicit in such exploitation. At first, she justifies herself, first to Rose, then to her father, by saying that the world has changed and people must adapt – to precarious jobs, to the drastic reduction of labour rights, to an economic structure operating outside the law, to outright exploitation – and that what she is providing is a service from which everybody is profiting: if she does not do it somebody else will. Even as she sinks deeper into immoral and illegal dealings, the text counterbalances our growing antipathy towards her ways with her generosity towards Iranian refugee Mahmoud (Davoud Rastgou) and his family, for whom she provides shelter and work, and her difficult predicament as a single mother. Since we are constantly aligned with her, there is no escaping from evaluating the moral choices she makes. Since she exhibits many of the trappings of a contemporary heroine and there is much to like and admire in what we see, our moral choices are often complicated because our familiarity with and admiration for her enable our understanding even if we gasp at some of the decisions she makes.

Recognition – Smith's first level – is also relevant to our analysis of the film's exploration of gender dynamics. Angie is recognizable first and foremost as a product of global capitalism, deregulation and, crucially, the gains of second-wave feminism, the cultural backlash that came as a response and the ambiguous dynamics of post-feminism. Further, as we have seen, this early-twenty-first-century femininity is compounded by her working-class origins and her aspirations of social climbing in a context in which the traditional class system is under pressure, not least from the realities of globalization and massive migratory movements. She is, in sum, a familiar social type bound to a specific historical moment, and one on which cosmopolitan and feminist concerns converge. Before things start happening to her and she starts reacting to them in growingly questionable ways, her cultural value is, for the spectators, already firmly in place through recognition. Rose, who is not free of contradictions, is a much more traditional figure of allegiance. When she decides to break up with Angie, after the latter reports a group of undocumented workers, including Mahmoud, to the immigration authorities so that she can replace them with a new batch of illegally brought-in migrants, most spectators will sympathize with Rose. Yet *It's a Free World...* accomplishes the difficult task of luring spectators into shadowy moral areas. We find it easy to accept Rose's and Angie's father's positions but they remain secondary characters, with whom we are not allowed to become narratively involved so readily. Conversely, Angie is presented as the movie's clearest agent of the excesses of neoliberalism and unchecked economic globalization, an ideology that comes under unambiguous attack in the course of the story, yet she is the main recipient of our sympathy. At the end, the narrative does not punish her for her appalling decision: the final scene, rhyming with the opening one, finds her still at the helm of her recruiting agency, now without Rose, still taking advantage of the possibilities offered by the deregulation of the economy and exploiting those who are at the bottom of the social ladder. Her saving grace is, from the point of view of spectatorial involvement, that her class and her gender turn her into a victim of a system that she needs to navigate in order to survive and to give an opportunity to her son.

Borderwork and femininity

Angie is a citizen and an active agent of the borderlands. She inhabits what Nyers calls 'the mezzanine spaces of sovereignty', those spaces that are in between the inside and the outside of the state (2003: 1080). Her actions transform some of those spaces and even create new ones. This is the case of the pub backyard, where she starts her business as a recruiting agent. This is not only where she and other citizens of the state meet the migrant other, but also a temporal borderland: the front of the pub, half-empty the only time we get a glimpse of it at the beginning of the movie, is the old territory of the working class, to which Angie herself, Rose and Andy belong – or, at least, used to belong. Conversely, the empty backyard is a creation of the new woman of the global borderland, the hidden no man's land from which she hopes to attain a more favourable position in the new social system. As I suggested above, this is one of the anonymous-looking, almost invisible spaces of the new economy where social, cultural and personal exchanges take place in the global cities. Out of nothing it soon becomes a busy site of the new deregulated economy, where Angie and Rose, combining harshness and sensitivity, toughness and understanding, ruthlessness and compassion, hospitality in the Kantian sense and rejection of the other, provide a service whose main goal is to get rich in as short a time as possible by trading in social precariousness and human despair.

On the one hand, Angie is not interested in the workers as human beings but as cheap labour that will allow her the social and economic position to which she feels she is entitled by her apparent ability to navigate the difficult waters of the new economy. In this sense, she represents the use of borders as a mechanism of control of the flow of labour. This dimension of borders is her ticket to wealth. At the same time, her physical attraction to Polish worker Karol (Leslaw Zurek) and her kindness to Mahmoud suggest that she has the potential for openness that the borderlands also foster, that she is better equipped than most for cosmopolitan hospitality. Perhaps in keeping with some of the working-class protagonists in Loach's earlier movies, such as

George in *Carla's Song*, David in *Land and Freedom* and, arguably, also Roisin in *Ae Fond Kiss…*, her social origin facilitates her relationship with the other: working-class people find openness to migrants easier, hospitality to foreigners more natural, Loach's imaginary seems to say. Yet *It's a Free World…* suggests that, in the borderlands, cosmopolitan openness and closedness go together and are not easy to tell apart. Mahmoud and his family, for example, are both the beneficiaries and the victims of Angie's borderwork, simultaneous objects of her ingrained hospitality and of her readiness to exploit others if she feels she has to. Angie uses borders pragmatically and ambivalently: once she has learned to navigate them on a daily basis, they become what she needs them to be, whether sites of exclusion, discrimination and injustice or porous membranes that are not only negotiable but also help people to become better, more understanding and more humane individuals. She embodies Ian Woodward and Nina Høy-Petersen's contention that practices of ethical cosmopolitanism often exist alongside conflicting objectives of self-protection (2018: 664), thus engendering what they call 'messy cosmopolitanism', in which cosmopolitan ethics are often inseparable from anti-cosmopolitan tendencies (ibid., 669).

Angie's ambiguous position as an agent of borderwork and her messy version of cosmopolitanism are narratively connected to the fact that she is a woman and a mother. She is willing to go to any extremes and take advantage of the system for the sake of her son Jamie (Joe Siffleet). She momentarily gains privileged access to the group of Polish workers through her sexual relationship with Karol. Her dealings with middlemen and factory managers are facilitated by her femininity. She benefits from their feelings of protection and even patronizing attitude towards her. At the same time, she is permanently seen as a sexual object, and this sometimes leads to harassment and violence. When she is betrayed by her bosses and the migrant workers feel betrayed by her, she is both savagely beaten up and threatened when Jamie is briefly kidnapped. While the migrants are oppressed and taken advantage of as second-class citizens without rights, Angie is discriminated against because of her condition as a woman and as a mother. Yet the danger in which her condition as woman and mother constantly puts her is, for her, perfectly compatible with capitalist ruthlessness and apparent disregard for others, even those she has previously helped. For example, when Rose feels guilty about the money they have made from renting rooms illegally to undocumented workers and suggests that they should use it to pay the wages they owe to the Polish workers, Angie urges her friend to divide their earnings in two halves. Rose can do what she likes with her money: it's a free world. But we know that the film's title is heavily ironic, particularly when it is a woman that utters that sentence.

Angie, therefore, embodies the ambivalent position occupied by women in the new global capitalist regime: children of second-wave feminists, they have grown up believing in equality and, unlike their mothers, apparently equipped to fend for themselves and 'make it' in a hostile world. Yet they continue to be victimized by the system and discriminated against, even if in subtler ways than before. In the film's rhetoric, this dynamic seems to exist in a convoluted relationship with Angie's capacity for openness and empathy with the other: as an enthusiast of the new economic system, she is closed to the other and the border is exclusively a source of opportunity for her to profit; but as a woman she retains what the film seems to present as an innate cosmopolitan potential even as her working-class background appears to allow her to cross borders without the burden of the racist and xenophobic misgivings that the film associates with other social classes. Her position at the centre of the urban borderlands endows her with a series of unresolved contradictions, alternatively empathetic and ruthless, victim and perpetrator, open and closed to the other. These contradictions are linked to her femininity in a global world that, in general, continues to be a man's world. Our complex allegiance to her (or lack thereof) reinforces – even actively constructs – this contemporary discourse on femininity. The film's closing moments summarize the dual view of the borderlands as simultaneously fraught with dangers and possibilities, openness and closedness.

In the final scene, we see Angie arriving in Kiev, now her own boss, recruiting workers illegally and charging them for her services, the fee she gets from them going directly into her pocket, without intermediaries. She sits opposite a nervous Ukrainian woman, Ludmila (Ludmila Borysh), who is travelling to England and leaving her children behind in search of an opportunity. Like Sassen's female migrant workers, this woman may find a degree of economic freedom in the UK while at the same time becoming even more disempowered than she is now in her own country. For her part, superficially at least, Angie does not seem to have changed much after betraying the migrants at the camp. She certainly seems to have achieved her goal, at least temporarily. In narrative terms, to the credit of the filmmakers, she has not discernibly become a monster after her fall from grace. At the same time, we perceive a certain heaviness and weariness in her demeanour. We see her take the woman's money almost reluctantly and ask to know her name, almost against her will.

As an agent of borderwork, she is aware of the importance of the question: this micro-moment of such borderwork means shifting her perspective and seeing the other as an individual, as a woman and a mother, like her, one that she will probably still exploit but whose face and name she will not forget easily. This final exchange, presented through a classic shot/reverse shot with a little table separating them (Angie and the Ukrainian translator on one side, Ludmila on the other) is one of the most charged border moments in the movie (Figure 6.2). The text forces the spectator to literally stand on the invisible line and consider the complexity of the impact of globalization on these two women, who are both clearly separated and brought together at this cosmopolitan moment. Angie and Ludmila may be seen as global women who, by dint of their existence in the borderlands, are permanently exposed to cosmopolitan experiences and react to them in complex ways. They do not occupy the same position, as underscored by the table that separates them, but, at least in the rhetoric of the film, the frail link that is established between them once Angie learns Ludmila's name is based on their experience as women. Angie has become an ambiguously cosmopolitan woman who understands the plight of the other woman, while Ludmila, also a mother, also willing to

Figure 6.2 Angie and Ludmila: Global women at the border in *It's a Free World...* directed by Ken Loach © Sixteen Films 2007.

make sacrifices, probably even moral ones, shares a flash of recognition. Exploitation remains the central ingredient of their emerging relationship, even as Angie performs cosmopolitanism, to borrow Woodward and Skrbiš's term, but the border can foster cosmopolitan solidarity and mutual recognition between the women even as the social separation between them is reinforced. This gendering of the border does not prevent border dynamics from happening, just as the borderlands produced by globalization do not erase gender differences. Angie, in her contradictions and the complexity of her construction as a character, embodies the charged meanings of the border, the various ethical ambiguities of cosmopolitan practices and the ambivalent place of women in this brave new world.

Engaging borders

The contradictory patterns of spectatorial engagement with Angie underscore both the complexity of borders and the multiplicity of attitudes and performances encompassed by a cosmopolitan perspective on the realities and representations of globalization. Angie may be described as a cosmopolitan citizen and, more specifically, as a cosmopolitan woman, in the precariousness of her position vis-à-vis work relations and gender relations, in her effortless openness to the other, in her ability to sit on the border and look both ways with equal interest, in her compassion and hospitality, in her ruthlessness and her appropriation of global capitalist practices, and in her quick disdain of others even as she sympathizes with them. In the context of Loach's oeuvre, she stands out as a character with whom engagement in Smith's model is particularly complex. We may be critical with the male protagonists of *Carla's Song*, *Land and Freedom* and *Bread and Roses*, as with other Loach working-class heroes, but our difficulty of allegiance in these cases is more an external ideological critique of the texts than a scenario consciously offered by them – the films do not invite this critique. Within the logic of the films, these are characters for whom we should not have any difficulty feeling allegiance, just as we are unproblematically aligned with them. The two protagonists of Loach's female-centred movies, Joy in *Poor Cow* and Maggie in *Ladybird, Ladybird*, approximate Angie in the difficulties spectators find to support them morally, even as we are aligned with them, but these are far less complex characters and, as I suggested above, are constructed almost exclusively as victims of an oppressive system, even though our recognition of them as social types offer important insights into their historical and geographical contexts. Casim and Roisin in *Ae Fond Kiss…* are, on the other hand, easier for the spectator to sympathize with. We see the choices they make as brave and compassionate even if the pressure of their respective social groups brings constant tensions to their relationship. But the romcom generic context helps Loach ensure the spectators' allegiance.

Perhaps the character that most approximates Angie in the films discussed here is Rosa (Elpidia Carrillo), Maya's older sister in *Bread and Roses*. She welcomes her sister into her home after the latter has crossed the border; she in fact pays the coyotes for her crossing; she prostitutes herself to secure Maya a job in the building where she works as a janitor; with her husband, sick and unable to work, she is the only provider in her family. Yet, at a climactic moment, she betrays the other janitors, including her sister, to the boss, as a result of which they are fired and she is promoted. We initially side with Maya in her shock at her sister's betrayal, yet, after learning about the sacrifices Rosa has made in the course of the years for the sake of everybody around her, she easily regains our sympathy. Her decisions are finally consistent in moral terms. In the case of Rosa, the turbulences of allegiance are only temporary. Angie is a more extreme case. By the story's end she remains unrepentant even as she continues to be an enlightened agent of borderwork. Her predicament, her personality and our response to it illustrate the multifaceted nature of the border and, further, women's unstable position in it.

Conclusion

Border movies constitute an ideal scenario to explore the effects of globalization and transnational exchanges as the social forces that best characterize twenty-first-century experiences and, from a theoretical perspective, become the most obvious space for the deployment of a cosmopolitan methodology. Within the growing corpus of this group of films, *It's a Free World…* occupies an important position. In a way, perhaps comparable to the later changes in the thematic concerns of the Dardenne brothers' oeuvre, as illustrated by the surfacing of borders in *Le silence de Lorna* (2008), *La Fille inconnue* (2016) and *Le Jeune Ahmed* (2019), it underscores the relevance of Loach's oeuvre as a space in which some of the most crucial social changes of the last half-century are played out. *It's a Free World…*, on the one hand, confirms what we could describe as a turn to the cosmopolitan in the director's movies, which had already started in certain films of the previous decade. On the other hand, it combines its multilayered cosmopolitan perspective with a much-needed acknowledgement of the gendered experiences afforded by the border and of the specificities of women's agency as citizens of the borderlands. *It's a Free World…* is not the only border film that highlights the role of women in a global world, but it is part of a sub-trend within border films that are responsive to such gender specificities. As a consequence, Angie becomes an overdetermined symbol at the intersection between traditional class concerns, contemporary gender politics and a cosmopolitan vision, a cocktail that may go a long way towards explaining the charged meanings and cultural value of the border.

Works cited

Anzaldúa, Gloria ([1987]1999), *Borderlands/La Frontera: The New Mestiza*, San Francisco: Aunt Lute Books.

Balibar, Etienne (1998), 'The borders of Europe', in P. Cheah and B. Robbins (eds), *Cosmopolitics: Thinking and Feeling beyond the Nation*, 216–29, Minneapolis: University of Minnesota Press.

Beck, Ulrich (2002), 'The cosmopolitan society and its enemies', *Theory, Culture & Society*, 19.1–2: 17–44.

Beck, Ulrich, and Natan Sznaider (2006), 'Unpacking cosmopolitanism for the social sciences: A research agenda', *British Journal of Sociology*, 57.1: 1–23.

Calhoun, Craig (2008), 'Cosmopolitanism and nationalism', *MAC/SLGS*, 23 September: 209–42.

Cooper, Anthony, and Chris Rumford (2011), 'Cosmopolitan borders: Bordering as connectivity', in M. Rovisco and M. Nowicka (eds), *The Ashgate Research Companion to Cosmopolitanism*, 261–76, London: Ashgate.

Davis, Mike (2000), *Magical Urbanism: Latinos Reinvent the U.S. City*, London: Verso.

Delanty, Gerard (2006), 'The cosmopolitan imagination: Critical cosmopolitanism and social theory', *British Journal of Sociology*, 57.1: 25–47.

Delanty, Gerard (2009), *The Cosmopolitan Imagination: The Renewal of Critical Social Theory*, Cambridge: Cambridge University Press.

Delanty, Gerard (2012), 'Introduction: The emerging field of cosmopolitan studies', in G. Delanty (ed.), *Routledge Handbook of Cosmopolitan Studies*, 1–8, London: Routledge.

Derrida, Jacques (2001), *On Cosmopolitanism and Forgiveness*, trans. Mark Dooley and Michael Hughes, London: Routledge.

Fine, Robert (2009), 'Cosmopolitanism and human rights: Radicalism in a global age', *Metaphilosophy*, 40.1: 8–23.

Høy-Petersen, Nina, and Woodward, Ian (2018), 'Working with difference: Cognitive schemas, ethical cosmopolitanism and negotiating cultural diversity', *International Sociology*, 33.6: 655–73.

Kureishi, Hanif (2017), 'Birdy num-num', *Sight & Sound*, 27.10: 42–5.

Massey, Doreen (1991), 'A global sense of place', *Marxism Today*, June: 24–9.

Massey, Doreen (2005), *For Space*, Los Angeles: Sage.

Massey, Doreen (2007), *World City*, London: Polity.

Mezzadra, Sandro, and Brett Neilson (2013), *Border as Method*, Durham, NC: Duke University Press.

Mignolo, Walter D. (2012), 'De-colonial cosmopolitanism and dialogues among civilizations', in G. Delanty (ed.), *Routledge Handbook of Cosmopolitan Studies*, 85–100, London: Routledge.

Nyers, Peter (2003), 'Abject cosmopolitanism: The politics of protection in the anti-deportation movement', *Third World Quarterly*, 24.6: 1069–93.

Papastergiadis, Nikos (2012), 'Aesthetic cosmopolitanism', in G. Delanty (ed.), *Routledge Handbook of Cosmopolitan Studies*, 220–31, London: Routledge.

Reilly, Niamh (2011), 'Cosmopolitanism and feminism', in M. Rovisco and M. Nowicka (eds), *The Ashgate Research Companion to Cosmopolitanism*, 367–86, London: Ashgate.

Robertson, Alexa (2012), 'Media cultures and cosmopolitan connections', in G. Delanty (ed.), *Routledge Handbook of Cosmopolitan Studies*, 178–87, London: Routledge.

Rumford, Chris (2012), 'Bordering and connectivity: Cosmopolitan opportunities', in G. Delanty (ed.), *Routledge Handbook of Cosmopolitan Studies*, 245–53, London: Routledge.

Sassen, Chris ([1991]2006), *Cities in a World Economy*. Thousand Oaks: Pine Forge Press.

Smith, Murray (1995), *Engaging Characters: Fiction, Emotion and the Cinema*, Oxford: Oxford University Press.

Woodward, Ian, and Zlatko Skrbiš (2012), 'Performing cosmopolitanism', in G. Delanty (ed.), *Routledge Handbook of Cosmopolitan Studies*, 127–37, London: Routledge.

Youngs, Gillian (2009), 'Cosmopolitanism and feminism in the age of the "war on terror": A twenty-first century reading of Virginia Woolf's Three Guineas', in M. Rovisco and M. Nowicka (eds), *The Ashgate Research Companion to Cosmopolitanism*, 145–59, London: Ashgate.

7

Marie Antoinette (2006), fashion queens and Hollywood stars

Sara Pesce

The contemporary cult of celebrity, strongly encouraged by the digital media, includes a wide range of strategies of self-promotion and multiplying virtual arenas that give potentially any individual an opportunity to reach public acclaim, set a trend, gather a high number of aficionados and become a celebrity. This is a context in which the feminine has become the target of ambivalent attitudes to women's 'degenerate pleasures' such as excessive preoccupation with clothing, cosmetics, luxury items and cosmetic surgery. Hollywood imagery and promotional strategies participate dynamically in this phenomenon, a fact that includes many forms of criticism made by show business insiders, including filmmakers. An interesting example is Sofia Coppola's *Marie Antoinette*. Its story and style create a metaphor of the Hollywood dream of stellar acclaim, embracing the contradictions inherent in this dream in the new millennium. The film also reveals Coppola's ambivalent vision, both nostalgic and critical, of the very notion of celebrity. As an heir to the New Hollywood's revolution of classic stardom, Coppola perpetuates and at the same time updates the previous generation's capacity to renovate the hierarchies of values attached to the cinematic icons, celebrating as non-conventional some kind of personalities that might, instead, appear as subdued to a political or cultural establishment. She tells a story of female self-positioning, setting it at a historical moment of change in power relations, tastes and publicity: the fall of the *Ancien Régime*. This self-positioning is tentative and innovative at the same time, interpreted by a Kirsten Dunst who is transformed from the girl next door into a star.

I will therefore discuss *Marie Antoinette* as a phantasmagoria of the Hollywood female star, whether it be the actress (Dunst) or the filmmaker (Coppola). The film draws on the widespread vilification of the last queen of France as an emblem of the decadence of the Ancien Régime as well as her celebration as an icon of style and beauty. While King Louis XIV has been historically accused of excesses in terms of absolutist power and ego inflation, Marie Antoinette has become a paragon of vast unpopularity due to her secluded though much rumoured indulgences concerning her self-adornment and bodily pleasures. By depicting Marie Antoinette as both a disreputable and seductive figure in a colourful apotheosis of style, as well as highlighting the pressure of conforming to the conventions set by the Court, the film evokes the rules Hollywood Studio stars have long undergone, as well as the scandals affecting their reputations.

Coppola's parallel between Marie Antoinette and the contemporary Hollywood star questions the status of contemporary celebrities: is a celebrity imitable, is she privileged, is her upbringing all important? Coppola's *Marie Antoinette* prompts reflection on our mixed feelings about the fashionable elite and the cult of celebrity. I will therefore set the film against the background of the contemporary fashion industry and celebrity culture. The notion of celebrity has been discussed intensely in the past twenty years. Entertainment industry insiders and scholars have scrutinized the subject from multiple perspectives. A number of scholars have reflected on the public addiction to celebrity: relating it to the rise of public society (Rojek, 2001), highlighting the role played by the mass media (Cashmore, 2006) or analysing fandom, the blurry notion of authenticity[1] and the economy of celebrity in the digital era (Turner, 2013). The '*celebrisation*' of society has been interpreted as a mode of consumption. Fashion has been acknowledged as a crucial component of leisure and style in our celebrity-thirsty society (Church Gibson, 2012). The film foregrounds splendour, style and leisure in a way that is very telling of the prestige of high fashion in contemporary society and has autobiographical overtones since Coppola has long been involved in the milieu of high fashion. In this sense, fashion substantiates the film's elitist imagery, its implicit celebration of an Olympus of taste perpetuated by Hollywood filmmaking.

The problem of leisure

The prologue of *Marie Antoinette* contains a provocative comment on leisure spending as a status symbol. The young queen is openly enjoying her relaxation and privilege. This scene displays Dunst both as a fictional character – the last queen of France – and as a Hollywood star. Resting gently in an armchair, dressed in white satin and enveloped in the pastel colours of the turquoise and pink furnishings, she wears a hairdo that is recurrent in the official eighteenth-century portraits of the queen, very high and decorated with showy white ostrich feathers. Her privileged upbringing comes to the fore: she is showing off her privileges, although with a touch of humour, revealed by her crafty smile. Coppola surrounds her with symbols of a luxurious lifestyle: decorated cakes, pastries of every kind, rose petals and adorable little shoes that a maid is fitting on her feet. In a flirty gesture, she winks at the audience. What we see is the disclosure of an enactment of the queen.

Yet the short duration of the scene, the intimate setting and the wink are also reminiscent of contemporary personal fashion blogs, both confidential and self-publicizing, where young women regularly post pictures or videos of themselves to document their outfits. In the extraordinary flourishing of this kind of blogging since the new millennium, self-portrait is the predominant mode of communication and the computer screen is used as a mirror (Rocamora, 2013: 114). Dunst as Marie Antoinette also reminds us of the Manhattan society girls like Tinsley Mortimer, Genevieve Jones, Fabiola Beracasa and Zani Gugelmann who became media phenomena in the early 2000s, making their appearance in fashion shows, charity galas and boutique openings (Agins, 2014: 68). These young women were charming in public. Fashion brands' publicists 'plied them with designer clothes and fine jewellery to get photographed in' (ibid.). They soon realized that they were far more than spectators of fashion and started to start fashion lines themselves. This prologue contains, therefore, many components of the contemporary culture of celebrity, where the consumption of fashion plays a pivotal role. It synthesizes new modes of self-assertiveness allowed by myriad forms of the 'democratisation of fashion',[2] among which fashion blogging represents an emblem of new spaces of identity construction, 'a panoptic gaze that reproduces women's position as specular objects, but also a space of empowerment' (Rocamora, 2013: 114). Coppola articulates here a woman's problematic control over her own public image. A set of alternative visions of femininity, a different mode of circulation of these modes are hinted at in her portrait of Marie Antoinette, wittingly sustained by the refined work of Milena Canonero, the film's costume designer.

On the other hand, this scene is a critical commentary on the absence of rank or class that characterizes fame today, a phenomenon that includes a variety of forms of self-promotion and self-broadcast of ordinary people on and off the web or in TV reality shows – many of which display or discuss trendy styles and fashionable outfits (Cashmore, 2006; Van Krieken, 2012). The film's overture is indeed an ironic celebration of aristocratic leisure as opposed to the commodification of leisure today – where 'the meaning and value of leisure comes to be identified with the purchase, possession, and control of material goods' (Weiermair and Mathies, 2004: 112). The equation between conspicuous consumption and leisure is underlined here, reinforced by a soundtrack ('Natural's Not in It', Gang of Four, 1979) that is an explicit commentary on 'the problem of leisure' and what to do with it. The pleasure afforded by new purchases can be considered at the same time enticing and disreputable. The film might indeed echo the different criticisms, old and new, addressed to stars and celebrities that focus on the economic issues of surplus, waste and on the moral question of excess, vanity and self-centeredness.[3] Gossip and publicity, in the press, TV programming and the web (especially publications and programs at their outset, eager to grab the reader's attention) indulge in denigrating narrations about celebrities. Even the managers of celebrities are ambivalent towards denigrators, who can, in some instances, induce the public to adopt an indulgent attitude towards the celebrity's fragility (Ricci, 2013: 37). In particular, the use of negative gossip to relaunch stars is very revealing if we consider *Marie Antoinette*: dwelling on the dark side of a personality is fundamental to the construction of the myth of a star, and Coppola capitalizes on Marie Antoinette's bad reputation and spending power to construct an unusual tale of fame.

Bodily concerns

Counterbalancing the denigration of Marie Antoinette, the film also highlights the liberating potential of bodily concerns. What comes to the foreground is the pleasure derived from sparkling, jubilant appearances, an escape from utilitarian concerns. These pleasures bring about a personal, if not political, empowerment.[4] To the viewers, this extreme lifestyle appears at the same time desirable and perilous, considering Marie Antoinette's well-known final punishment. The contradiction is seductive, particularly because Marie Antoinette's glamour, emphasized by the film especially in the intimate depicting of the queen's private spaces, evokes the paradox between the extraordinary and ordinary that the film star has embodied since the beginning of the Hollywood Star System, and which propagates in different directions in the contemporary mediascape. According to Richard Dyer (1998: 49), the star lives a luxurious life but should not be transformed by it. She/he ought to remain a simple person so that the public can identify with her/him. This paradox was reprised in the many celebrity reality TV series that started appearing in the early 2000s, like *The Osbournes* (MTV, 2002–5) and *The Simple Life* (Fox and E!, 2003–7). These shows further develop the paradigm of the TV franchise *Big Brother*, whose viewers know that the reality contestants are people like them. They have been familiarized with them at the beginning of the program, before contestants become famous. They have witnessed step by step their transformation into celebrities during the show. The backstage has allowed viewers to keep their private lives under observation. It is thus easy to identify them as ordinary people. In *Newlyweds Nick and Jessica* (MTV, 2003–5), for example, the protagonists Nick Lachey and Jessica Simpson are ordinary people living an extraordinary life since they are both rock stars. They confront thousands of fans at concerts and are shown inside luxury environments, especially hotels. At the same time, they are also shown at home, as the show follows their marriage, displaying before our eyes Simpson's naive personality and playing on the popular stereotype of the dumb blonde.

In Coppola's film, too, the ambivalence between ordinariness and extraordinariness is displayed, since the ordinary core of Marie Antoinette is constantly preserved. Marie Antoinette's transformation happens before our very eyes. It is a passage marked by the language of the body and dress. From the naive Austrian girl who knows nobility in terms of caste but is inexpert regarding etiquette and style, Marie Antoinette undergoes an evolution imposed by the rules of Versailles, which flattens the separation between subjectivity and publicity. The film describes this evolution in successive steps: saying goodbye to her friends, leaving behind all objects and items of clothing of the homeland, learning the rituals of dressing before the nobles appointed to assist her, serve her and without doubt observe her. In this process, the positive or negative feedback of the courtiers is the mark of her conquests or failures. A number of elements pertaining to star narratives converge here: the blended personal and public identities, the appropriateness of the roles interpreted, the stars' style in relating to the public, their being exposed to the fans' sneaking into the most intimate spheres of their life.

Marie Antoinette therefore emerges as a model of behaviour where self-adornment plays a pivotal role and is used, although not openly or politically, against gender constraints.

Marie Antoinette belongs to the category of biographical films – lately financed by European production houses – depicting famous women. These biopics offer an alternative vision of feminine destiny as compared to the so-called new woman's film, because they address the role of women in the public arena (Radner, 2017: 160). Yet, *Marie Antoinette* also draws on the 'new woman's film' by focusing on female self-gratification, inaugurated by the 1990s 'chick films' and 'smart-chick films' such as *Pretty Woman* (Marshall, 1990), *Clueless* (Heckerling 1995), *Legally Blonde* (Platt, 2001) and *The Princess Diaries* (Marshall, 2001). It also contains the ironic vision of the woman's fate typical of this subgenre, 'a sense of uncertainty about the possibilities for fulfilment that contemporary society offers to women with its twentieth-century progenitors' (Radner, 2017: 8). Coppola's portrait of the last queen of France is not merely that of an unfortunate victim of her class and time, as opposed to the novel from which it was adapted (Antonia Fraser's *Marie Antoinette: A Journey*, 2001). On the contrary, the film's emphasis on Marie Antoinette's fashion statements unveil the queen's spheres of agency, an *authorship* in designing her public role and her destiny.[5]

Fashion in Coppola's film is a vehicle of feminine celebration: through fashion, the victimized woman is seen to exercise a degree of agency over her fate and finally triumph (Radner, 2017: 158).

Empowering fashion: An aristocratic phantasy

Marie Antoinette's use of clothing makes her prominent and publicizes joyously her agency, her influence as a young woman confronted with the conservative milieu of the royal court. The film was released in 2006, when in the world of high fashion repeating old trends was the norm and successfully underwriting a designer's private fantasy had become very rare: a period when 'more and more designer clothing looks standard-issue, cut from the same linens and cottons, using the same sewing' (Horyn, 2009). Considered in this perspective, Marie

Antoinette's capacity to make her personality visible through clothing smacks of nostalgia for a time when the old nobility had the privilege of being dressed by *couturiers* of exquisite creativity. A nostalgia towards the daring inventiveness of *couture* – a culture which had definitively flagged by the 2000s (Agins, 2014). Marie Antoinette is, therefore, not merely a brand, as an insightful response to the film has already underlined.[6] She can rightfully be seen as the pinnacle of a lost world imbued with caste privilege.

Marie Antoinette was not an enormous success in the United States, but it was in Europe, where, at the start of the 2000s, knowledge about the big names of fashion was wider, and *couture* was more directly associated with aristocracy. Whether in France, Italy or England, Coppola–Canonero's updated and trendy imagery of the queen of France (Diamond, 2011: 203–31) could be appreciated precisely because it added a special Hollywood touch to an idea of fashion design associated with personality and because it enriched a bulk of non-cinematic imagery and discourse relating to this historical figure. A characteristic of Marie Antoinette that historian Caroline Weber underlines was her special ability to raise her own visibility both figuratively and literally in the social eye. This can be deduced from the large amount of images, clandestine or overt, surrounding the queen and commenting on her behaviour during the years of her reign. Her public persona was marked by extremes: extreme overdress and extreme underdress. She learned from an early age that fashion was a matter of political power (Weber, 2007).

The film reprises this ability to raise the queen's visibility through extreme outfits. Let us consider, for example, the *pouf* (Figure 7.1). Marie Antoinette's use of extremely high hairdos began at a time when she was not very welcome in the French kingdom, due to her Austrian origins and the fact that she was not giving the kingdom an heir. At Versailles the king was the one who dazzled, commanding all attention. The queen provided heirs. Probably because she could not do her job as heir-giver, for a few years, Marie-Antoinette used fashion to uphold royal standards, gaining the allegiance of Parisian

Figure 7.1 The pouf in *Marie Antoinette* directed by Sofia Coppola © Columbia Pictures 2006.

couturiers and stylists. The public opinion of the time nurtured an appetite for knowing what Marie Antoinette was wearing at any public appearance: balls, promenades, the coronation. Her trips to Paris showed her that outside Versailles there was a world where she could be adored, worshipped. She began to cultivate her image as a queen of fashion,[7] assisted by fashion ministers, as they were called. Marie Antoinette's trademark look was a plain pouf accessorized with ostrich feathers, which appears also in Elisabeth Louise Vigée Le Brun's portraits (such as *Marie Antoinette en grand habit de court*, 1778). Marie Antoinette's poufs could be accessorized with fresh vegetables (*le pouf à la jardinière*) or other objects to express her feelings or her awareness of specific political issues (*le pouf à la circonstance*). The film emphasizes the queen's dedication to these elaborate hairdos, also showing her being assisted by an eccentric hairdresser. It also draws on one political event that inspired Marie Antoinette's decorative creativity – a battle during the American war of independence – portraying the partying queen with a headdress shaped as a fully rigged naval vessel. That specific hairdo reproduces the historical pouf worn by Marie Antoinette to make her public statement. By means of these strategies of self-decoration, Marie Antoinette could carve her own new territory: what a queen should look like and how she should express her states of mind. She used a code that was public, visible, strictly feminine. A code that also gave direct access to her intimate thoughts, a crucial element of contemporary celebrity culture. This search for a fulfilling feminine code of self-expression in the public arena is a crucial theme of Coppola's work, especially relating to the Hollywood milieu, of which the court of France can be seen as a metaphor. Versailles appears indeed as a historical arena reverberating present-day established territories of identity negotiation and power display.

Nostalgia for Hollywood royalty

While contributing to the development of a canon of women as historical figures, *Marie Antoinette* applauds the role of the 'established Hollywood' in creating this canon.

Inside Hollywood, Coppola occupies a position in between the mainstream and 'Indiewood', according to Geoff King (2009). She therefore introduces innovation, critical insight and auteurism, while at the same time embracing the industry's commercial agenda. As a knowledgeable insider of Hollywood's commercial dealings and a close witness to the commodification of its stars, Coppola endows her film with an awareness of the contradictions of the contemporary cult of celebrity. The film especially underlines Marie Antoinette's 'performance of the self': a self-aware, ambiguous and unsatisfactory mode of female life and social relations. It does so using visual codes so accurate – as the choice of specific and recurrent colour nuances – and vigorous – creating a correspondence between costumes, decorations and the queen's states of mind – that they surpass dialogue or action (Lewis, 2019: 190). The portrait of Marie Antoinette's identity juxtaposes, on the one hand, self-denial and the cult of privacy, through the many indoor private scenes pervaded by a sense of self-protection, and, on the other, self-exposure as an inescapable social duty, in outdoor sequences, encounters with the courtesans and the rituals of everyday life.

Why is Marie Antoinette such a meaningful figure for Sofia Coppola and what makes her so topical today? For centuries, Marie Antoinette has been at the centre of a deprecatory discourse on the excesses of the Ancien Régime and has been blamed for the collapse of a political system. Marie Antoinette's reputation echoes that of the Hollywood milieu, regularly attacked for its lavish lifestyle and its self-centredness. The film's historical outlook makes reference not so much to the European aristocracy as to another, very American, aristocracy, that of show business. It is not by chance that Coppola picked an emblematic period in the history of female visibility, when conflicting forces paraded on the battlefield of the presentation, decoration and commodification of the self. At the end of the eighteenth century, 'the great era of ornateness (wigs, powder, brocade, cod-pieces, beauty spots) beg[an] to decline' and came to be labelled as trivial. Historically, the decline of adornment in a person's public reputation coincides with the end of the Ancien Régime, when the ornate and the plain started to be culturally and politically gendered: 'ornateness being associated with the female … and its value discounted, and plainness, correlated with the male, comes to signify dignity and power' (Spiegel, 2011: 184).

Marie Antoinette's story as squanderer and fashion queen makes her the emblem of the contemporary dream of fame and of the price of celebrity. It reverberates and expands Hollywood fancy, its history of stardom, acclaim and decline. 'Marie Antoinette's fairy tale turned tragedy has spawned biographies, fictionalisations, operas, plays, ballets and memoirs' (Covington, 2006). Even her hairdresser and her executioner published ghostwritten recollections. And, like her marvellous wardrobe, the queen's story became perfectly suitable for Hollywood's sparkling style since 1938, when the film *Marie Antoinette* was acclaimed as a triumph of costume design. Similarly, Coppola's film, with Canonero's colourful and coquettish emphasis on modernized decorations, emphasizes the queen's extravagance while also celebrating Hollywood as 'a dream factory'.

The circumstances of this particular queen's notoriety, and the means she used to construct her public persona, can be appreciated in the post-feminist American context:

> A globalised, neoliberal, female lifestyle economy in which gender is highly commodified has emerged as a dominant feature of Western women's cultural life. (Lewis, 2019: 192)

Some traits of Marie Antoinette's behaviour – her blasting consumption habits, creative social adaptability and oscillation between extreme privacy and extreme publicity – fulfil a neoliberal ideal of femininity based on the ability to manage one's own lifestyle, to self-train and develop 'techniques of the self' supported by experts or coaches – often found watching TV shows (Ouellette and Hay, 2008) – and finally use the web for self-promotion. Marie Antoinette's behaviour can be seen as the story of an influencer. The historical queen exploded Versailles' dress codes by bending them to her creativity, she blasted the aristocratic pleasures and sophistications and created a personal environment at the Petit Trianon – an historical fact recently made attractive to the general public by the restoration of the queen's palace inside Versailles. As I will discuss later, it is not incidental that this restoration took place in the same years of the film's production. All the queen's lifestyle choices, which the film praises, echo the mode of 'adaptable femininity' (Ouellette and Hay, 2008) typical of the American post-feminist era, where contradictory dynamics occur between fantasies of escape and desires of extreme visibility.

This adaptable femininity can be seen especially in the cult of celebrity. Marie Antoinette's special ability to raise her visibility can be seen as an epitome of modern celebrity, a form of fame that has largely replaced the archaic concept of renown. 'Renown … was once assigned to men of high accomplishment in a handful of prominent and clearly defined roles. [It] brought honour to the office not the individual, and the public recognition was not so much of the man himself as of the significance of his actions for the society' (Inglis, 2010: 4). It is historically a category applied to men, although illustrious female examples do exist. Take, for instance, the detailed record of the *Royal Progresses of Elizabeth I*. In her case, the royal ceremonials had the meaning of pledging the monarch to the people and vice versa (ibid.). Marie Antoinette constructed her own ceremonials around her attire and a set of rules concerning the spaces of the Court, which called attention only to herself, not to her royalty. The display of Marie Antoinette was certainly spectacular (as much as that of Elizabeth I), but the meaning the spectacle dramatized was not the same. 'Elizabeth is renowned for being the monarch; Her fame is conferred by her people on behalf of God and England; the enacted theory of her rule partakes equally of her pious receptiveness and her subjects' supplication and approval' (ibid., 6) Comparatively, Coppola does not portray a queen from a historical or political perspective. Rather, she expresses her personal fascination for the young queen's way of negotiating her position, using visibility and not accomplishment, sacrifice or heroism as a way of ordering the world – as Nick Couldry puts it – of being at the centre of things (,2000). A new notion of hierarchy, separating those who have access to image-making and the rest (Biressi and Nun, 2005), was born precisely with the collapse of the Ancien Régime.

The sins of celebrity: Forgery and commodification

Marie Antoinette's politics of public visibility epitomizes a historical period of cultural and economic shift in the circulation of fame. Marie Antoinette was consigned to a terrible reputation by pamphlets and by caricature images, by the spoofing of her clothes and hairdos and the endless repetition of her famous phrases, like 'Let them eat cake'. The circulation of her fame expanded therefore to non-official environments outside the court. In this respect, the fame of Marie Antoinette can be seen as successfully reverberating that of the contemporary Hollywood star, threatened by a flattening of the distinctions between stars, celebrities and personalities. Over the last three decades, the Hollywood star's monopoly of attention, traditionally sustained by a persistent industrial policy of marketing, promotion and publicity, has been threatened by alternative forms of celebrity (Church Gibson, 2012), based on strategies of self-branding and blogging – fashion bloggers like Chiara Ferragni, hybrid personalities like Kim Kardashian and multitudes of web personalities, so-called microcelebrities, among which are the media fans transformed into media professionals (Marwick, 2015), momentary appearances (e.g. the 'celetoids' analysed by Chris Rojek) allowed by multiplying platforms of visibility, especially on the web, that outstrip the official channels of communication. The effect is a levelling of differences and hierarchies, which the Hollywood elite, here represented by Coppola, perceives with alarm. This preoccupation is detectable in the crepuscular tone of Coppola's film and her emphasis on the young queen's aloofness, her detachment and lack of purpose. It is 'a lament about the decline of status and value which attends modern celebrity' (Redmond and Holmes, 2007: 6), which can be read as a lament about the challenge to Hollywood's hegemony (Vincendeau, 2000; Babington, 2001). Film stardom faces competition from other kinds of celebrities in a production and distribution system where the big screen does not necessarily hold primacy and a vast range of media sites make the circulation of fame less unique (Redmond and Holmes, 2007).

Coppola's film adumbrates the perils of contemporary celebrity culture. Indeed, it stains Marie Antoinette with the greatest sin of this culture: inauthenticity. At a diegetic level, the theme of counterfeit emerges when Kirsten Dunst is proposed as a posed fake in the film's overture – a modern one, as the rock soundtrack underlines. However, forgery and commodification can be found even more clearly in the film's paratext. The whole promotional campaign, the expansion of the film's imagery into the realm of fashion publicity (as in *Vogue* magazine's use of Dunst and the memory of her regal interpretation in the magazine's September issue of 2006) and the impact on merchandizing and tourism at Versailles have transformed Marie Antoinette into an icon of wearable luxury (Horyn, 2009) and have tested her capacity to become a brand.

Coppola's film participates, for example, in the myth surrounding Marie Antoinette's space of retirement, set within the grounds at the limits of the palace of Versailles: the Petit Trianon. In 1786, Marie Antoinette began building the Hameau de la Reine, an extravagant retreat near the Petit Trianon in Versailles where she could exclude the larger court nobility. It became a symbol of Marie Antoinette's extravagance and self-indulgence. The social life she organized there induced suspicion. Palace gossip spun outrageous tales about scandalous and perverse goings-on at the Trianon, giving anti-monarchist pamphleteers material for salacious underground cartoons. The queen's private residence at Versailles was restored between 2000 and 2008, when it reopened to the general public, generating renewed interest and reshaping her fame through a re-aestheticization of her image. This space has been transformed into an extraordinary target of fashion tourism, a very profitable strategy that has transformed the historical Marie Antoinette into a modern commodity. Each year millions of visitors flock to Versailles and Fontainebleau, where the queen maintained a second palace, to admire her exuberant tastes in furniture and décor (Covington, 2006). Marie Antoinette's use of the Petit Trianon to escape the palace protocol is explicitly mentioned in the film. It is associated with a change in style that underlines Marie Antoinette's inventiveness and capacity to be a trendsetter. Her outfit in the little white dress, shown in the bucolic scenes of the film, was much more practical and simple than court dresses (Figure 7.2). It was a lot less expensive. Although it was meant for her endeavours to withdraw, it was widely copied by contemporaries, from aristocrats to prostitutes.[8] And Coppola's film displays it in a dreamy atmosphere. The scenes in the white dress offer an alternative view of the queen's intimacy, of her ordinariness. Her simple dress and unpowdered hair demonstrate, in fact, that social difference is no longer visible in someone's clothes. No sign of royalty is inscribed in Marie Antoinette's appearance, contrary to her historical paintings: no bourbon lilies, no crown, no fancy jewellery. Less official portraits, like *La reine en gaulle*, painted by Madame Vigée Le Brun in 1783, offer a glimpse of her passion for this outfit in white

Figure 7.2 Bucolic scene in *Marie Antoinette* directed by Sofia Coppola © Columbia Pictures 2006.

muslin, known as the *gaulle*, much plainer and more comfortable than the formal court gowns. This was a revolution in fashion that made prostitutes look like queens.

The Petit Trianon scenes are particularly telling of the importance of Dunst to the escapist meaning of the queen. The film indeed helped the actress rise to stardom after her debut success in *The Virgin Suicides* (Coppola, 1999), and Dunst is instrumental to the depiction of the queen as a teenager. In the same years of Coppola's discovery of the actress, Dunst's fresh-faced interpretations were also tinged with a rock aesthetic of intensity and romantic rebellion, as in *The Crow: Salvation* (Nalluri, 2000). Except in star vehicles like *Spider-Man* and *Spider-Man 2* (Raimi, 2002, 2004), Dunst's angelic persona and eroticism can be nostalgic of a familial order, like the lap-dancing angel of *Lucky Town* (Nicholas, 2000), or of a scandalous time in Hollywood's history (*The Cat's Meow*, Bogdanovitch, 2001), and are often substantiated by pop music themes (*Bring it On*, Reed, 2000). Coppola exploits her film persona as a candid provincial American girl to update Marie Antoinette's fascination, adding a hint of immaculate charm seasoned with American country-rock resonances.

Versailles and the unstable destiny of the ascribed celebrity

The contemporary celebrity is an industrial product, subjected to market forces, yet in the era of social media the celebrity can take shape as a 'bottom-up' phenomenon due to the multiplication of platforms of personal visibility. Personal appeal has undergone changes under the pressure of expanded modes of access to luxury products and lifestyles, where the fashion market is a driving force. Over the years, the blurring of lines involved in the *celebrification* of society has been widely acknowledged: film culture has become well aware of how social media have determined the idiom through which public life and subjectivity are constructed (Marshall, 2001). Because celebrity 'is constituted discursively, by the way in which the individual is represented' (Redmond and Holmes, 2007: 12), fashion can be seen as crucial to these discursive means. Fashion trends, brands and promotion have emerged as substantial driving forces in the imagery of screen celebrities and also in the process of their creation. Fashion is playing a crucial role in the interactive, authoritative, creative behaviour of their fans (Bruzzi and Church Gibson, 2013). The Hollywood industry (including cinema and television) participates dynamically in this phenomenon with its strategies of promotion of female stardom.

While participating in this ambivalent process of the celebrification of society, Hollywood has developed many forms of internal criticism. A number of Coppola's films, such as *Somewhere*, *Marie Antoinette* and *The Bling Ring*, are interesting examples of this. While creating narratives on – or metaphors of – the Hollywood dream of stellar acclaim, these films offer a meaningful example of the ambiguities of the empowerment of the star.

Marie Antoinette can be seen as a phantasmagoria of the Hollywood female star precisely because Versailles activates contemporary fantasies and consumption habits related to sophistication. The historical legacy left by Marie Antoinette is certainly related to Versailles' opulence and capacity to shape a newcomer into a public personality in every detail of attire and behaviour. Coppola's film establishes a convincing link between monarchy and cinematic stardom, made explicit in the scenes of the regulated codes of dressing, and dinners in front of the courtesans. As historians have underlined, in Versailles, Marie Antoinette learned to look the part of the royal every minute of every day. To a contemporary eye, that place is pungently reminiscent of Hollywood's combination of exclusivity and ostentation. The rituals and conventions set by the Court are reminiscent of Hollywood Studios' impositions on the star's duties, body, behaviour and identity. This has long been the price of fame that the star is supposed to pay, though not often willingly.

The behavioural protocols, the marketing and publicity of the Hollywood industry create a monopoly of attention around the star, with exorbitant rewards. Royalty, Rojek indicates, is one of the few modes of celebrity that is determined by blood. It is 'ascribed celebrity' (2001: 17). Contrary to Rojek's argument that the royal celebrity is safe from many of the vicissitudes that the celebrities from the entertainment industry undergo (a stability of status, a guarantee of privilege), Coppola's 'allegory' extends the equation between royalty and stardom in their unstable destiny: Marie Antoinette is perceived today as a precarious figure as much as the Hollywood starlet.

Coppola's Marie Antoinette, with her adolescent self-absorption and her totalizing style-oriented vision of life, serves a need for narratives about fame capable of negotiating royal celebrity with two centuries of democratic culture. This character resonates with 'the same kind of involvement with publicity and public relations that we might associate with party politics or the movie industry'; not unlike contemporary royals, she is an aristocrat offered for public consumption.[9]

Conclusion: Coppola queen, Coppola Star

Marie Antoinette is a portrait conceived by a filmmaker who sees herself as an heir of 'the magnificent Hollywood'. The model of celebrity that

Hollywood applauds, fearing the attacks of contemporary competitors like television and the web, is nurtured by fantasies of regality inspired by the absolute monarchies, despite their elitism and closed-mindedness. These fantasies of sumptuous ostentation and absolute power inspired the Hollywood pioneers at the time they were building the industry. In these 'Hollywoodian monarchies', so to speak, those at the forefront in terms of representation, of splendour, of celestial admiration, are the stars, who are, according to Danae Clark (1995), 'a privileged class within the division of actors' labour' (MacDonald, 2013: 5). Therefore, stardom in Hollywood is a category of labour and class, a social and economic category. Telling a story about the highest of classes – royalty – and the 'labour' performed by that class (ruling over the norms of behaviour and etiquette, influencing courtesans and people, setting new fashions), ennobles and at the same time mourns Hollywood stardom.

In this sense, Coppola's film exposes the false democracy of contemporary celebrity culture, where only the elite can set a trend or make powerful statements. Notwithstanding the guillotine – which is absent from the narrative – the film celebrates Marie Antoinette's success while revealing its complexities; a success that strongly confirms the perception of privilege – the 'Let them eat cake' transferred to Haute couture (Browne, 2006). Ultimately, it conveys the uniqueness of the Hollywood star, traditionally used as a marker of distinction (The Star-as-brand according to Paul MacDonald (2013: 41–64)), and whose high quality is proposed as essential and not fabricated. This notion of caste inherent in Hollywood stardom reverberates also in the very real stigma attached to endorsements within the Hollywood milieu, testifying to an idea of stardom as something 'which exists outside of commerce, a social contract without an economic contract' (Turner, 2013: 106).

Finally, through Marie Antoinette's stylistic emancipation and pleasures, Coppola celebrates herself as a filmmaker unafraid to take risks with style and subject matter (Cook, 2007: 480–1). She celebrates her high profile, her glamour. Coppola belongs to the class of Americans that reconciles Bohemian sensibility with that of the bourgeois (Lewis, 2019: 194), which has the cultural function of maintaining the status quo in the face of the democratization of celebrity. Coppola's *Marie Antoinette* prompts a reflection on our mixed feelings about democracy and high castes, where 'democracy perpetually fails to deliver what it promises, and arguably, this failure is most cruelly exposed in the limitations of its elected leaders' (Rojek, 2001: 181). The conflict between the ideally universal accessibility to fame and the menace of celebrity degradation or dissipation is enacted by a story of seductive femininity in which not only youth and invention but also means and bloodline allow the woman's survival in a demanding environment. It perpetuates the dream-factory-ideal according to which Hollywood is still the place where a woman's makeovers, negotiations and constructions of identity take place, albeit painfully. It includes in the celebrity portrait the current neoliberal climate which encourages women to consume ever more fashionable goods and leads them to excessive self-exposure, followed at times by shame and solitude, while avoiding any depiction of the woman's cruel destiny – the well-known death of Marie Antoinette.

Notes

1 The two edited volumes of Su Holmes and Sean Redmond, *Stardom and Celebrity: A Reader* (2007) and *Framing Celebrity: New Directions in Celebrity Culture* (2010), gather many of these critical perspectives on celebrity culture in the new millennium.

2 Concerning the new democratization of fashion in the twenty-first century, due to new industrial politics, the impact of the media and the globalization, see Thomas (2007), Warner (2014), English (2013) and Agins (2000).

3 As Chris Rojek (2012: 5) underlines, this kind of criticism is more often addressed to television wannabe stars. It can also manifest in 'star paranoia', which derives from sentiments of resentment towards celebrities for getting ahead in some way that is commonly deemed to be unreasonable. A specific discourse on excess is at the core of the success of some

televisual celebrities, epitomized in Paris Hilton. Discourse and enactments concerning fashion consumption have become the core of televisual programs, from reality shows to docu-fiction. Discourse on the star's body can offer the occasion to attack the star and her/his decline, as in the case of Nicole Kidman, who in 2010 became one of the paragons of negative comparison regarding facelifts.

4 See Diana Diamond's comments on how *Marie Antoinette* epitomizes the 'third wave of feminism' (2011: 208).

5 In this respect, see Thomas (1997 and 2004). See also the film *Farewell, My Queen* (Jacquot, 2012).

6 Fashion journalist Alix Browne (2006) maintains that Marie Antoinette is officially a brand.

7 The film does not put much emphasis on the pouf, sticking mostly to official portraits of the queen, although a coquettish appearance is always around Marie Antoinette. Surprisingly, poufs are to be found more easily on other aristocrats, at the theatre and during celebrations.

8 As Weber underlines, an impressive number of women started to imitate Marie Antoinette. This was the birth of modern fashion magazines. Evidence comes from contemporary prints of her attire in the company of women similarly dressed. Official portraits show her the way she ought to appear in official ceremonies (like the coronation of the king), whereas prints showed what she actually looked like: girly, thrilling, coquettish.

9 Graeme Turner (2013: 106) analyses the notion of 'royal celebrity' in contemporary society.

Works cited

Agins, Teri (2000), *The End of Fashion: The Mass Marketing of the Clothing Business Forever*, New York: HarperCollins.

Agins, Teri (2014), *Hijacking the Runaway: How Celebrities Are Stealing the Spotlight from Fashion Designers*, New York: Gotham books.

Babington, Bruce (ed.) (2001), *British Stars and Stardom: From Alma Taylor to Sean Connery*, Manchester: Manchester University Press.

Biressi, Anita, and Heather Nunn (2005), *Reality TV: Realism and Revelation*, London: Wallflower Press.

Browne, Alix (2006), 'Style: Let them wear couture', *New York Times*, 26 February. Available online: https://query.nytimes.com/gst/fullpage.html?res=9C03EFDA113EF935A15751C0A9609C8B63 (accessed 28 July 2018).

Bruzzi, Stella, and Pamela Church Gibson (eds) (2013), *Fashion Cultures Revisited*, London: Routledge.

Cashmore, Ellis (2006), *Celebrity Culture, Key Ideas*, London: Routledge.

Church Gibson, Pamela (2012), *Fashion and Celebrity Culture*, London: Bloomsbury.

Clark, Danae (1995), *Negotiating Hollywood: The Cultural Politics of Actors' Labor*, Minneapolis: University of Minnesota Press.

Cook, Pam (2007), *The Cinema Book*, 3rd edn, London: BFI.

Couldry, Nick (2000), *Inside Culture: Reimagining the Method of Cultural Studies*, London: Sage.

Covington, Richard (2006), 'Marie Antoinette', *Smithsonian Online Magazine*, November. Available online: https://www.smithsonianmag.com/history/marie-antoinette-134629573/ (accessed 28 June 2018).

Diamond, Diana (2011), 'Sofia Coppola's Marie Antoinette: Costumes, girl power, and feminism', in A. Munich (ed.), *Fashion in Film*, 203–30, Bloomington: Indiana University Press.

Dyer, Richard (1998), *Stars*, London: BFI.

English, Bonnie (2013), *A Cultural History of Fashion in the 20th and 21st Centuries: From Catwalk to Sidewalk*, London: Bloomsbury.

Holmes, Su, and Sean Redmond (eds) (2010), *Framing Celebrity: New Directions in Celebrity Culture*, London: Routledge.

Horyn, Cathy (2009), 'Just a bunch of hayseeds, dressed by Lagerfeld', *New York Times*, 6 October. Available online: http://www.nytimes.com/2009/10/07/fashion/07REVIEW.html (accessed 28 June 2018).

Inglis, Fred (2010), *A Short History of Celebrity*, Princeton, NJ: Princeton University Press.

King, Geoff (2009), *Indiewood, USA: Where Hollywood Meets Independent Cinema*, London: I.B. Tauris.

Lewis, Caitlin Yunuen (2019), 'Cool postfeminism: The stardom of Sofia Coppola', in Su Holmes and Diane Negra (eds), *In the Limelight and Under the Microscope: Forms of Female Celebrity*, 174–98, New York: Continuum.

MacDonald, Paul (2013), *Hollywood Stardom*, Malden: Wiley-Blackwell.

Marshall, David P. (2001), *Celebrity and Power: Fame in Contemporary Culture*, Minneapolis: University of Minnesota Press.

Marwick, Alice E. (2015), *Status Update: Celebrity, Publicity, and Branding in the Social Media Age*, New Haven, CT: Yale University Press.

Ouellette, Laurie, and James Hay (2008), *Better Living through Reality TV: Television and Post-Welfare Citizenship*, Malden, MA: Blackwell.

Radner, Hilary (2017), *The New Woman's Film. Femme-Centric Movies for Smart Chicks*, London: Routledge.

Redmond, Sean, and Su Holmes (eds) (2007), *Stardom and Celebrity. A Reader*, Los Angeles: Sage.

Ricci, Oscar (2013), *Celebrità 2.0: Sociologia delle Star nell'epoca dei New Media*, Milano: Mimesis.

Rocamora, Agnès (2013), 'Personal fashion blogs: Screens and mirrors in digital self-portratits', in S. Bruzzi and P. Church Gibson (eds), *Fashion Cultures Revisited*, 112–27, London: Routledge.

Rojek, Chris (2001), *Celebrity*, London: Reaction.

Rojek, Chris (2012), *Fame Attack: The Inflation of Celebrity and Its Consequences*, London: Bloomsbury.

Spiegel, Maura (2011), 'Adornment in the afterlife of Victorian fashion in film', in A. Munich (ed.), *Fashion in Film*, 181–201, Bloomington: Indiana University Press.

Thomas, Chantal (1997), *The Wicked Queen: The Origins of the Myth of Marie-Antoinette*, New York: Zone Books.

Thomas, Chantal (2004), *Farewell, My Queen: A Novel*, London: Weidenfeld & Nicolson.

Thomas, Dana (2007), *Deluxe: How Luxury Lost Its Luster*, New York: Penguin.

Turner, Graeme (2013), *Understanding Celebrity*, London: Sage.

Van Krieken, Robert (2012), *Celebrity Society*, London: Routledge.

Vincendeau, Ginette (ed.) (2000), *Stars and Stardom in French Cinema*, London: Continuum.

Warner, Helen (2014), *Fashion on Television: Identity and Celebrity Culture*, London: Bloomsbury.

Weber, Caroline (2007), *Queen of Fashion: What Marie Antoinette Wore to the Revolution*, New York: Picador.

Weiermair, Klaus, and Christine Mathies (eds) (2004), *The Tourism and Leisure Industry: Shaping the Future*, New York: THHP.

Part Three

Women protagonists in mainstream television and blockbusters

8

Voice-overs: Renewing gender representations in American TV series

Anaïs Le Fèvre-Berthelot

In an episode of *Cougar Town* (ABC, 2009–15) inspired by *The Breakfast Club* (Hughes, 1985), the protagonist and her son discuss the use of voice-over in TV and film:

Jules: And why does every movie and TV show need so much voice-over? I mean I hate thinking. Why do I want to listen to someone else do it?

Travis: Voice-overs are a great storytelling device. You can get out exposition fast, plus you get to see inside a character's head. (s04e13)

A sequence with a voice-over follows this dialogue, to let the audience hear what is inside Jules's head. Today, voice-overs do seem ubiquitous on American TV and female voice-overs do not sound extraordinary to viewers. However, it has not always been the case: few (if any) female voice-overs were heard on American TV serial fictions before the 1980s. Not only does this sequence underline the omnipresence of voice-overs in contemporary American TV, but it also points to the various functions of this device and to some of the debates about its use in audiovisual media.

The voice-over has been studied – in itself or in relation to specific films – from three main perspectives.[1] Borrowing from semiology and narratology, an essentially descriptive approach raises issues of taxonomy.[2] A second approach is heavily influenced by Lacanian theories and their later adaptations by feminist film theorists; it focuses on the figure of the subject and on the possible meanings of the disembodied voice.[3] Finally, semio-pragmatic or cognitive approaches take into account the experiences of audience in their diversity.[4] The approach adopted here is historical and ideological; it follows Amy Lawrence's observation that obstacles to the presence of women's voices on screen are 'a tangle of technological and economic exigencies, … suffused with ideological assumptions about woman's "place"' (1991: 32). By focusing on the production and reception of women's voices in US TV series, this chapter aims to illustrate how the changing uses of the voice-over on TV go with an evolution of the representations of women (and men) on screen and behind the scene. Gender is key to understand the perception of voices and voice-overs in audiovisual media and the hierarchy between the audio and the visual. A gendered perspective also underlines the evolution of voice-overs in American TV serial fictions. The growing number of female voice-overs on contemporary American TV shows points to an evolution in gender representations. This evolution will be studied by focusing on production through an analysis of the opinions about sound and voice-over conveyed in writing manuals, interviews and the trade press, and by analysing contents through a survey of key TV serial fictions that have used voice-over since the 1950s.

Showing versus telling: A gendered hierarchy

Because it is associated with language, voice in film and television is often the object of criticism anchored in what Rick Altman calls the 'ontological fallacy', whereby cinema is essentially considered as a visual medium 'and the images must be/are the primary carriers of the film's meaning and structure' (1992:14). The traditional dismissal of the voice-over is rooted in theoretical debates linked to the introduction of synchronized sound in cinema (Le Fèvre-Berthelot, 2013). The view that favors showing over telling still underlies the practice of many screenwriters. Many authors of screenwriting manuals urge their readers to be very wary of voice-over. Linda Seger writes, 'Sometimes screenplays use a voice-over or an expository statement to express inner conflict. Unless these are used carefully, they can easily make a story talky' (1994: 166). Christina Kallas describes the voice-over as 'a narrative tool that is difficult to master and is often used awkwardly by screenwriters'. But she also acknowledges that 'the off-screen narrating character has become an object of experimentation and variation' (2010: 64). Screenwriters who use this narrative device are aware of this perception of the voice-over. Stephanie Savage, co-executive producer of *Gossip Girl* (The CW, 2007–13) and *The Carrie Diaries* (The CW, 2014), two series using female voice-overs, acknowledges this bias: 'People often dismiss [the voice-over] as a crutch – a way of telling instead of showing the story – but it doesn't have to be that way' (Le Fèvre-Berthelot, 2015: 57–63). The dismissal of dialogue and voice-over often goes hand in hand with a gendered perspective associating sound and speech to the feminine. Sarah Kozloff writes, 'Films that are "talky" come with the connotations "trivial" and "idle" and, ultimately, "female." Visual images and physical activity, which in the history of cinema came first (as Adam preceded Eve), are associated with masculinity and "naturally" given precedence' (2000: 13).

In the history of radio and cinema, the exclusion of the female voice was justified by three types of arguments: 'the myth of woman's "naturally" less powerful voice, technical deficiencies, and … "cultural" distaste for women's voice' (Lawrence, 1991: 29). Often, women's voices were said to be too high or even too shrill for the first microphones. On screen, the issue of women's voices is reflected in *Singin' in the Rain* (MGM, 1952). The film illustrates the complex relation between the female voice, the body and the technical means of sound reproduction. The acclaimed star of the silent era is ridiculed as soon as she opens her mouth and her voice is heard.

Since the technical devices of the 1930s were able to record female speaking voices (Hilmes, 1999: 25), the real issue is not linked to the technique but to the culture that uses it and chooses to caliber microphones for male voices. Anne McKay and Michele Hilmes both studied a debate launched by Jennie Mix of *Radio Broadcast* magazine in 1924 (McKay, 1988: 187–207; Hilmes, 1999). A phonograph record dealer wrote to say that clients did not buy recordings featuring women speakers because 'when the speaker is not seen in person, and if that speaker be a woman, her voice is very undesirable, and to many, both men and women, displeasing'(Hilmes, 1999: 22). When Mix asked several station managers for their thoughts on the topic, 'two of the managers dismissed outright the idea of women's unsuitability, citing the many women on radio and improvements in the reproduction of higher-pitched sound. But most agreed that women announcers and lecturers suffered from a variety of handicaps' (ibid., 23), including stiffness or a lack of distinct personality. This controversy suggests that the issue of female voices, of their reproduction and their circulation was central in the 1920s and 1930s, when the structures of audiovisual industries emerged. The myth of the incompatibility of women's voices with recording and broadcasting techniques is part of a socio-technical apparatus that assigns women to the private sphere and denies them the right to speak in public.

Women were excluded from the public and political spheres, and in the audiovisual media they were restricted to specific genres. The emergence of gendered genres, such as the woman's film of the 1940s, participated in ambiguous representations of gender. For instance, Joseph L. Mankiewicz's *A Letter to Three Wives* (Twentieth Century Fox, 1949) uses a female voice-over. Addie Ross, a mysterious woman who remains invisible throughout the film, tells three women stuck on a boat that she is running away with one of their husbands in a voice-over that speaks out the content of the letter that appears on screen. She also comments on the actions and declarations of the protagonists as an omniscient narrator. The voice-over calls out to the viewers and seems to control the movements of the camera. This type of female voice-over is quite rare, but it remains crucial because it offers an example of a woman who shapes her destiny and the fate of the three main characters, until the ending that restores the status quo. Addie Ross is a woman who despises the patriarchal society she lives in and wishes to escape the alienation of marriage. Even though female voice-overs appeared in films of the 1940s, it took another forty years to hear them in fictional TV series. Despite theoretical oppositions to the use of voice-overs, TV screenwriters have used male voice-overs in fiction since the 1950s. As for the obstacles to the rise of female voice-overs, they seem to have been lifted in the 1980s, as new representations of women emerged on American TV screens. The evolutions of voice-overs and the representations they convey suggest that the hierarchical dichotomy between male and female voices is disappearing.

The voices of those who see and know all

The first examples of TV series using first person narrators were cop shows. At the beginning of *Dragnet* (NBC, 1951–9), the TV show adapted from the radio serial, an announcer tells the viewers that the story they are about to see is true and that the names have been changed to protect the innocent. The first episode opens with an aerial shot of Los Angeles with a male voice-over explaining,

> This is the city, 150 square miles of it, 150 thousand acres, a big place, six thousand miles of streets, two million people. In my job you get a chance to meet 'em all. I'm a cop. This is the City Hall, the base is 476 feet on its longitudinal axis, the tower goes up 452 feet above the level of Main Street. They put it up to stay. Lime stone from France, marble from Tennessee, grey Californian granite. It was Tuesday, November 15. It was cold in Los Angeles. We'd been working the early watch out of central division of the detective bureau. I got an emergency call to check back in at the office. An entire block in the heart of the city was facing sudden total destruction. We had twenty-six minutes to try and stop it. This is the story of those twenty-six minutes. (*Dragnet*, s01e01)

This example is reminiscent of Mark Hellinger's voice at the opening of *The Naked City* (Dassin, Universal DCA, 1948): 'This is the city as it is, hot summer pavements, the children at play, the buildings in their naked stone, the people without makeup.' These omniscient voices are didactic and informative. They can be associated with the 'voice of God' originally found in the documentary genre (Wolfe, 1997: 149–67).

The voices heard in detective shows inspired by film noirs, such as *Mickey Spillane's Mike Hammer* (Syndication, 1958–60), illustrate this twofold purpose. The tone, the timbre and the accent of Mike Hammer (Darren McGavin) build his hard-boiled detective ethos.

> I had a hunch it was gonna be one of those days when I might as well have stayed in bed. The kind of a day when the telephone doesn't ring, and there's nothing but bills and advertisement in the mail. But I was only half right. The telephone didn't ring, but the mail contained something besides bills and advertisements. The envelope was soiled and smudged and smelled of lubricating oil, my name and address had been printed with a pencil, the letter had been mailed in Manhattan the night before, but there was no return address. (*Mickey Spillane's Mike Hammer*, 'Park the Body')

Such voices offer a distanced perspective on the facts. They also support the association of masculinity to rationality, critical distance and cold-bloodedness.

Male voice-over narrators also tend to inscribe their TV narratives within a larger American story. Several series use the voice-over to describe a typically American space such as the megalopolis or the South. Thus, the pilot of *The Dukes of Hazzard* (CBS, 1979–85) opens with the heroes chasing a police car in their red muscle car nicknamed 'General Lee' with a confederate flag on the roof. The scene is commented by 'the Balladeer' (Waylon Jennings):

> Welcome to Hazzard County. You probably noticed there's something different here. Well, this is Hazzard County. They do things different here. This is Bo Duke and Luke Duke, they're cousins, they fight the system. (*The Dukes of Hazzard*, s01e01)

Here, the male narrator is a guide in a new territory and provides his own interpretation of the situation – Bo and Luke are not roughnecks nostalgic for the Confederate rebellion; they are resisting against institutions that threaten individual liberties. Therefore, the narrators do not simply tell a story: they frame it. The audience is told about the social rules of the space where the scene is set and about the ethical dilemmas that the characters face in this situation.

When male voice-overs are first-person narrators, they often bear a retrospective dimension. The voices of older men often tell the stories of their younger selves. In *The Waltons* (CBS, 1972–81), the voice of Earl Hamner Jr., the series' creator, frames the episodes. It is the voice of John-Boy, the main character, after he has become a writer. His cues tell the story of an idealized youth, in a home where the values of the agrarian republic are central:

> A mountain has no need for people, but people do need mountains. We go to them for their beauty, for the exhilaration of standing close to mysterious skies, for the feeling of triumph that comes from having labored to reach a summit, and I remember a day in the 1930s when I went to Walton's Mountain in search of manhood.
>
> I became not a hunter but a writer and I hope a source of some pride to my father. For to be a good hunter or a good writer one must know why he hunts or why he writes. And the why-of-it-all for me lies in that house and in the memory of voices that rise in the night and will sweetly haunt my life forever. (*The Waltons*, s01e05)

The edifying dimension of the narrative is reinforced by the voice-over that points to the transmission of a certain model of masculinity.

A retrospective dimension also characterizes the voice of Ted Mosby explaining to his children how he met their mother (*How I Met Your Mother*, CBS, 2005–14). Bob Saget was hired as the narrator (whereas the character on screen is played by Josh Radnor), thus creating a different Ted: one that is a father and wants to share his experience with his children – maybe one that is not very different from the widowed father from *Full House*, played by Bob Saget, as some fans have suggested.[5] These voice-overs open and close most episodes, constructing male characters who are entitled to share the knowledge and wisdom granted by experience.

Here, male voice-overs are voices of men who know what they are talking about. Their position in space, time and in the narrative grant them authority. While the device has been associated with authority, here the characterization of the narrators is more important than the device itself. Producer, writer, detective, father – the men who speak are defined by the authority society bestows on them. Male voice-overs are traditionally inscribed in the gendered hierarchy they reinforce.

A feminine 'I'

One of the first series to feature a female voice-over is *Little House on the Prairie* (NBC, 1974–83). Laura Ingalls (Melissa Gilbert) is the first-person narrator of the pilot of this series adapted from Ingalls Wilder's autobiographical books. However, the narration is not retrospective since it is the child's voice that tells the story mostly for exposition purposes. The next notable example is the pilot episode of another period drama about a woman going West. In *Dr. Quinn, Medicine Woman* (CBS, 1993–8), Michaela Quinn (Jane Seymour) tells her story in the first person. From the 1970s onwards, the representation of women on TV changed: characters such as Mary from *The Mary Tyler Moore Show* (CBS, 1970–7), or later Murphy Brown from the eponymous CBS sitcom (1988–98), brought independent professional women to the fore. And yet female voice-overs did not appear in these sitcoms celebrating the new 'new women' but rather on shows that presented pioneer women who wrote a page of the narrative of the conquest of the American West. Laura's and Michaela's voices link the personal journeys and the national quest in one narrative. These early examples of female voice-overs opened the pilots, but they did not become part of the narrative structure of the following episodes. Still, they were signs of the emergence of feminine subjectivity on television.

My So-Called Life (ABC, 1994–5) was the first show to regularly use a female voice-over, in a way that was central to the construction of the narrative. Angela Chase (Claire Danes), a fifteen-year-old teenager, shares her thoughts, her feelings and her doubts in voice-over monologues that remind the audience of a diary. In an interview, the writers explained that they wanted to convey what was going on in a teenage girl's mind.[6] Although it only lasted one season, the series inaugurated the trend of teenage shows and had a lasting influence on the way television represents adolescence. In 1998, a slightly older young woman, Felicity Porter (Keri Russell), recorded her story on tapes sent to her friend Sally thus providing the voice-over narration for the drama *Felicity* (The WB, 1998–2002). These examples are indebted to nineteenth-century autobiographies, diaries and epistolary novels. They suggest that the inspiration for the first female voice-overs in TV series came from literature and were associated with subjective narratives focusing on personal experience. Suzanne Ferris and Mallory Young argue that narrative techniques such as journaling, correspondence or simply first-person narrative assimilate a large corpus of work written by women to the chick-lit genre (Ferriss and Young, 2006: 4). The first examples of female voice-over in TV series were anchored in this gendered cultural tradition.

What is at stake in the use of female voice-overs is the elaboration of a 'genuine' representation of intimacy. Internal focalization and the emphasis on the characters' intimacy and interpersonal relationships are part of the definition of feminine media genres – many examples of female voice-overs since the 1990s fit this description. Ally McBeal's interior voice, for instance, revealed to the audience what the character could not say out loud. Carrie Bradshaw's narrating voice in *Sex and the City* (HBO, 1998–2004) focused only on the four characters' intimate life.

The renewed success of primetime soaps accelerated this trend. In the framing voice-over monologues of *Grey's Anatomy* (ABC, 2005–), Meredith Grey spells out the theme of the episode (superstition, anger, communication, etc.). These monologues often use 'we' to include the audience in the existential musings of the protagonist. But sometimes the commentary calls out to the audience, as in Season 5's finale: 'Did you say it? "I love you. I don't ever want to live without you. You changed my life." Did you say it? Make a plan. Set a goal. Work toward it, but every now and then, look around. Drink it in 'cause this is it. It might all be gone tomorrow' (*Grey's Anatomy*, s05e24). Paired with music in a moment of great narrative tension, the voice-over here is greatly indebted to melodrama.

In a much lighter way, contemporary comedies use the voice-over as a reflexive and meta-narrative device. *The Mindy Project* (Fox, 2012–15; Hulu, 2015–17) regularly plays with the convention of chick culture. The main character, Mindy Lahiri (Mindy Kaling), is addicted to romantic comedies and romance novels. In several scenes, she comments on her life in voice-over:

> Met in an elevator, my hair came undone, are you kidding me? I am basically Sandra Bullock! And then, it happened –

Before the commentary becomes synchronous and reveals that Mindy was in fact telling her story to another character.

> – We were stuck in the elevator for twenty minutes, and I moved into his apartment two months later. (*The Mindy Project*, s01e01)

The character consciously plays the role of the romcom heroine and interprets her life through the prism of movies such as *When Harry Met Sally* (Reiner, Columbia Pictures, 1989), *Sleepless in Seattle* (Ephron, Tristar Pictures, 1993) or *Bridget Jone's Diary* (Maguire, Universal Pictures, 2001). Open references to these romantic comedies stress the meta-narrative dimension of the voice-over. They also point to the show as the heir of a tradition of films – from the women's films of the 1940s to the romcoms of the turn of the century – that have shaped representations of femininity and gender relations. The way *The Mindy Project* uses the voice-over emphasizes how strongly this way of publicizing private thoughts has become associated with cultural and media products targeting women.

New voice-overs and renewed gender representations

At the beginning of the twenty-first century, male voice-overs started using the first person. Thus, they went beyond their traditional function and manifested the intimacy of the male characters. The most striking example of this change was J.D.'s voice-over in *Scrubs* (NBC, 2001–8; ABC, 2009–10). The sitcom used the voice-over to convey the thoughts and feelings of a young medical intern played by Zach Braff. Contrary to most male characters in twentieth-century TV series, J.D. was full of doubts and flaws as he tried to figure out the world he lived in. Everything in the show was seen from J.D.'s perspective, and J.D.'s thoughts were conveyed not only by the voice-over but also through visual effects. Creator Bill Lawrence explained,

> What we decided was, rather than have it be a monotone narration, if it's going to be told through Zach's voice, we're going to do everything through J.D.'s eyes. … It opened up a visual medium that those of us as comedy writers were not used to. (Weisman, 2009)

The different audiovisual devices used to convey the character's feelings are similar to those used in *Ally McBeal* (Fox, 1997–2002). The focus on J.D.'s feelings goes with a feminization of the character. For instance, in one scene where the camera pans around a bathroom and the voice-over says, 'Living with Eliot was certainly different. Every inch of her apartment was filled with girly stuff. There were lavender scented candles, pink robes, bath salts. It – was – awesome' (*Scrubs*, s05e07). When the voice-over pronounces 'awesome', the camera focuses on J.D. enjoying a bubble bath, his head wrapped in a pink towel turban. Later in the episode, J.D. is nicknamed Dorothy, a joke that relies in part on the repetitive questioning of J.D.'s sexual identity and orientation by his friends and colleagues. The show conjures up stereotyped gender representations and undermines them through the voice-over. *Scrubs* introduced a male voice-over that was not supposed to convey objectivity nor authority. Instead, it expressed a male character's subjectivity and relied on the empathy it generates in the audience.

The notion of empathy is central to the reception of *Dexter* (Showtime, 2006–13), a drama whose eponymous hero is a serial killer. Dexter's thoughts are spoken in first-person voice-over, often conveying cynical comments that bring out the protagonist's double identity. The voice-over plays on traditional gender and genre codes and on their subversion.

> Dexter's originality lies in the 'normality' of the serial killer. Even though Dexter is a vocational killer, he is only a man who blunders, makes mistakes and tries to do the right things. This presentation of the serial killer, together with his role as executioner of bad guys, determines the complicity the character generates. (Santaularia, 2010: 69)

The voice-over in *Dexter* helps build an ambiguous character. In the first episode, Dexter introduces himself in this way:

> My name is Dexter. Dexter Morgan. I don't know what made me the way I am, but whatever it was left a hollow place inside. People fake a lot of human interactions, but I feel like I fake them all and I fake them very well. And that's my burden, I guess. (*Dexter*, s01e01)

Because the voice-over shares Dexter's secrets, it positions the members of the audience as accomplices. They witness the actions and thoughts of a character who is presented as a likeable monster. This uncomfortable position is made even more so since Dexter immediately reveals that he can fake human interactions, and therefore the voice-over might be unreliable.

Both dimensions are also found in *Desperate Housewives* (ABC, 2004–12). Viewers learn to trust the narrating voice of Mary Alice Young (Brenda Strong) during the first season. Her soothing tone suggests a gentle character whose secret could not be so terrible. And yet, the season finale reveals that Mary Alice was the author of a gruesome murder. In both series, the voice-over is unsettling, because it gives the audience access to the thoughts and feelings of a 'monster' and forces them to be accomplices. In *Dexter*, the character's ability to feign social relations forces the audience to decide whether or not to trust what the voice-over says, for instance, when he declares about his parents' death: 'I didn't kill them, honest' (*Dexter*, s01e01). The audience is also encouraged to trust Mary Alice even after her crime and lies have been revealed. As Mary Alice keeps on narrating the next seven seasons, the viewers have no choice but to rely on her.

Male voice-overs are used in TV series that target a large 'neutral' (male by default) audience. *Dead Like Me* (Showtime, 2003–4) is the main example of a series that does not specifically target women but uses a female voice-over. Male voice-overs can also be present in series whose target audience is mostly women. One example of this is the 'Latin Lover Narrator' in *Jane the Virgin* (The CW, 2014–19). In this series adapted from a Venezuelan *telenovela*, the main character is a young woman, whose story is told by a voice-over whose position is not clear. The narrator (Anthony Mendez) speaks with a heavy Spanish accent and first seems to be a typical omniscient narrator controlling what is seen on screen. But as the first season moves on, the Latin Lover Narrator becomes more and more important, so much so that the character and the actor generated a lot of interest from fans and the press (Bradley, 2015; Friedlander, 2015; Hill, 2015). His status evolves in the first season. For instance, he conveys Jane's thoughts when he exclaims 'OMG! It's him, it's him!' when the cell phone of the heroine rings (*Jane the Virgin*, s01e07), but he also voices the reaction of the audience when he comments on the discovery of a secret passage: 'Oh, wow! An unexpected twist.' In the same episode he concludes by addressing the audience directly: 'I told you the drama was just getting started' (s01e09). The voice-over blurs the boundaries of the narrative and plays a central role in the reflexive dimension of the show. The influence of *Sex and the City* on the series is made obvious when the narrator says, 'It's hard not to get all Carrie Bradshaw' (s01e15). *Jane the Virgin* plays with the boundaries of fiction and the metanarrative dimension is crucial throughout the series: Jane is an aspiring writer who loves *telenovelas*, romance novels and magical realism; Jane's second novel ends on the characters' story being turned into a *telenovela*, and in a final plot twist the viewers discover that the narrator is in fact Mateo, her son who grew up to become a voice-over actor (*Jane the Virgin*, s05e19, Figure 8.1). While the first male voice-overs were used mostly for exposition purposes and the first female voice-overs conveyed the thoughts and feelings of female protagonists, the reflexive use of the voice-over allows writers to play with genre and gender representations.

Figure 8.1 *Jane the Virgin*, S05e19, 'Chapter One Hundred', developed by Jennie Snyder Urman © The CW 2019.

Women's voices have come a long way since the 1920s and comments that questioned their place in audiovisual media. As the industry started to openly target the 'niche' female audience in the post-network era, female voice-overs emerged as key elements in fictional TV series at the turn of the twenty-first century. The renewed emphasis on the characters' feelings and thoughts played a role in the more general evolution of TV series towards what Jason Mittell calls 'complex TV' (Mittell, 2015). As this chapter suggests, the evolution towards more complex narratives and towards stories that focus on the characters' inner turmoil is linked to the influence of devices and genres traditionally coded as feminine. The creative uses of voice-over by women-centred series have had an influence on the evolution of male voice-overs. Voice-overs are no longer limited to omniscient and objective narration; they are often used to highlight the flaws and contradictions of the characters and they sometimes upset traditional gender representations. The growing use of voice-over in various TV formats went hand in hand with the confusion of the public and private spheres. The creation of TV series based on characterization rather than action encouraged writers to foreground emotions, reflection and decision making. Female and new male voice-overs epitomize the complexity of contemporary serial TV narratives. In terms of gender representation, such voice-overs subvert traditional narrative rules and give more importance to emotions and behaviours that are culturally coded as feminine. These voices are part of a larger trend that allows audiences to hear more diverse stories.

Notes

1 For a more detailed review of the literature on this topic, see Le Fèvre-Berthelot (2013).
2 See Percheron and Butzel (1980: 16–23), Chion (1982) and Kozloff (1988).
3 See Bailblé (1978: 54–9), Chion (1982), Doane (1980: 33–50) and Silverman (1985: 57–69; 1988); for a more critical take on the psychoanalytic perspective, see Sjogren (2006).

4 Châteauvert (1996), Boillat (2007), Jost (2004) and Jullier (2000: 8).
5 See *How I Met Your Mother*; Browne (2014).
6 MSCL.com.

Works cited

Altman, Rick (1992), 'Introduction: Four and a half film fallacies', in Rick Altman (ed.), *Sound Theory, Sound Practice*, 35–45, New York: Routledge.

Bailblé, Claude (1978), 'Programmation de l'écoute (1)', *Les Cahiers Du Cinéma*, 292: 54–59.

Boillat, Alain (2007), *Du Bonimenteur à La Voix-over: Voix-Attraction et Voix-Narration Au Cinéma*, Lausanne: Editions Antipodes.

Bradley, Laura (2015), 'Why Latin Lover Narrator is the best character on *Jane the Virgin*', *Slate*, 11 May. Available online: http://www.slate.com/blogs/browbeat/2015/05/11/jane_the_virgin_s_narrator_is_the_best_thing_about_the_cw_show.html (accessed 16 July 2015).

Châteauvert, Jean (1996), *Des Mots à l'image: La Voix over Au Cinéma*, Québec: Nuit blanche éditeur.

Chion, Michel (1982), *La Voix Au Cinéma*, Paris: Cahiers du Cinéma, Éditions de l'Étoile.

Doane, Mary Ann (1980), 'The voice in the cinema: The articulation of body and space', *Yale French Studies*, 60: 33–50.

Ferriss, Suzanne, and Mallory Young (2006), 'Introduction', in *Chick Lit: The New Woman's Fiction*, Londres: Routledge.

Friedlander, Whitney (2015), '"Jane the Virgin" narrator Anthony mendez woos his fans', *Variety*, 6 September. Available online: http://variety.com/2015/tv/news/jane-the-virgin-latin-lover-anthony-mendez-voiceover-1201514664/ (accessed 16 July 2015).

How I Met Your Mother Wiki, 'Future Ted'. Available online: http://how-i-met-your-mother.wikia.com/wiki/Future_Ted (accessed 7 July 2017).

Hill, Libby (2015), 'How *Jane the Virgin* is redefining TV narration', *Vulture*, 5 December. Available online: http://www.vulture.com/2015/05/jane-the-virgin-is-redefining-tv-narration.html (accessed 16 July 2015).

Hilmes, Michele (1999), 'Desired and feared: Women's voices in radio history', in Mary Beth Haralovich and Lauren Rabinovitz (eds), *Television, History, and American Culture*, 17–35, Durham, NC: Duke University Press.

Jost, François (2004), 'Un Continent Perdu: Le Son à La Télévision', in Dominique Nasta and Didier Huvelle (eds), *Le Son En Perspective: Nouvelles Recherches/New Perspectives in Sound Studies, 213–22,* Bruxelles: P.I.E. – Peter Lang.

Jost, François (2011), *De Quoi Les Séries Américaines Sont-Elles Le Symptôme?*, Paris: CNRS éditions.

Jullier, Laurent (2000), 'Etre Devant, Etre Dedans. Son et Parole à La Télévision d'un Point de Vue Cognitiviste', 1–8, Séminaire Téléparoles, INA/Université de Metz. Available online: http://laurent.jullier.free.fr/TEL/LJ2000_DevantDedans.pdf.

Kallas, Christina (2010), *Creative Screenwriting: Understanding Emotional Structure*, trans. John Howard, New York: Palgrave Macmillan.

Kozloff, Sarah (1988), *Invisible Storytellers: Voice-Over Narration in American Fiction Film*, Berkeley: University of California Press.

Kozloff, Sarah (2000), *Overhearing Dialogue*, Berkeley: University of California Press.

Lawrence, Amy (1991), *Echo and Narcissus: Women's Voices in Classical Hollywood Cinema*, Berkeley: University of California Press.

Le Fèvre-Berthelot, Anaïs (2013), 'Audio-visual: Disembodied voices in theory', *InMedia. The French Journal of Media and Media Representations in the English-Speaking World*, 4. Available online: http://inmedia.revues.org/697.

Le Fèvre-Berthelot, Anaïs (2015), 'Ecoutez Voir. Revisiter Le Genre Par Les Voix Des Femmes Dans Les Séries Télévisées Américaines Contemporaines', Sorbonne Nouvelle, Paris 3.

McKay, Anne (1988), 'Speaking up: Voice amplification and women's struggle for public expression', in Cheris Kramarae (ed.), *Technology and Women's Voices: Keeping in Touch*, 187–207, New York: Routledge & Kegan Paul.

Mittell, Jason (2015), *Complex TV: The Poetics of Contemporary Television Storytelling*, New York: New York University Press.

MSCL.com, 'So-called scripts 2002 bonus DVD interview'. Available online: http://www.mscl.com/scripts/dvdinterview.html (accessed 14 July 2015).

Percheron, Daniel, and Marcia Butzel (1980), 'Sound in cinema and its relationship to image and diegesis', *Yale French Studies*, 60: 16–23.

Santaularia, Isabel (2010), 'Dexter: Villain, hero or simply a man? The perpetuation of traditional masculinity in *Dexter*', *Atlantis*, 32.2: 57–71.

Seger, Linda (1994), *Making a Good Script Great,* 2nd edn, Hollywood: Samuel French Trade.

Silverman, Kaja (1985), 'A voice to match: The female voice in classic cinema', *Iris*, 3.1: 57–69.

Silverman, Kaja (1988), *The Acoustic Mirror: The Female Voice in Psychoanalysis and Cinema*, Bloomington: Indiana University Press.

Simpson Browne, Kit (2014), 'The dark secret behind the *How I Met Your Mother* Finale', *Movie Pilot*, 4 April. Available online: https://moviepilot.com/posts/1317577 (accessed 7 July 2017).

Sjogren, Britta (2006), *Into the Vortex – Female Voice and Paradox in Film*, Urbana: University of Illinois Press.

Weisman, Jon (2009), 'Genre jumping pays off', *Variety*, 23 March. Available online: http://web.archive.org/web/20090323235123/http://www.variety.com/awardcentral_vstory/VR1117936723.html (accessed 16 July 2015).

Wolfe, Charles (1997), 'Historicising the "voice of God": The place of vocal narration in classical documentary', *Film History*, 9.2: 149–67.

9

Moving into the mainstream: Pregnancy, motherhood and female TV action heroes

Anne Sweet

Lead female heroic characters in American TV action-drama series have caused multiple debates about female empowerment and feminism (or the lack thereof) at least since their breakout success on shows like *Wonder Woman* (CBS/ABC, 1975–9) and *Charlie's Angels* (ABC, 1976–81) that debuted during the sexual revolution and the second wave of feminism. These characters can be defined as 'female action heroes', as Frances Early and Kathleen Kennedy note that the use of the word 'hero' rather than heroine denotes a woman who has particular heroic agency and power at the centre of a popular culture narrative, such as that of an action drama (2003: 3–4).[1] While these characters were once rare and exceptional, in the post-2000 era, they have become an accepted and integral part of the TV landscape – both in women-centred dramas like *Rizzoli & Isles* (TNT, 2010–16) and as part of ensemble casts such as *Once Upon a Time* (ABC, 2011–18) and *Lucifer* (Fox/Netflix, 2016–21). However, even if female action heroes have moved into the mainstream, they nevertheless continue to be vehicles for gender discourses that both undermine and empower them as symbols of feminist progress, and this can especially be exemplified in the way motherhood and pregnancy are depicted in TV series that feature them. On TV, showing pregnancy was once taboo, and televised depictions of pregnancy and motherhood have been fraught with controversy as they have raised questions about the representation of women's bodies, sexuality, sexual identity and right to choose. Amanda Lotz maintains that in interpreting mediatized gender messages,

> emphasis must be placed on the constancy of struggle and perpetual reassertion of dominant perspectives, and a medium such as popular television is an important site to examine because of the way its stories contribute to the ideological state apparatus – social institutions such as family, churches, education systems and the media that teach and enforce 'proper' ways of being, thinking and believing within society. (Lotz, 2014: 41)

TV series featuring female action heroes continue this 'struggle', and Lotz furthers notes that in these media productions, which continue to be produced in a male-dominated industry,[2] there are competing patriarchal and feminist ideologies and discourses.

Representations of women in the media from the 1990s onwards are often linked to 'third-wave feminism' or 'post-feminism'.[3] However, the ambiguity and changing definitions of these terms have led Lotz to dismiss them as 'too fraught with contradictory meanings to be useful' in analysing gender on TV series, thus leading her to favour the expression 'post-second-wave', as contemporary gender representations are 'more clearly an outcome of second-wave activism – albeit long in fruition – than a result of more nascent feminist generations or their endeavours' (Lotz, 2014: 23). Female action heroes can thus be analysed as 'post-second-wave' representations and examined in terms of the way they represent and reflect social changes effected through the second wave's efforts to achieve female equality.

Lead female heroic characters in action dramas are generally depicted as young, conventionally attractive, aspirational models of success, which, according to Hannah Sanders, 'epitomizes the postfeminist dialectic of "having it all", the assumption that feminism's goals have been achieved and all that modern women have to do is choose a lifestyle from the endless range of options now available to them' (Sanders, 2007: 74). But in fact, female action heroes are rarely allowed to truly have it all. Moreover, pregnancy and motherhood are often portrayed quite negatively in series which feature them, which would seem to be at odds with the feminist progress presented by the series. This will be demonstrated by an analysis of the gender discourses and meanings being produced by series featuring female action heroes in terms of pregnancy and motherhood through the prism of the following recurrent narrative tropes:

1. Pregnancy is often disempowering for the heroines, as it involves a loss of mastery over their bodies, their moods and thus their minds, which is often depicted for comedic effect. They are notably the victims of hormones, unwanted pregnancies and/or uncontrollable bodily functions.
2. Childbirth is associated with extreme trauma and/or accompanied by violence, and can even quite literally be portrayed as horrific through the use of horror film tropes and/or the 'monstrous womb' as described by Barbara Creed in her research, which draws upon Julia Kristeva's ideas of the abject feminine. As Creed notes,

    > the womb represents the utmost in abjection for it contains a new life form which will pass from inside to outside bringing with it traces of its contamination – blood, afterbirth, faeces. The abject nature of the womb, and the birth process caused the Church fathers to recoil in horror at the very idea that man should be born of woman. The horror film exploits the abject nature of the womb by the depicting the human, female and male, giving birth to the monstrous. (1997: 49)

3. Motherhood is depicted as being extremely problematic for heroic mothers, and it is often complicated by the fact that they have to defend their progeny from specific threats. To wit, action-drama heroines often give birth to 'special babies' who have extraordinary destinies to fulfil and/or are being hunted by villains for some nefarious purpose. While maternity is often used as a way to explain and justify both TV and film heroines' violence (Tasker, 1998: 69), in contemporary TV action dramas, it is also used to

illustrate their issues with work/life balance and demonstrate the incompatibility of being a hero and a mother.

4. When present in the series, the mothers of female action heroes are rarely depicted in a good light, reflecting a potential bias against older women in media representations. Representations of the 'monstrous-feminine' also apply to the mothers, as they are often depicted as transgressive or evil characters who are either absent or dead. When living, they are often failures in life, and rarely, if ever, aspirational characters or role models.

These recurring tropes can be found in some of the most successful series to feature female action heroes as mothers in lead roles, such as *Xena: Warrior Princess* (Syndicated, 1995–2001), *Charmed* (WB/CW, 1998–2006), *Once Upon a Time* (ABC, 2011–18) and *Wynonna Earp* (Syfy, 2016–21). They also exist in varying degrees in ensemble series from the 1990s and early 2000s, like *Star Trek: Deep Space Nine* (Syndicated/UPN, 1993–9), *The X-Files* (Fox, 1993–2018) and *Alias* (ABC, 2001–6). Moreover, they have carried through into modern series like *The Blacklist* (NBC, 2013–), *Rizzoli & Isles* (TNT, 2010–16), *Jessica Jones* (Netflix, 2015–19), *Lucifer* (Fox/Netflix, 2016–21), the *Charmed* reboot (WB, 2018–) and *Bones* (Fox, 2005–17). Many of these series belong to the genre Lotz categorizes as 'female-centred action dramas', which include both fantasy and more realistic series: 'Such series feature protagonists that can be characterised as action heroines in the most extreme cases, but at least as females possessing extraordinary physical, intellectual or mystical power' (2006: 32). Thus, for the purposes of this study, the category 'female action heroes' will include female characters with leading roles in action-drama series whose heroism puts them in danger and forces them to use violence, a category that features women in a variety of heroic roles including warriors, police officers, forensic scientists, crime-solvers and witches.

TV is an interesting object of study in terms of gender discourses as it has often been considered more progressive in feminist terms than film. This is notably due to TV executives' early awareness of the importance of creating content to attract well-educated female consumers whose university educations made them aware of and interested in the feminist movement, and whose disposable incomes made them a desirable target demographic for advertisers and lucrative audiences for whom to create content (Douglas, 1995; Rabinovitz, 1999). Then, after the rise of cable channels, TV producers began conceiving programmes that would appeal specifically to women and audiences in niche markets, which allowed them to be more innovative and daring in terms of gender messages (Lotz, 2006). In order to understand the push-pull of the feminist and patriarchal discourses at play in action dramas featuring female TV action heroes, the discourses will first be contextualized to see how representations of televised pregnancy, and female action heroes, have moved from the margins into the mainstream. Then, the recurring narrative tropes will be analysed in more detail in order to examine the ways in which the negative representation of maternity potentially represents a form of containment to the empowerment and agency of TV female action heroes.

Moving from the margins to the mainstream: Pregnancy on TV and the rise of mothers in action dramas

Well after the controversy raised by the depiction of Lucy's pregnancy in *I Love Lucy* (CBS, 1951–7), the representation of pregnancy and sexuality were still thorny issues when the female action-hero-drama genre began on the small screen in the 1970s, in the wake of the sexual revolution and the second wave of feminism. 'Network programming executives initially became interested in "feminist programming" because it was good business,' notes Lauren Rabinovitz (1999: 145). At this time, advertisers were trying to reach a new, younger generation of women who were more independent than their elders (ibid., 145–6; D'Acci 1994: 63–104). Nevertheless, Julie D'Acci sees the 1970s as a time when TV and film representations 'were highly contradictory' and calls the mid-70s the '"jiggle" era' of TV, with a shift from programmes that mostly featured domestic characters (mothers, housewives, etc.) to series like *Wonder Woman* (CBS/ABC, 1975–9) and *Charlie's Angels* (ABC, 1976–81) that tapped into women as sex objects and exploited their bodies as 'spectacle' (D'Acci, 1994: 13–14). These women were not mothers, but single women, whose charm was based partly on their sexual availability: it would have been too scandalous to show their pregnancy at the time. Yet, *Charlie's Angels*, notably, did find a backhanded way around this by having one of its main characters, Kelly, pose undercover as an expectant mother who wants to give her baby up for adoption. Having characters go undercover, or assume another identity through various plot devices, has often been a way for producers to explore subjects that might be considered too 'shocking' or taboo for networks, their sponsors and/or viewers. The 'unreality' of the situation allows it to be brushed off as a one-off, not really the character's true self or the show's real stance on an issue.[4]

If the 1980s were considered by Susan Faludi (1991) to be a moment of 'backlash' against feminism, notably in the media, an important exception can be found in *Cagney & Lacey* (CBS, 1982–8), which was not only exceptional for having two female police officers in lead roles at a time when there was a dearth of strong women's roles, but also for addressing important social issues. Similarly to *I Love Lucy*, the decision was made to incorporate a pregnancy into the storyline in order to accommodate the real-life pregnancy of one of the stars. The depiction of this pregnancy was also considered a delicate matter, even if the social mores had changed and pregnancy had become much more commonplace on television. A detailed *New York Times* article from the time, entitled 'The Pregnant Detective', describes the production team's struggle to hit just the right note when Mary Beth Lacey became pregnant with her third child (Stabiner, 1985). Acknowledging overtly that a lead female character was having sex or could get pregnant was no longer problematic, but producers now had to address such thorny issues as unplanned pregnancies and abortion, for example. They were worried about how the pregnancy storyline would resonate with the show's 20.7 million viewers, especially with women viewers – its target demographic. The *New York Times* underlines the stakes involved:

> CBS has structured its Monday night line-up with women in mind, to offer an alternative to ABC's 'Monday Night Football'. In its crucial 10 P.M. time slot, 'Cagney & Lacey'– forced by events to tackle the story of how a 38-year-old working woman decides when and whether to have a child, and how to juggle family and career – could well strengthen CBS's standing by addressing issues that have lately become a national obsession. (Ibid.)

The article further reports that in discussions with staff on how to handle the pregnancy, the executive producer, Barney Rosenzweig, understood the power and importance of his series as a platform to explore women's changing roles in society and evolving social mores, and it notes that he 'posed his standard query: "What are we saying to the women of America?"' (ibid.). The producers did not want to ignore the issue of abortion in light of its social importance, but they did not necessarily want to show one either, which could be controversial and unpopular with many viewers. A compromise was thus decided upon: Lacey would be desirous of her current pregnancy and keep the baby but would mention that she did have an illegal abortion in the past in an episode called 'The Clinic' (5.6) in which, heavily pregnant, she investigates the bombing of an abortion clinic. The matter of the show's position on abortion was considered of such import that the production team had the National Organization for Women and National Abortion Rights Action League screen 'The Clinic' prior to broadcast and asked for their support (Gendel, 1985).

By the 1990s, the gender issues that were considered as pushing the envelope had changed. In the 1980s, the producers of *Cagney & Lacey* were concerned about the lead protagonists being perceived as lesbians, to the point that one of the lead actors was replaced at the beginning of the series by a more 'feminine' version in a move the press considered to be 'a tactic to squelch gay implications CBS apparently is convinced viewers associate with scenarios in which women work seriously together' (D'Acci, 1994: 41). But in the 1990s, the producers of *Xena: Warrior Princess* actively encouraged the idea that the characters of Xena and Gabrielle were gay through a subtext that included 'relatively subtle hints' like taking a bath naked together, in order to please fans who enjoyed reading them as a couple (Helford, 1999: 139). The 'father' of Xena's baby Eve was a woman, as Xena was impregnated in an immaculate conception by the soul of her arch-rival, the female warrior Callisto. She co-parented the baby with her sidekick Gabrielle, so that Xena became a gay icon, even if the producers were not allowed to officially 'out' her as it was considered risky in terms of viewers and sponsors at the time (Figure 9.1).

In the years post-2000, the diversification of media distribution has led to increasingly varied and edgy content, yet contradictory and competing patriarchal and feminist discourses in terms of the representation of women have not been eliminated. While some aspects of the depictions of women on TV have changed for the better, notably in terms of richer and more inclusive representations of women of different ethnic, gender and sexual identities,[5] negative representations of women's reproductive and maternal functions have survived, especially in action-drama series, which can be evidenced through an examination of recurring narrative tropes in series containing female TV action heroes.

Figure 9.1 Xena with charm and baby in *Xena: Warrior Princess*, S05e13, 'Eternal Bonds', developed by John Schulian and Robert Tapert © Studios USA Television Distribution 1999.

Disempowerment through loss of body control and the spectacle of the unruly pregnant woman

Female TV action heroes are usually both physically and mentally competent, which makes these representations quite empowering and explains in part why they are popular with many viewers. If the TV series in which they are featured can be praised for their depictions of pregnant women who continue to be active and who do not turn into fragile flowers, pregnancy also undermines them, robbing them of their mastery of themselves, both physically and mentally. A first indicator pointing to loss of body control is the fact that most female TV action heroes' pregnancies are not planned. In addition, the women are often unaware that they are pregnant for a while and/or their pregnancies are often a surprise. They are often told about their pregnancies and what is happening in their bodies by someone else: a friend, a relative, a co-worker or even a stranger. For example, the FBI-agent-turned-fugitive Liz from *The Blacklist* was not aware for a few months that she was pregnant, while Red, her informant, says he suspected it:

Liz: I'm pregnant.
Red: Yes. I've known for some time.
Liz: How?
Red: Everything. Your body, your skin, the look in your eyes. Different tastes for different foods. Nausea, distracted, moody.
Liz: (Laughs) Yes. With everything that was happening, I just – I mean I guess I knew, but I just couldn't – I bought a pregnancy test three weeks ago, and I threw it out before I took it. I mean, I was okay facing the Cabal, but those two red lines – I just could not handle that. ('The Vehm' 3.12)

Not only does Liz find criminals easier to manage than being pregnant, but she has her pregnancy symptoms explained to her by a male criminal informant who at this time is positioned as a father-like figure to her. In many cases, such as in this example, being pregnant subordinates the female action hero to the people around her, who have to explain her own body to her,[6] which undermines the usual competence and authority she exhibits in most other matters as well as her feminist heroic potential. Furthermore, some aspects of getting pregnant seem too taboo or uncomfortable to handle. For example, while most female action heroes are sexually active, birth control is rarely discussed before or during intercourse. In the rare cases when a pregnant female hero says she was 'being careful', we see that she nevertheless has no control when it comes to pregnancy.

Not only are there natural surprise pregnancies like Liz's, but babies can even be 'womb invaders', especially in supernatural or science fiction series, in which demonic or technologically induced pregnancies are forced upon the heroines, like when Agent Scully from *The X-Files* is impregnated as part of alien experiments in collaboration with human co-conspirators in the US government. Despite the element of surprise involved in many of their pregnancies, most female action heroes decide to remain pregnant and abortion is generally a non-issue, which likely represents – as in the case of *Cagney & Lacey* – the producers' anxiety over potentially upsetting viewers and thus alienating the series' networks and financers in a country where there is a very important conservative and Christian resistance to a woman's right to choose. Yet some pregnancies do not end in healthy babies. For those that do, the female action heroes often do not end up raising their children due to various plot devices, and motherhood is often denied to them.

While pregnant, female action heroes become the victims of their hormones, which make them unable to control their own bodies or their moods (and thus their minds). In contrast to previous eras, the taboo on intimately discussing bodily functions related to pregnancy has been lifted, which can represent a certain form of social progress. Yet pregnant action heroes are often figures of fun and their pregnancy symptoms are played for comic effect, featuring the women either overtly discussing or experiencing the following issues: gas, vomiting, sneezing, frequent urination, uncontrollable crying, mood swings, hormones and/or unusual food cravings.[7] Thus, the fact of being pregnant can turn female action heroes into transgressive figures, as they lose control of their body mastery and thus their sex appeal, displaying what once might have been considered very 'unladylike' behaviour, and at times devolving into a version of the 'unruly woman' described by Kathleen Rowe who writes, 'Through body and speech, the unruly woman violates the unspoken feminine sanction against 'making a spectacle' of herself' (1997: 76). In this way, then, these somewhat comic representations of the 'reality' of pregnancy are subversive by daring to depict women as unattractive or even repulsive. Thus, pregnancy often represents a departure or a diversion from the female action heroes' character and character arc when, as soon as they become pregnant, the usually serious and in-charge heroic saviours are presented as the comic relief, with their bodies being the one thing they cannot control.

The pregnancy of a female action hero is often the result of the real-life pregnancy of the actor, and thus various plot devices are developed to work around the fact that the actors may not be as available or active as usual. If an actor is pregnant in real life, different filming techniques may be used so as not to reveal her pregnant stomach. For example, in *The X-Files*, Gillian Anderson's real-life pregnancy involved changing the way the series portrayed and filmed her character, Dana Scully. As Linda Badley notes,

> the 'story arc' was founded in, and would prove always in some sense to be about, Anderson's biology and Scully's body absence, and it was plotted in an obviously gendered way. Even the camera work and the mise-en-scène took their shape from disavowal of Anderson's anatomy, turning Scully into an X-File, a denaturalized, fractured body. (2000: 77)

For example, to film around Anderson's pregnant stomach, the camera was more focused on her face, so as not to show her growing stomach, which Badley notes had the effect of 'abstracting her into a "sexily" disembodied head' (ibid., 79). She was featured more prominently in her role as a scientist, allowing the camera to focus on her upper body as she used different kinds of lab technology and tools.

Being pregnant also often means that female action heroes, who are usually dressed to be attractive, even sexually beguiling, are for once covered up, often in bulky garments. Thus, their bodies are less available to be ogled as a sexual spectacle, although in some cases, the pregnancy-amplified breasts are still an important visual spectacle. For example, when Phoebe is turned evil by the demonic baby she is carrying in *Charmed* (and the actor is not pregnant in real life), she is styled to be sexier than usual. In this case, Alison Peirse notes that 'excessive femininity is aligned with anomalous behaviour' and her increased sexiness is thus meant to illustrate that the pregnancy has made her transgressive (2007: 122). A sexy pregnant woman, is thus, in this case, an evil one, and Peirse notes that in the series, 'power and femininity are invested with monstrosity' (ibid., 124).

The female action heroes' wombs may also become a different sort of spectacle or symbol, as Badley notes is the case in *The X-Files* during the alien abduction plotline that was created to accommodate the actor's real-life pregnancy. She deconstructs how Scully's male partner, Fox Mulder, envisions her pregnancy:

> In 'Ascension' [2.6], Mulder imagines Scully's experience on an alien operating table under blinding white light. A drill descends, the next shot framing Anderson's wondrously swelling abdomen. Vicariously, Mulder experiences what he has always wanted: her/his body filled with an alien presence, impregnated with the alien Word. Touched by the sky gods, implanted with a microchip, having immaculately conceived, Scully is transfigured, Mulder is enraptured. (Badley, 2000: 77–8)

The name of the episode, 'Ascension', with its religious connotations, is highly symbolic. Scully is seen in a white room, wearing white, almost as if she were in heaven. Mulder's vision of a technological immaculate conception foreshadows how Scully becomes a Virgin Mary figure[8] who creates life both mysteriously and against her will, as it is later discovered that she was abducted as part of a series of experiments led by a patriarchal male shadow government to create human-alien hybrids. Thus, the spectacle of the close-up of Scully's womb being penetrated by a giant drill, a violent representation of the phallus, symbolizes the ultimate loss of body control, with the female hero falling victim to the patriarchal forces that wish to control her, her body becoming a site of fantasy for her male partner.

Over and over again, in multiple action-drama series featuring female action heroes, the female hero is robbed of her body mastery and heroic agency by pregnancy. She becomes less bright, a figure of fun, a spectacle and a victim of bodily functions, hormones and even patriarchal forces. Female action heroes not only lose autonomy due to their pregnancies, which are generally not chosen, but also undergo trauma during and after childbirth, as their children often become monstrous beings.

Traumatic childbirth, horrific motherhood and the monstrous womb

Creed suggests that when pregnancy is depicted as horrible or even literally horrifying, it is related to anxiety about sexual difference and women's power to reproduce:

> The fact that the womb is still represented in cultural discourses as an object of Horror tends to contradict the argument that the reason for this is ignorance. A more probable explanation is that woman's womb – as with her other reproductive organs – signifies sexual difference and as such has the power to horrify woman's sexual other. (1997: 57)

While pregnancy is often played for comedy in action-drama series, in contrast childbirth is often a moment of trauma, and is even at times depicted using tropes from horror films. The female action hero is generally under duress during childbirth, or portrayed as a victim in some way while it is happening. The babies are often born in the midst of a battle, or while the mother is under threat. The fact that childbirth is rarely a 'normal' (even if perhaps painful) moment in life, but one when something terrible, or even completely horrifying, happens, is another way in which maternity is portrayed in a negative light in many series featuring female TV action heroes.

A case in point is the pregnancy of Gabrielle in *Xena: Warrior Princess*, which is a striking example of the deployment of the 'monstrous womb' horror trope, with Gabrielle carrying a demonic baby after she is raped by the god Dahak. Gabrielle's pregnancy is unnaturally quick, and the baby, both in and outside the womb, grows at an accelerated rate. When Gabrielle gives birth, an ensemble of unusual phenomena (a freak storm and animals going insane as she gives birth in a stable under threat from a religious order of knights on a mission to kill her baby) indicate the evil nature of her child, despite being called 'Hope' by her mother. At first, Gabrielle gives her up for her own protection but then has to kill her after Hope murders her soulmate Xena's son. Motherhood for these two particularly empowered female heroes, who usually conquer all, is filled with pain, tragedy and horror, a situation that is not unique to this series but is recurrent in other action dramas.

To wit, another significant traumatic maternity arc featuring the 'monstrous womb', which spanned over twenty years, is the one involving the abduction of Scully in *The X-Files*. As a monstrous womb, Scully has a potentially unlimited number of alien offspring living out in the world. Furthermore, when she discovers and begins to care for her offspring, they die, as in the case of her supposed daughter Emily. Badley notes that the abduction narrative arc and resulting offspring 'left Scully with the most traditional of roles: that of the monstrous and sorrowful mother, her body out of control, unconsciously proliferating, belatedly discovering and then grieving her children on the way' (2000: 84). She further notes that Scully's representation is an example of *The X-Files* 'making a feminist statement and retracting that statement in the same gesture' (ibid.). Scully was considered a trailblazer in terms of female agency on TV – with heroes like Xena and Buffy following directly in her wake – and yet she is also a victim, especially as pertains to maternity and her reproductive functions.

The recurrent narrative tropes of traumatic childbirth, horrific motherhood and the 'monstrous womb' are certainly, as Creed notes, linked to the patriarchal conception of women as 'other' and disdain for the abject as it pertains to their reproductive functions. These tropes show no sign of letting up, as evidenced by Season 8 of *The X-Files* which focuses on a horrific assisted-reproduction facility and Scully giving birth under the watchful eye of alien soldiers. More recent series have followed suit, like *Once Upon a Time*, with its many traumatic birth scenes including pregnancies that are magically and horrifyingly accelerated, and a hero giving birth while in prison chains, and *Wynonna Earp*, where Wynonna fears she is pregnant with a demon's baby and her baby keeps growing whilst she is under a sleeping spell. Thus, the female action hero, a symbol of female empowerment, is often depicted as being particularly powerless when it comes to maternity and motherhood, both of which are often shown to be incompatible with the work of a hero.

Maternal protection, progeny under threat: Work-life balance and the incompatibility of motherhood with female heroism

Allison Futrell notes that in classical heroic narratives '"heroines" exist as mothers and nursemaids of heroes and gods, fulfilling at most a supporting role' (2003: 13–14). Female action hero narratives in contemporary popular culture – by placing women at the centre of the action – are thus innovative for their break with conventional representations of women in heroic narratives. Yet Yvonne Tasker notes that positioning them as mothers defending their offspring in cinematic representations is one way to justify their 'otherness': 'The maternal recurs as a motivating factor, with female heroes acting to protect their children … or in memory of them' (1998: 69). In a similar manner, if TV female action heroes are actually allowed to be mothers, they often must defend their children from some threat. However, as TV programmes' serial narratives play out over years, and we follow the day-to-day lives of women who happen to also be heroes, this trope is also used to illustrate that the work-life balance of being a mother and being a hero is particularly complicated and that the two are generally incompatible.

In TV series, female action-drama heroes' children are often exceptional in some way and/or are desired by evildoers for one nefarious purpose or another.[9] Keeping them safe can give rise to and justify female heroism, and even in some cases, violence. For example, in *Charmed*, Piper's child, Wyatt, is supposed to be the most magical child ever born and thus is sought after by the forces of darkness who would use his magic for their evil goals. Piper becomes more powerful and violent than ever when protecting her children and it becomes a significant motivator for her actions. However, as a witch, she feels her 'otherness' acutely and wishes to be a 'normal' mother, thus rejecting her heroism. She falls into the category of what Lotz terms to be 'reluctant heroines', who feel that they must use their agency or their powers in order to save others, but who consistently 'articulate a desire to be "normal"' (2006: 81), which thus represents of form of containment of their heroism. This can notably be seen in the episode 'Desperate Housewitches' (8.4) in which Piper, who has assumed a new identity and is trying to live a normal life, helps her young son Wyatt participate in a school play. She expresses frustration over the fact that her witch duties have interfered with her maternal duties and her mastery of the domestic arts, and she feels like a failure compared to another mother, Mandi, who seems to be perfect. However, Mandi turns out to be possessed by a demon who is collaborating with The Source of All Evil to get to Wyatt, which forces Piper out her retirement to use magic to defeat her. Yet Piper still has her moment of blissful 'normalcy' at the end of the episode when she and her spouse Leo express their contentment at being allowed to watch Wyatt's play like 'normal' people. The red-haired, preppy, perfect housewife Mandi is clearly inspired by *Desperate Housewives'* (ABC, 2004–12) alpha housewife, Bree Van de Kamp, whom Niall Richardson asserts is a campy send-up of a 'Stepford Wife'[10] and who highlights the nature of 'idealised feminity' as performance in a patriarchal society (2006: 92). He notes,

> Bree acknowledges that she is in a 'desperate situation' but that she will counteract it by 'playing' her allocated role to its very limit. Bree will be the ultimate Stepford Wife, thus showing, through the campiness of her performances, that she is playing a socially constructed role within an oppressive culture. (Ibid.)

However, the feminist message in the *Charmed* episode 'Desperate Housewitches' is an ambiguous one. Piper ultimately rejects the 'idealized femininity' represented by Mandi, which aligns her with second-wave feminism's rejection of what Tatjana Takševa terms the 'oppressive dimensions of the mother role as defined by Western patriarchy' and its accompanying obligation to be a perfect wife and mother and a virtual slave to one's nuclear family (2018: 181). Yet, as a prime-time show and a commercial media product geared to appeal to mass audiences, *Charmed* aligns itself with rather mainstream values, and none of its protagonists go so far as to reject motherhood completely as some radical second-wave feminists did, or even exhibit any sort of extreme feminist positioning, which is also the case for most female action heroes in drama series.[11] Piper remains a 'reluctant heroine' and seems to aspire to be more like the perfect housewife Mandi. In fact, Piper's lifestyle corresponds to the embrace of motherhood as a voluntary choice rather than a form of oppression, which are values that Takševa (2018) underlines are linked to discourses of third-wave feminism, or post-second-wave feminism in first-world countries.[12]

In many action-drama series, being a woman of action does not seem compatible with being a mother. There is usually no happy resolution to this problem, reflecting an exaggerated version of the difficult work/life balance many women face. For example, through various plot devices, these women are often not allowed to keep their babies. For example, in a particularly tragic scene, Officer Rizzoli of *Rizzoli & Isles* is beaten violently in the stomach in the line of duty, which causes a miscarriage, reflecting a very literal presentation of the incompatibility of heroism with motherhood. If the children manage to be born, they may be killed, kidnapped or given away for safety (*Xena: Warrior Princess*/*The X-Files*/*The Blacklist*/*Wynonna Earp*) – or through supernatural plot devices, the child becomes an adult without the parents actually aging (*Xena: Warrior Princess*/*Once Upon a Time*). This means that the mothers in question are deprived of both the work and the pleasure of raising their children, with whom they are only reunited as adults. This is presented in the series as traumatic because the female heroes express the desire to raise their children themselves and are denied the experience. Those who do manage to keep their children and raise them tend to retire from their work as heroes at the end of the series. For example, the lead female characters of *Alias* and *Charmed* essentially withdraw from active heroism to raise children, thus purposely disempowering themselves. Being a devoted wife and mother is shown to be the 'happy ending' to both series. This would stand in contrast with what Sara Crosby outlines as the ultimate goal of many male heroes: a rise to power and agency. She maintains that female heroes are often blocked in attaining political agency in popular culture narratives because tough women are seen as threatening the patriarchy (2004: 154). Thus, in the cases of *Alias* and *Charmed*, the fact that motherhood is incompatible with being an action hero demonstrates the failure of 'having it all' and the realization of mainstream feminist objectives. Power and agency are often denied to the female hero in popular culture narratives through voluntary renunciation of heroism, self-sacrifice and self-disempowerment, which Crosby notes often result in the heroine's suicide or death, like Xena or Prue in *Charmed* (ibid., 153–78), to which could be added the self-sacrifice of motherhood.

Negative depictions of older mothers and the dearth of aspirational second-wave mother figures

Sanders laments 'popular feminism's lack of visibly older women' (2007: 82) and links this 'lack' to a bias against older women due to the consumerist and capitalist imperative to promote 'attractive' aspirational TV characters who will draw female viewers towards materialistic overconsumption. Series featuring female action heroes are no exception, which can be seen in the way their mothers are represented. Few are actually present in their daughters' lives, or even still alive. They are frequently depicted as either being less savvy or 'with it' than their young daughters, and they are certainly never shown as aspirational role models to be emulated. Mothers are divorced, broke, meddling or even criminals: Rizzoli's mother on *Rizzoli & Isles* lives in her friend's guesthouse after her divorce, while Bones's mother is dead and was a criminal. On *The Blacklist* as well as on *Alias*, the female protagonists' mothers were presumed dead Russian spies. In many cases, mothers are portrayed as transgressive or evil, thus representing not only a bias against older women, but also against older versions of femininity and feminism.

For example, Sanders notes that the *Charmed* sisters' mother, Patty, who has 'the most feminist potential in the show' (2007: 82) as a representative of second-wave feminism, is also notable by her absence. A divorced working mother, Patty was killed by a demon when her children were small. While she does come back as a ghost, she is much more absent than the girls' grandmother, Grams, both in life and from beyond the grave (they are both dead when the series begins). Sanders notes that 'Patti (sic.) is discredited as the "bad mother," unruly because she is divorced and rather footloose yet autonomous within the show, a trope well traversed in the iconography of popular witches' (2007: 82). Moreover, Karin Beeler hypothesizes that *Charmed* tries to distance itself from previous generations and second-wave feminism, not only through the absence of older women but also through the demonization of older female human characters and 'older versions' of femininity as represented by various mythological and supernatural figures. She notes,

> Patty and Penelope Halliwell remain ghosts in the series, and may symbolize the image of second-wave feminism as a movement from the past. Grams is further demonized in a mythic and in a feminist sense; she is presented as a crone /wolf figure (under the influence of the evil witch's spell). (2007: 110–11)

Thus, older female characters are not just portrayed as being evil or transgressive, but they can also be literally demonized by being transformed into actual embodiments of the 'monstrous feminine' through supernatural plot devices.[13]

Negative depictions of older women in action-drama series have carried on into recent series, showing very little progress in depicting older mothers in a positive light. For example, in *Jessica Jones* (Netflix, 2015–2019), Jessica's adopted mother is abusive. Jessica's real mother, Alisa, was originally presumed dead in a car crash when Jessica was an adolescent. However, Jessica later discovers that her mother was saved by a mad scientist whose experimental work on her caused her to become a biologically enhanced, mentally unstable, remorseless killer. As one critic notes, Alisa is an embodiment of rage:

> Alisa is consumed by the rage of knowing she never lived up to her own potential. She gave up her own dreams as a mathematician to placate her husband and handle duties at home. This resentment has built up for decades – about the years apart from the daughter who believed her dead, the experimentation that robbed her of autonomy, the terrifying nightmares, the way her life went awry in her previous marriage – and when her chances of happiness and peace are threatened, she isn't afraid to kill. (Bastién, 2018)

Alisa Jones's anger and violence are thus partly a response to her failure at 'having it all'. Her story brings to light, and is a platform for, feminist issues, as she is the embodiment of a woman from the second wave who was unable to achieve a fulfilling life, despite feminist progress. There is no happy end for this character who is tragically killed off.

Thus, the lack of living and/or aspirational older mothers (or even grandmothers) in many series featuring female action heroes can be perceived as a particularly negative facet of these programmes even as they display other progressive attributes, and represents a possible backlash against the second wave.

Conclusion: Patriarchal production values and post-second-wave feminist inspirations

If female TV action heroes are part of the conflicting and contradictory patriarchal and feminist discourses surrounding representations of women's social progress in popular culture, it is interesting to note that, while women are involved in the production of the TV shows mentioned in this study, most of the series cited have men – or in some cases, exclusively men – as showrunners and executive producers in an industry still dominated by men.[14] A press article about *The X-Files* reboot, 'Gillian Anderson Calls Out The Lack Of Women Behind "The X-Files"' (Cheng, 2017), notes that, up to the end of Season 10 in 2016, only two women had ever directed an episode of *The X-Files* and only nine women had ever received a writing credit in over two hundred episodes. Therefore, the question could be raised if the lack of women in charge is partly or even wholly responsible for some of the patriarchal and 'backlash' discourses in certain series featuring female TV action heroes: pregnancy as comedy, wombs as mysterious and monstrous, childbirth as traumatic and motherhood as potentially incompatible with female heroism. Yet, when *Bones* officially ended its twelve-year run recently, it did so on a high note, with the three lead female characters, despite their struggles during the series, essentially 'having it all': married, with children and intent on continuing to be crime-fighters. This ending stands in contrast with those of many of its predecessors where the mothers either gave up their babies or their heroic activities. The positive portrayal of a successful post-second-wave scientist on *Bones* has been an inspiration to women, as notes a recent CNN article, 'How "Bones" Bred a New Generation of Female Scientists', which contains an interview with Emily Deschanel who played Bones. The article explains,

> The way women are portrayed on television has power. Deschanel pointed to 'The Scully Effect' as an example from the past. The phrase refers to the increased number of women encouraged to enter the law

> enforcement, science and medical fields thanks to the success of Fox's 'The X-Files' and the popularization of Dana Scully (Gillian Anderson). 'I love continuing that,' Deschanel told CNN. (Gonzalez, 2017)

The executive producer, Jonathan Collier, credits the female writers on staff for crafting interesting stories for the characters and affirmed that 'the show always remained "respectful" of the fact that they were portraying three diverse female scientists – a rare combination. When crafting arcs for the characters, "Bones" writers aimed to give them stories that went "beyond men"' (ibid.). These words show a consciousness on the part of the producers to send a positive image of women that viewers connect with, yet Gillian Anderson's words in the previous article show that equality both in front of and behind the camera are imperfectly realized. Moreover, the continued negative representation of women's reproductive and maternal functions in recent and contemporary TV series (like the monstrous wombs in *Once Upon a Time* or the monstrous mothers in *Jessica Jones*) indicates that some aspects of TV depictions are slow to change and demonstrates that feminist progress in contemporary TV series is somewhat contained, despite the vision of empowerment that they strive to offer.

Notes

1 See also Marianne Kac-Vergne (2016) and Christine Cornea (2007) who also use the term 'female hero' to denote a female character at the center of the action – versus one on the sidelines – who takes on what could formerly be considered the male's role (or the hero's role) in leading a heroic narrative. Cornea notes that Yvonne Tasker's original use of 'action heroine', or later 'female action hero', at first denoted a muscular, 'masculine' and violent female hero, like Ripley in *Alien* (Scott, 1979) (Cornea, 2007: 160; see also Tasker, 1998). However, in TV action dramas, the female heroes are not typically as violent or as physically strong as their action-film counterparts. In fact, the interest for viewers in watching TV action dramas often lies as much, if not more, in following

rich, ongoing narratives about the female heroes' personal lives than in seeing them perform acts of heroism. In this chapter, the term 'heroine' will nevertheless be used when it conforms to an author's use of the term.

2 See also Martha Lauzen (2020) whose annual 'Boxed In' study gives key data on women working in TV for The Center for the Study of Women in Television and Film at San Diego State University and demonstrates the lack of gender parity in the entertainment industry. Specific information on the production of each series, which can be found at www.imdb.com, would seem to indicate that series featuring female action heroes are no exception (accessed 19 August 2021).

3 The second wave of feminism is defined by Karin Beeler as 'the movement of the 1960s to the 1980s' that 'has been understood as a debate about equality, feminist activism, "equal access to the workforce" and criticism of patriarchy' (Beeler, 2007: 102–3). The third wave, which was not a political movement per se, is often used to categorize a moment in the 1990s–2000s, when there was an emphasis on and awareness of individual choice for women and an emphasis on empowerment in the media, which was linked to consumerist discourses (see Beeler, 2007; see also Sanders, 2007). It is sometimes associated with the term 'post-feminism', which has become controversial as it seems to indicate that the goals of feminism have been achieved (Tasker and Negra, 2007: 2). Most of the messages about motherhood and work/life balance are linked to the second-wave discourses and thus Lotz's terminology, 'post-second wave', would seem to be the most relevant.

4 For further examples, see e.g. Sweet (2012: 209–24).

5 See e.g. Valerie Frankel (2019 and 2020) whose collected works examine the evolving representations of women on screen, notably in terms of female action heroes.

6 Other examples include Xena, who becomes more aggressive due to her pregnancy-related mood swings and is told by a male character, Joxer: 'You're pregnant. That's the way pregnant women are' (5.11). Like in the aforementioned *Blacklist* episode, it is a man who explains pregnancy symptoms to a woman. During her second pregnancy, the genius scientist Bones of the series *Bones* seems to be almost comically unaware of, and refuses to accept, how far along her pregnancy is, with various characters commenting on it.

7 In 'The Memories in the Shallow Grave' (7.1), Bones begins crying while examining a dead body, even though she is usually calmly rational. The usually stoic police detective Jane Rizzoli from *Rizzoli & Isles* is shown getting violently nauseous, throwing up in a sink when faced with a body in the morgue. Piper from *Charmed* burps 'bubbles' – or little puffs of white magic. In *Xena: Warrior Princess*, Xena and Gabrielle have unusual food and disgusting cravings during their respective pregnancies.

8 The fact that Scully never seems to have sex, as she is in a will-they-or-won't-they relationship with her partner Mulder, is key to her character representation. Even when they do become a couple, evidence of a physical relationship remains scarce.

9 Examples include *Xena: Warrior Princess*, since Xena's child, Eve, is a product of Immaculate Conception, prophesized to bring about the end of the Greek gods. On *Wynnona Earp*, evil beings called 'The Widows' want to use Wynonna Earp's baby to resurrect their dead husbands. On *The Blacklist*, a criminal who believes he is Liz's child's grandfather kidnaps her, as he needs to find a blood relative for medical purposes in order to cure a rare disease.

10 In the horror film, *The Stepford Wives* (Forbes, 1975), which was released during the second wave of feminism, the lead character discovers that all the perfect housewives of the town to which she just moved are actually robots created by the men in the town to submissively serve them as ideal homemakers.

11 Bolder or more daring gender or feminist messages may be told through supporting characters, metaphors or through use of fantasy; see e.g. Sweet (2012).

12 While the mainstream women's liberation movement in the United States was supportive of motherhood during the second wave, certain more radical second-wave feminists rejected motherhood as it was linked to patriarchal oppression in the form of 'compulsory parenthood' and the societal obligation for women to be mothers, which was linked to 'the nuclear family as a nexus of female oppression' (Takševa, 2018: 181). Yet Adrienne Rich argued for nuance in the way motherhood was considered and Tatjana Takševa notes that Rich's work *Of Woman Born* (1976) 'makes the crucial distinction between the patriarchal institution of motherhood and the experience of mothering, which is not inherently oppressive'

(Takševa, 2018: 182). Takševa underlines that Rich's ideas were surely key to a shift in thinking about motherhood, underlining that the experience of certain white middle-class women who felt oppressed by the patriarchy as slaves to their husbands and children is not a universal experience and that mothering can even be an empowering or community experience for some.

13 Interestingly enough, the *Charmed* reboot, which launched twenty years after the original in 2018, does not seem to be any sort of beacon of progress on this issue, as the lead characters' mother is killed in the first episode to be later reincarnated and inhabited by a demon in another. Moreover, it is interesting to note what qualifies as an 'older woman' in Hollywood, as the actor who plays the mother was born in 1976 and is only eight years older than one of the actors playing her daughter. Source: *Charmed* IMDB page, https://www.imdb.com/title/tt6394324/ (accessed 31 September 2020).

14 For key numbers concerning gender parity in TV production, see Gibson (2014) or Lauzen (2020).

Primary corpus

Alias (2001–6), [TV programme]: ABC.
Bones (2005–17), [TV programme]: Fox.
Cagney & Lacey (1982–8), [TV programme]: CBS.
Charmed (1998–2006), [TV programme]: WB.
Jessica Jones (2015–19), [TV programme]: Netflix.
Once Upon a Time (2011–18), [TV programme]: ABC.
Rizzoli & Isles (2010–16), [TV programme]: TNT.
The Blacklist (2013–), [TV programme]: NBC.
The X-Files (1993–2018), [TV programme]: Fox.
Xena: Warrior Princess (1995–2001), [TV programme]: Syndicated.
Wynonna Earp (2016–21), [TV programme]: Syfy.

Works cited

Bastién, Angelica Jade (2018), 'What *Jessica Jones* understands about female rage', *Vulture*, 15 March. Available online: https://www.vulture.com/2018/03/jessica-jones-season-2-female-rage.html (accessed 1 September 2020).

Badley, Linda (2000), 'Scully hits the glass ceiling: Postmodernism, postfeminism, posthumanism, and The X-files', in Elyce Rae Helford (ed.), *Fantasy Girls: Gender in the New Universe of Science Fiction and Fantasy Television*, 61–89, Lanham, MD: Rowman & Littlefield.

Beeler, Karin (2007), 'Old myths, new powers: Images of second-wave and third-wave feminism in *Charmed*', in Karin Beeler and Stan Beeler (eds), *Investigating* Charmed: *The Magic Power of TV*, 101–11, London: I.B. Tauris.

Cheng, Susan (2017), 'Gillian Anderson calls out the lack of women behind "The X-Files"', *Buzz Feed*, 30 June. Available online: https://www.buzzfeed.com/susancheng/gillian-anderson-women-xfiles?utm_term=.lsKpqOgYw#.ggAAmVB0D (accessed 18 July 2017).

Cornea, Christine (2007), *Science Fiction Cinema: Between Fantasy and Reality*, New Brunswick: Rutgers University Press.

Creed, Barbara ([1993] 1997), *The Monstrous-Feminine: Film, Feminism, and Psychoanalysis*, London: Routledge.

Crosby, Sara (2004), 'The Cruelest Season: Female Heroes Snapped into Sacrificial Heroines', in Sherrie A. Inness, *Action Chicks: New Images of Tough Women in Popular Culture*, 153–78, New York: Palgrave Macmillan.

D'Acci, Julie (1994), *Defining Women: Television and the Case of Cagney and Lacey*, Chapel Hill: University of North Carolina Press.

Douglas, Susan J. ([1994] 1995), *Where the Girls Are: Growing Up Female with the Mass Media*, New York: Three Rivers Press.

Early, Frances, and Kathleen Kennedy (2003), 'Introduction', in Frances Early and Kathleen Kennedy (eds), *Athena's Daughters: Television's New Women Warriors*, 1–10, Syracuse: Syracuse University Press.

Faludi, Susan (1991), *Backlash: The Undeclared War Against American Women*, New York: Anchor Books.

Frankel, Valerie Estelle (2019), 'Introduction', in Valerie Frankel (ed.), *Fourth Wave Feminism in Science Fiction and Fantasy. Volume 1. Essays on Film Representations, 2012–2019*, 1–8, Jefferson, NC: McFarland.

Frankel, Valerie Estelle (2020), 'Introduction', in Valerie Frankel (ed.), *Fourth Wave Feminism in Science Fiction and Fantasy. Volume 2. Essays on Television Representations, 2012–2019*, 1–17, Jefferson, NC: McFarland.

Futrell, Alison (2003), 'The Baby, the mother, the empire: Xena as ancient hero', in Frances Early and Kathleen Kennedy (eds), *Athena's Daughters: Television's New Women Warriors*, 13–26, Syracuse: Syracuse University Press.

Gendel, Morgan (1985), '"Cagney & Lacey" seeks help on abortion show', *LA Times*, 23 October. Available online: https://www.latimes.com/archives/la-xpm-1985-10-23-ca-14074-story.html (accessed 25 August 2021).

Gibson, Megan (2014), 'Here's a sliver of good news about women in television', *Time Magazine*, 16 September. Available online: http://time.com/3386285/women-television-boxed-in-study/ (accessed 21 July 2017).

Gonzalez, Sandra (2017), 'How "Bones" bred a new generation of female scientists', CNN, 27 March. Available online: http://edition.cnn.com/2017/03/27/entertainment/bones-tv-show-women-stem/index.html (accessed 21 July 2017).

Helford, Elyce Rae (2000), 'Feminism, queer studies, and the sexual politics of *Xena: Warrior Princess*', in Elyce Rae Helford (ed.), *Fantasy Girls: Gender in the New Universe of Science Fiction and Fantasy Television*, 135–62, Lanham, MD: Rowman & Littlefield.

Herbert, Kiran (2013), '"Charmed" Netflix success prompts CBS reboot', *Rolling Stone*, 25 October. Available online: http://www.rollingstone.com/tv/news/Charmed-netflix-success-prompts-cbs-reboot-20131025 (accessed 18 July 2017).

Kac-Vergne, Marianne (2016), 'Sidelining women in contemporary science-fiction film', *Miranda*, 12: 1–12. Available online: https://journals.openedition.org/miranda/8642 (accessed 23 August 2021).

Kristeva, Julia (2006), 'Approaching abjection', in Amelia Jones (ed.), *The Feminism and Visual Culture Reader* [2003], 389–91, London: Routledge.

Lauzen, Martha M. (2020), 'Boxed In 2019–2020: Women on screen and behind the scenes in television', in *Boxed In*, Center for the Study of Women in Television and Film, San Diego State University. Available online: https://womenintvfilm.sdsu.edu/wp-content/uploads/2020/09/2019-2020_Boxed_In_Report.pdf (accessed 19 August 2021).

Lotz, Amanda D. (2006), *Redesigning Women: Television after the Network Era*, Urbana: University of Illinois Press.

Lotz, Amanda D. (2014), *Cable Guys: Television and Masculinities in the 21st Century*, New York: New York University Press.

Peirse, Alison (2007), 'Postfeminism without limits? Charmed, horror and sartorial style', in Karin Beeler and Stan Beeler (eds), *Investigating Charmed: The Magic Power of TV*, 112–26, London: I.B. Tauris.

Rabinovitz, Lauren (1999), 'Ms.-representation: The politics of feminist sitcoms', in Mary Beth Haralovich and Lauren Rabinovitz (eds), *Television,*

History and American Culture: Feminist Critical Essays, 144–67, Durham, NC: Duke University Press.

Rich, Adrienne (1976), *Of Woman Born: Motherhood as Experience and Institution*, New York: W.W. Norton.

Richardson, Niall (2006), 'As Kamp as Bree', in Janet McCabe and Kim Akass (eds), *Reading Desperate Housewives: Beyond the White Picket Fence*, 86–94, London: I.B. Tauris.

Rowe, Kathleen K. (1997), 'Roseanne: Unruly woman as domestic goddess', in Charlotte Brunsdon, Julie D'Acci and Lynn Spigel (eds), *Feminist Television Criticism: A Reader*, 74–83, Oxford: Clarendon Press.

Sanders, Hannah E. (2007), 'Living a charmed life: The magic of postfeminist sisterhood', in Yvonne Tasker and Diane Negra (eds), *Interrogating Postfeminism: Gender and the Politics of Popular Culture*, 73–99, Durham, NC: Duke University Press.

Stabiner, Karen (1985), 'The pregnant detective', *New York Times*, 22 September. Available online: http://www.nytimes.com/1985/09/22/magazine/the-pregnant-detective.html?pagewanted=1 (accessed 17 July 2017).

Sweet, Anne Currier (2012), '"Unreal" gender messages in late 90s women-centered action dramas', *TV/Series*, 1: 209–24. Available online: https://journals.openedition.org/tvseries/1205 (accessed 28 August 2020).

Takševa, Tatjana (2018), 'Motherhood studies and feminist theory: Elisions and intersections', *Journal of the Motherhood Initiative*, 9.1: 177–94. https://jarm.journals.yorku.ca/index.php/jarm/issue/view/2311 (accessed 23 August 2021).

Tasker, Yvonne (1998), *Working Girls: Gender and Sexuality in Popular Cinema*, London: Routledge.

Tasker, Yvonne, and Diane Negra (2007), *Interrogating Postfeminism: Gender and the Politics of Popular Culture*, London: Duke University Press.

10

In the mouth of fearfulness: Women, power and the *vagina dentata* in contemporary American cinema

Charles-Antoine Courcoux

Indulging in historical speculation is always hazardous. However, it seems likely that, over time, 2017 will impose itself as a watershed year for the feminist struggle in general and in Hollywood in particular. From the Women's March in Washington, DC, on January 21 to the advent of the *#MeToo* movement and the growing global reckoning regarding violence against women, including sexual assault and harassment in the workplace, 2017 was replete with events, polemics and debates about sexual politics, free speech and gender equity that have, without presuming the outcome of these phenomena, contributed to the awareness-raising process that feminists have sought to encourage for decades.[1] In the field of American television and cinema, 2017 was also an important year for women, *off* screen as well as *on* screen. The female-produced HBO miniseries *Big Little Lies*, starring Nicole Kidman, Laura Dern, Reese Witherspoon, Zoe Kravitz and Shailene Woodley, which thematized the issues of rape, domestic violence, bullying and sexual harassment, won eight Emmys. Hulu's dystopian and feminist drama series *The Handmaid's Tale*, based on Margaret Atwood's 1985 novel, took home four Emmys, including Best Directing (Reed Morano) and Outstanding Lead Actress (Elisabeth Moss) in a Drama Series. In cinema, not only did the female-led *The Shape of Water* win four Academy Awards, including Best Picture, but the economic triumph of *Beauty and the Beast*, *Wonder Woman* and

Star Wars: The Last Jedi was a reminder that actresses could also lead the three biggest domestic box office successes of a year. This was a first since 1958, when a similar trio of female-led 'blockbusters' – namely the musical *South Pacific* (starring Mitzi Gaynor), the comedy *Auntie Mame* (starring Rosalind Russell) and the drama *Cat on a Hot Tin Roof* (starring Elizabeth Taylor) – last dominated the box office.

Obviously, whether in Hollywood or in American society at large, these phenomena are of very diverse origins, content and nature. They can therefore neither be seen as the fruit of a linear evolutionary process nor be associated with discourses of systematically 'feminist', 'progressive' or even homogeneous content. This is particularly true with respect to films and Hollywood. As Jeffrey A. Brown observed in his study of the new action heroines of films such as *The Girl with the Dragon Tattoo* (2011), *Snow White and the Huntsman* (2012), *The Hunger Games* (2012–15) and the *Divergent* (2014–16) franchises, 'the action heroine's dramatic increase in popularity through the first two decades of this century is an indication of changing cultural, gendered, and economic conditions' (Brown, 2015: 6). However, despite the sometimes transgressive representation these films offer of their heroines, the fact remains that, as Brown points out a little further on, 'factors like the preference for youthful heroines, their relations with central male characters, and the sometimes extreme levels of violence associated with [them] illustrate how the current wave of action heroines is redefining femininity through a struggle with stereotypical and historical ideas about womanhood' (ibid., 7). In other words, these films' discourses continue most often to appear contradictory or strongly ambivalent at best. Indeed, the supplement of agency given to the central female character is repeatedly repaid by discursive concessions or symbolic renunciations, which are not without consequence for the extent of this positionality and the plurality of the meanings potentially associated with femininity.

Of course, this discursive ambivalence and the 'containment strategy' that typify it, and even the polysemy of these films, are neither recent nor new. Diachronically, and apart from isolated exceptions, the films that have marked the history of the slow shift, for Hollywood actresses, from passive victims to main and more active roles, within traditionally 'male' genres, have almost always distinguished themselves by intensely ambivalent or, in some respects, problematic discourses. One well-known example is the *slasher* subgenre, where, according to Carol Clover, one of the first main female characters endowed with significant agency, the Final Girl, emerged in the mid-1970s (Clover, 1987: 187–228). However, as Clover also pointed out, in films such as *Halloween* (1978), *Alien* (1979), *Friday the 13th* (1980), *Hell Night* (1981) and *Aliens* (1986), the autonomy and the strength of this character were interrelated with the valorization of sexual control, the non-penetrability of the female body, her distinctiveness from other (more promiscuous) girls and her respect of normative values. This goes against some of the key claims (the fight for reproductive rights and exercising control of one's sexuality and the fight against systemic sexism) and principles (faith in solidarity and collective agencies) at the heart of the feminist movement of the late 1960s. As a character moving from a position of passive victim to that of active heroine free of any 'disturbing' female characteristics, it is not surprising that, as Clover astutely revealed, the Final Girl was also able to serve as an identifying surrogate for male spectators who formed part of the core audience of these films at the time.[2]

Nevertheless, as the police thrillers of the early 2000s can also attest (Gates, 2011: 257–98; Brown, 2011: 212–22), such ambivalence is not limited to *slashers* or the 1970s. In an attempt to identify the historical specificities of contemporary female heroism and its enduring discursive ambivalence in American cinema in recent years, I would like to postulate that if film heroines now appear as active, independent and often powerful women, even more so than the Final Girl of the 1970s, this new level of agency is possible only by, like the Final Girl, partially or completely repressing their sexuality. However, this repression does not transpire through the heroines' masculinization or even their fetishization – as was the case for some of the most famous heroines of the 1990s–2000s like Trinity (Carrie-Anne Moss) in *The Matrix* (1999),

Sydney Bristow (Jennifer Garner) in the *Alias* series (2001–6) or Selene (Kate Beckinsale) in the *Underworld* franchise (2003–16) – but instead through the mobilization of a motif that was relatively unexploited in the aforementioned films or the first wave of slashers: a toothed vagina functioning as the externalized expression of sexuality to be repressed. It is, of course, Barbara Creed who has most clearly shown that the 'vagina dentata' is a recurrent motif of female monstrosity in the codes of American horror films. In her renowned book *The Monstrous-Feminine*, Creed has inscribed the toothed vagina in the repertoire of bodily expressions that make it possible to portray women as abject monsters, both fascinating and horrifying (Creed, 1993: 105–21). The notion of *abject* is to be considered here in line with Julia Kristeva's theorization, which relates it to the disregard of limits, to ambiguity and the mixed. The author associates the abject more precisely with 'a collapse of paternal laws' in the Western world and with 'the feminine body, the maternal body, in its most un-signifiable, un-symbolisable aspect' (Kristeva, 1982: 20). For Creed, the toothed vagina symbolizes the castrating potential (both genital and symbolic) of women and their sexuality, a power assimilated in this case to gaping, greedy and destructive sexual organs that the heroine (or the hero) must control or neutralize, if (s)he wants to be able to affirm the normative dimension of her gendered identity. The recourse to this motif represents 'the female genitalia as a trap, a black hole which threatens to swallow [men] and cut them into pieces' (Creed, 1993: 106). It is, in short, the symbol of the deceitful and uncertain nature of woman who, in the patriarchal imagination, 'promises paradise in order to ensnare her victims' (ibid., 106). In the cinema, this motif comes in many forms, starting with gaping holes or mouths with sharp teeth, dangerous accesses, doors that can close at any time and narrow and suffocating corridors (ibid., 107–8).

To corroborate my hypothesis – besides considering *Teeth* (2007), which, by endowing its heroin with a toothed vagina, features the motif quite literally[3] – I will start by analysing a specific scene that involves the character of Rey (Daisey Ridley) in *Star Wars: The Force Awakens*

(2015). The content of this scene, the priority given by the film to its symbolic function and the generic codes that are exploited will lead me to study several successful productions from the horror genre. I will reflect on how the toothed vagina is used throughout the course of the films and how it is diversely hinged on the journey of a female character. I will then come back to the cursory analysis of a film outside of the horror genre to underline the general discursive convergence of these productions and initiate a reflection on their place in the history of the representations of powerful women in contemporary American cinema.

The toothed vagina awakens

To examine *The Force Awakens* seems relevant in this context, not only because it was the largest commercial success of 2015 but above all because the character of Rey is exemplary of the prominent place attributed to certain action heroines in contemporary high-budget productions, a genre that usually demeans women's roles. Let us consider the scene where the 'Rathtars' appear (43:05). Reminiscent of the *Alien* universe, the scene mixes the visual codes of science fiction and of horror films by displaying human characters chased by slimy and voracious monsters in the metallic, circular and dark corridors of a spaceship. Rey and Finn (John Boyega) have just escaped from the First Order fighters onboard the Millennium Falcon. Shortly after leaving the planet Jakku, they are captured by a massive cargo vessel that attracts their ship into its midst via what looks like a giant jaw. Once on board the cargo, Rey and Finn meet Han Solo and Chewbacca, who are struggling with rival squads of smugglers, to whom Han Solo has promised three monstrous creatures he has captured, the so-called Rathtars. To escape this difficult situation and save Han and Chewbacca, Rey flees with Finn through underground passages and tries to isolate the smugglers by closing the blast doors of the corridors by 'resetting the fuses'. Her attempt, however, fails and, at the same time, frees the Rathtars, who invade the corridors with their wide jaws in pursuit of all the men on board the spaceship. After ingesting members of the smugglers' crews, a Rathtar attacks Finn, grabbing him by the waist and legs with his tentacles. Rey first pursues the Rathtar in the hallway but, threatened by the range of its tentacles, is quickly distanced by the creature. She then stops in front of a control panel, follows on a monitor the trajectory of the monster holding Finn and succeeds this time in closing the blast doors of a corridor at the precise moment when the monster is passing through the doors. She thus cuts off the two tentacles that held Finn and frees him from the creature's grip. The two characters, ultimately joined by Solo and Chewbacca, board the Millennium Falcon and escape the Rathtars and the smugglers' fire together.

This visually rich action sequence illustrates the way in which contemporary cinema articulates the agency of its heroine with signs of the abject female body in order to signal the lethal potential of an autonomous femininity in terms of sexuality. This sexuality is metaphorized here by the Rathtars as an actualization of a toothed vagina, to better underline, via the neutralization of the monsters, the heroine's ability to control her sexuality. It is significant that it is precisely after Rey's first demonstration of strength that this sequence occurs. While the fighting scene on Jakku reveals Rey's independence (notably through her repeated refusal to take Finn's condescending hand), her combat ability, her tactical skills and her technological mastery, the following scene seems to have the sole purpose – as a typically 'masculine' paranoid projection – of showing that this level of agency does not come with sexual drives that could potentially undermine her male partner's agency. The fears expressed and resolved in this sequence are that if her power is likely to generate some sort of sexual hysteria (which *only* threatens men here), Rey is nevertheless able to control it.

In this respect, the Rathtars are incredibly consistent – both because of their physiology and the large number of motifs with which they are associated – with Creed's description of the toothed vagina in cinema. Three characteristics prevail in their appearance: a spherical and elastic body, a huge reddish mouth, set with several rows of teeth, and a multiplicity of long-range tentacles. Besides, in the script of the film, this caricature of a giant castrating Medusa, who made her tentacles the symbol of the penis/trophies she has castrated/won, is described as an insatiable octopus: an 'enormous, fierce and ravenous land octopus – slithers out of its cage!'[4] Moreover, the Rathtars' breakout from their containment cells, signified first by the exit of their tentacles from the cells, coincides with a change in the lighting tone of the corridors from a diffuse brown to a predominantly red colour. This change in lighting, which is particularly noticeable on Rey's and Finn's faces, evokes the danger associated with creature liberation but can also be more obliquely correlated with menstrual blood as an indicator of female sexual maturity. On a situational level, this scene also takes place entirely in corridors described in the script as 'narrow' and uses doors that, as Creed has pointed out, play a crucial role in evoking the castrating power of the toothed vagina.[5] Furthermore, the film articulates in a clear way the monstrous appearance and the devouring function of the Rathtars with Rey's mouth. It seems indeed symptomatic that it is after watching for the first time a Rathtar eating gang members that Rey, bewildered by what she sees, puts her hand in front of her open mouth. Obviously, the a priori anodyne nature of such a gesture could minimize its symbolic significance, but the fact that it is carefully scripted in the final draft of the scenario, and also in capital letters ('Rey COVERS HER MOUTH'),[6] makes it at least possible to note that it is not a trivial gesture in this instance. Additionally, from the beginning of the sequence, Rey is consistently associated with the Rathtars on a visual level. In this respect, the sequence is in line with a 'classical' narrative economy of the horror film. It evokes the monsters in several ways: first, on a verbal level; second, in a metonymic way (through the exposure of an orifice doubled by a suction cup in a porthole, then tentacles), third, metaphorically (with the appearance of the red lighting of the corridors when they are released) and, ultimately, fully, first in a wide shot then brought closer, when they start to devour the characters. However, just before the first partial visualisation of the monsters, Finn asks Solo where he keeps the Rathtars. Finn and Rey are framed in the foreground of a frontal two-shot, with the metal door's yellow window located between them, in the background. In the reverse close shot, Solo answers 'there is one' at the precise moment when a kind of sphere, in the shape of a suction cup, suddenly materializes on the window between Rey and Finn. This abrupt appearance drives a frightened Finn out of the frame, leaving Rey visually alone with the monster's first physical manifestation. Finally, whereas it is Han Solo, the ultimate representative of a benevolent patriarchy, who originally captured the Rathtars, it is Rey who frees them, and, in the end, neutralizes them. Their release, which is associated with a temporary lack of Rey's technological mastery, is ultimately compensated by a reaffirmation of this mastery. However, this regained control is directly articulated, as in the case of the hand on her mouth earlier, with Rey's aptitude to close an orifice which, opportunely, cuts the monster's tentacle that threatened her male partner's bodily integrity.

Obviously, as always in the context of the analysis of a sequence's symbolic dimension, especially when based on a psychoanalytical interpretation, one could argue that this is a free association that invests these images, motifs and characters with far-fetched meanings. In response to this objection, I would like to make three short arguments. First, this treatment is in line with the symbolic economy characteristic of the *Star Wars* saga, in which sexuality is systematically shown to be dangerous and the Jedi status associated with the renunciation of all sexuality.[7] Second, my interpretation of the Rathtars as a 'toothed vagina' is not isolated. In his analysis of *The Force Awakens* at the mythological level, Glen Robert Gill (2019) writes,

> The real archetypal significance of this episode, however, is found in the group's defeat of the monstrous Rathtars that escape their pens and threaten to consume them: in these round, snake-tentacled, gaping-mawed creatures it is possible to see the outlines of the mythical Medusa, a demonic incarnation of the yonic symbol that Freud called the 'vagina dentata'.

Finally, as a follow-up to Gill's analysis, I would claim that the metaphorical interpretation of this sequence is not only based on the framing and editing, but that this symbolic function even takes precedence over its narrative function, which is almost non-existent here. Indeed, this sequence's contribution to the development of the narrative is nearly insignificant, except possibly for the solidarity it creates between the characters of Rey, Han, Finn and Chewbacca. Besides, the terminology used in the film's script and writing style makes this symbolic function even clearer. For example, when the Millennium Falcon is caught by the cargo ship, it is described as 'powerless' and its capture mode is depicted via an oral and animal comparison in all capital letters: 'ITS GIANT HANGAR OPEN LIKE A HUGE MOUTH WHICH SWALLOWS THE FALCON LIKE A WHALE!'[8] In *The Force Awakens*, Rey's agency, which refers to the subsequent awakening of the Force within her (and thus to the possibility for a woman to control a power previously only held by men), is therefore coupled with her reassuring control over a caricatured female sexuality in the form of a mouth/toothed vagina. Moreover, this correlation goes beyond this one scene since throughout the film, Rey's warrior skills are clearly associated with a slit pattern, be it the scar she inflicts on Kylo Ren's face (Adam Driver) during their duel[9] – 'A LARGE BURN SCAR SLASHED ACROSS HIS FACE!'[10] – or the appearance of the crevasse which, at the end of the duel, splits the ground in two and ends the confrontation by separating the opponents.

I will very briefly come back to Rey's aptitude to open and close orifices at the end of this essay, but I would now like to suggest that *The Force Awakens*' limited use of the toothed vagina to alleviate fears related to the depictions of potent female protagonists is not a unique case in current Hollywood productions. The anchoring of this sequence in horror film visual codes is even indicative of the fact that it is, once again, in this genre that this motif finds its privileged expression. In order to further explore its depictions and meanings as a 'containment strategy', I propose to look at *Evil Dead* (2013), directed by Fede Álvarez, which is a fascinating case. Unlike *The Force Awakens* or other films such as *The Thing* (2011), *10 Cloverfield Lane* (2016), *The Shallows* (2016) or *Jurassic World: Fallen Kingdom* (2018), where the symbolism of the toothed vagina is exploited in specific and sometimes limited ways, in *Evil Dead* this motif structures the entire iconographic work of the film and, hence, its thematic progression.

Making sure the *Evil* is dead

A remake of Sam Raimi's famous homonymous film (1981), *Evil Dead* tells the story of a group of young friends – Mia (Jane Levy), her brother David (Shiloh Fernandez) and their friends Olivia (Jessica Lucas), Eric (Lou Taylor Pucci) and Natalie (Elizabeth Blackmore) – who go to an isolated cabin in the woods to spend a weekend in order to help Mia overcome her drug addiction. As Mia struggles with the craving, the four friends discover an old witchcraft manuscript in the cabin's basement: *The Book of the Dead*. Driven by curiosity, Eric reads it and involuntarily summons an evil force that will possess not only Mia but also Olivia and Natalie and cause everyone's death apart from Mia. The fight between Mia and this evil, protean and incomprehensible force continues until she finally manages to destroy it with a chainsaw in a rain shower of blood. From the expository scenes, Mia's addiction is tacitly associated with the trauma of enduring her mother's developing dementia, cancer and death, in the absence of the reassuring figure that her brother David usually represented. In this way, the film articulates Mia's psychic feverishness, her instability, to what will later be described as David's cowardice, a cowardice that the character eventually overcomes to exorcise his sister from the evil female spirit that is possessing her, by first killing her, then burying and ultimately resurrecting her. David, however, sacrifices himself a moment later trying to eliminate the evil again before Mia has to take over, replace David and truly end the beast.

The opening scene establishes the film's stakes at a symbolic level. A teenage girl (Phoenix Connolly) is chained to a wooden pillar in the basement of a house, in front of a few people who appear curious and fascinated, while her father (Jim McLarty) approaches her. An old woman, who is deciphering an ancient grimoire nearby, intimates to the man to 'do what he has to do'. The father, seemingly hesitant at first, approaches his daughter who, ostensibly frightened, asks him what she is doing here and where her mother is. He replies that she should know because she killed her. Incredulous, the young woman, with a terrified look and quivering voice, repeatedly begs her father to free her. This plea continues until the man is able to light a match to ignite the flammable liquid he spilled on her a moment earlier to purge her of the evil that, according to the old woman, inhabits the teenager's body. In accordance with this diagnosis, the young woman radically changes her attitude when she catches fire: her eyes turn yellow as she exclaims to her father, with a powerful voice, both raucous and deep: 'I will rip your soul out, you pathetic fuck! You motherfucker! I will fucking kill you like I killed your whore!' In an instant, the lamb turns into a beast. The father steps back at the sight of this screaming human torch and replies 'I love you baby', just before blowing her head off with a shotgun. The title of the film is displayed in scarlet-red letters, on a deep black background. This scene, in which evil displays the face of innocence before asserting itself as a hypersexualized young woman who has killed the feminine (her mother) and negated male authority (her father), lays the foundation for the film's central question: how to eradicate evil when it manifests itself as a feminine disorder associated, as in *The Exorcist* (1973) forty years earlier but also in 1981's *The Evil Dead*, with a hypertrophied female sexuality in a context marked by the lack of male authority? The low-angle close shots and contrasting lighting on the teenager's breasts when she is attached to the pillar at the very beginning of the film, initially point to the negatively sexualized nature of the young woman's body, while the emphasis on her mouth, the filthy and sexual terminology she uses and especially the gendered decoupling between her female face and the shift to a male voice emphasize her transgressive and excessive sexual nature. The shot that follows the title confirms the more general discursive concern raised by this scene, since it offers the view of a peaceful green forest landscape but turned upside down and dug in its middle by a furrow. This large slit, as a topographical expression of the unbridled female sexuality that has just manifested itself, potentially threatens to engulf the group of friends' vehicle that is advancing on the road. The fact that the teenager's condition in the first sequence is summarily related to her mother's murder and her father's weakness (a father who must be pushed into action by the old woman) is rather significant here: Mia's traumatic situation is correlated later on with the painful disappearance of her mother who has gone mad (a symbol of a lost female ideal), in the absence of men (in this case her brother). In *Evil Dead*, it is the male failures that mostly bear the responsibility for female deviance, which is actualized in the form of a devouring sexual drive. Consequently, the character of the young girl at the beginning of the film – who possesses Mia in the rape scene where she purges from her bloody mouth a kind of twisted vine that penetrates Mia through her genitals – imposes herself as the personification of a perverted femininity, a sexualized and undisciplined teenager, who killed her mother, and from which Mia (who looks very similar physically) must be able to differentiate/exorcise herself. This is only possible by externalizing this young girl's evil spirit (thanks to Mia's brother) and then destroying it by herself. In this respect, the case of Mia is both quite close and remote from Rey's. Despite the obvious differences in the two productions' tone, due to the film genres in which they are embedded – *The Force Awakens* is colourful and optimistic whereas *Evil Dead* is resolutely gloomy, wet and pessimistic – each must offer reassurance as to the female character's ability to control/annihilate the sexual impulses that, in the patriarchal imagination, are potentially let loose by women's increased agency. However, Rey's experience of power is more voluntarist and much less devalued than Mia's, since it is the circumstances, in this case her brother's absence, which force Mia to occupy this position. And if, in both cases, this power takes the form of a 'phallic symbol', this symbol is loaded with opposed connotations. Rey's spear is a rather simple, readable and positive weapon, which she masters, while the kind of giant penis that forms the entanglement of branches that penetrates Mia from below during the rape scene in the forest is a resolutely horrific representation: an evil vine that dominates her. This representation is in accordance with the iconography in the *Book of the Dead* consulted by Eric, where, a little like for the Rathtars, monstrosity is associated, on the model of the Medusa, with a hole accompanied by tentacles.

This amalgamation is important since it is a recurring trope in all the productions examined here and is, as such, indicative of the gendered nature of the bond that they condemn. In her famous 1984 article, 'When the Woman Looks', Linda Williams suggested that the woman's look at the monster, in the classic horror film, 'is more than simply a punishment for looking'; it is also 'a recognition of their similar status as potent threats to a vulnerable male power'. Subsequently, according to Williams, 'the woman's look at the monster offers at least a potentially subversive recognition of the power and potency of a non-phallic sexuality' (1984: 90). But in the lesser-known 'sequel' to this article, Williams reassessed the nature of this monstrous alliance to show, based on an analysis of *Psycho* (1960), that the horror that these films bring into play has in fact less to do with femininity than with 'the kind of absence of stable gender identity that would eventually become institutionalised as generic expectation in the slasher genre of the 70's' (Williams, 2001). I would argue that the type of threat expressed through the association between the toothed vagina and tentacles of all kinds in the films I'm considering is similar in nature to the one described by Williams: the manifestation of a 'gender trouble', that is, the alliance, designated as 'unnatural', between a distinctly feminine sexual organ and a phallic appendix that connotes power.

In this context, *Evil Dead*'s exploitation of the symbolism of the toothed vagina and all the motifs that are related to it according to Creed, appears more and more clearly as the narrative and thematic progression of the story unfolds. This is the case until Mia, during the final confrontation, calls the beast a 'motherfucker' and violently cuts it in half at its centre and gives it back the shape of what it should always have been: a swollen, threatening and bloody vulva, whose verbal referent says how much it carries the threat of the destruction of a female ideal that is both maternal and necessarily asexual. The discursive strategies are, in this respect, quite clear in the orientation of the film's iconographic choices and system of referentiality. This is seen in the film's propensity to exacerbate the danger of the group's or a character's engulfment by using shots that place the characters in the depth of a field, or in front of an entrance (of the cellar, the well, a burrow, a room), or filmed from inside the dark space that they are about to enter. This is further seen in the emphasis on (self)mutilation, bites, body orifices, dark and uterine doors or corridors, in the crescendo role of blood and mouths as a mode and site of contamination; and especially in the iconography of the bloody slit, with its sexual connotations and the fear of the loss of bodily integrity it embodies. The exploitation of this last motif – starting from the groove that, at the topographical level, breaks the inverted forest landscape in two at the beginning – is noteworthy because it gradually establishes itself as the privileged expression of the horror tied to the unleashed female sexuality explored by the film. The original *The Evil Dead* also explored the fear of castration through the overriding hysterical possession of the three female characters' bodies.[11] But the fact that its remake is centred on a heroine rather than a hero seems to have further contributed to the dramatic growth of this Freudian imagery. This is *Evil Dead*'s way of giving form to the infra-world of sexual impulses which, in the discursive logic of the film, governs the autonomous female body. Similarly, it is the shape that evil takes on as it infects the other human bodies via Olivia's cut cheek, Mia's tongue split with her cutter, Mia's bloody kiss on Natalie's mouth, the crack of the opening of the basement trapdoor when Mia tries to get out or the gaping and bloody mouth of the female humanoid monster at the end.

Moreover, in *Evil Dead*, just as in the original film, the gendered aspects of the evil entity are underlined by the fact that it is only women (all physically wounded) who are possessed and who attack and kill men for the most part during the film. At the end, while her brother has just died and the monster now manifests itself through the remains of a hysterical female body and a shower of blood, the heroine can be reborn purified by leaving the ground with her face immaculate (which is narratively unmotivated). She signals her acceptance of male law by 'castrating' herself (she cuts her hand), hanging the medallion given to her by her brother (which precisely symbolizes the internalisation of his authority[12]) and grabbing the chainsaw (a temporary phallic symbol) to finally chop the 'Abomination' (Alvarez and Menez, 2011: 100) in two. This last act is a sign of the definitive repression of her sexual drive and its necessary return to the infra-world. Indeed, it is underground that the defeated creature ultimately returns. While the beginning of the film located the heroine at ground level, sitting backlit on an old car frame, wearing a sweatshirt that tended to masculinise her silhouette, the concluding scene represents her standing upright in a red dress. Thanks to the camera's final upward movement and the tonal emphasis on the rising sun's warm light, the shot emancipates the character from the earth's materiality and her physicality through a kind of divine gesture.

Stranger (sexual) *Things*

The articulation between sexual threat and female power through the mobilization of the toothed vagina can be observed in several other successful contemporary film and television productions, which also attest to the importance of the use of this motif as a containment strategy. Let us take a brief look at the parent cases of the film *It* (2017), the second adaptation of Stephen King's homonymous novel (1986), and the *Stranger Things* series (created in 2016), both of which have been the subject of considerable popular interest. Without going into their plots in detail, one can note that their narrative framework is based, in both cases, on the adventures of a gang of young boys labelled 'losers' whose lives are suddenly disrupted by the concomitant arrivals of an intelligent and potent young girl – who introduces a rupture in the group's homosocial unity – and of an omnipresent and extremely dangerous monster figure, who threatens to decimate the group.[13] Moreover, and once again, the creature is associated with a network of underground galleries, which, here, in either case, could be considered as a metaphor for the types of dangers parents frequently associate with teenagers' use of the internet: it is represented as an attractive, complex and rhizomic underground space, which is dangerous for teenagers because it is located outside the sphere of parental scrutiny and control. Finally, whether in *It* or *Stranger Things*, the female character in question – Beverly 'Bev' Marsh (Sophia Lillis) and Eleven (Millie Bobby Brown), respectively – not only has a short haircut and superior abilities to the boys of the gang but is also significantly related to the motif of blood, which in both cases echoes the character's sexual maturity. Power and bleeding are associated in Bev's spectacularly bloody bathroom scene in *It*, while it is a recurrent motif in *Stranger Things* since Eleven has nosebleeds every time she uses her paranormal abilities. Contrary to *The Force Awakens* and *Evil Dead*, in which the question of the sexuality of Rey or Mia is never thematized, these two stories rest on a prominent 'coming of age' narrative framework. Considering these patterns, it appears as symptomatic that the monstrous creature(s) find, in both cases, a privileged situational anchoring in dark and uterine corridors whose claustrophobic and castrating connotations are exploited by these productions. Moreover, it is indicative that the monsters all have gaping jaws – red or pink in colour, ovoid and generously serrated – that morphologically echo the iconography of the toothed vagina. The various written descriptions of Pennywise's jaw (Bill Skarsgård), *It*'s killer clown, in the film script even more than in King's novel,[14] are strongly evocative in this respect: 'his mouthful of razor-like teeth'; '[his] smile begins to grow, as his jaw becomes unhinged. Revealing rows and rows of teeth right before'; 'his jaw full of large razor sharp teeth, dripping with saliva'[15] (Figure 10.1). The binary gendered dimension of the relationship to danger that emerges from the particular expression of these phenomena for girls and boys is easily perceptible in *Stranger Things*' second season, where the cavities that threaten to engulf the young boys tend to be anus-shaped, while

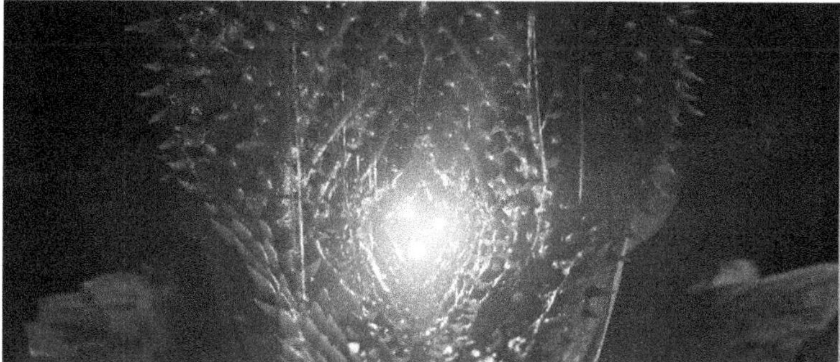

Figure 10.1 Pennywise's jaw as a toothed vagina in *It* directed by Andy Muschietti © Warner Bros 2017.

the one that Eleven seeks to shut off at the end of the last episode of the season – notably entitled 'Chapter Nine: The Gate' – is a gigantic vulva with, again, a tentacle upright in her direction. Furthermore, the words used by the character of Dr. Brenner (Matthew Modine), in his threatening speech to Eleven in flashback and mostly voice-over, during this final confrontation, clearly reveal the sexual nature of the power against which he warns her: 'You have a wound, Eleven, a terrible wound. And it's festering. And it will grow, spread. And eventually, it will kill you.' Moreover, it is only when she manages to halt the growth of the tentacle moving menacingly towards her and to close, by using the force of her mind and by bleeding abundantly from her nose, the monumental slit from which this phallic appendix emerges that Eleven succeeds in triumphing over the monster that threatened to swallow everything. This victory over her outer as well as inner wound translates, in subtext, into a victory over the supposed irrepressible and devouring components of her sexuality. If, as I have indicated, *It* and *Stranger Things* open up the possibility of the physical potentialities of affective relationships between teenagers, these potentialities lead to a resolutely sentimental and minimal expression. Indeed, just like Bev who exchanges a kiss with Bill (Jaeden Lieberher) in *It*'s very last scene, Eleven's 'sexuality' during the last scene of the series is confirmed but also contained by the fact that she integrates the reassuring canvas of traditional heterosexual *romance* by dancing and chastely kissing her partner at the school party.

Despite their differences, in the cases of *It*, *Stranger Things*, *Evil Dead* as well as *The Force Awakens*, the stigmatization of unbridled female sexual impulses is part of a broader discursive containment strategy ultimately aimed at reassuringly legitimizing the power and autonomy given to certain female characters (heterosexual and white), by entirely or partly decoupling them from sexuality.

But as the Rathtars sequence suggested earlier, this strategy is not confined to horror, even if it is in this genre that it has found its most wide-ranging manifestation. The character of Lisbeth Salander in *The Girl in the Spider's Web* (2018) is a telling example. In *The Girl with the Dragon Tattoo* (2011), a remake of the Swedish adaptation (2009) of Stieg Larsson's famous novel, Salander (Rooney Mara) represented the quintessential 'phallic girl' theorized by Angela McRobbie, that is, a 'girl' that, among other traits, 'perform[s] masculinity, without relinquishing the femininity which makes [her] so desirable to men' (McRobbie, 2009: 84). In this remake, Salander is indeed represented as a phallicized, dark, tough and attractive young hacker who can sew up the wound of her partner, Mikael Blomkvist (Daniel Craig), as well as initiate having sex with him. Seven years later, *The Girl in the Spider's Web*'s Salander, played by Claire Foy this time, is similar to the one performed by Mara in terms of ingenuity, use of violence and phallic power. But she differs significantly from her predecessor in terms of sexuality. In this adaptation of the fourth novel of the series (taken up by David Lagercrantz after Larsson's passing), Salander indeed renounces sexuality outside of a visually concealed sapphism, which is suggested early in the film by the presence, in her bed, in the morning, of a young woman she had met the day before at a nightclub. Her only physical relationship with Blomkvist (Sverrir Gudnason) is a stitching session, with a stapler, of the bleeding wound that runs through her back's dragon tattoo (1:08:00). The suturing of this wound is interesting in two respects. On the one hand, the bleeding wound, to which the film returns at regular intervals ((30:03), (1:07:53),

(1:40:26)), metaphorizes the mixture of greed, incestuous sexuality and castrating power embodied by the film's antagonist, namely Salander's sister Camilla (Sylvia Hoeks). The wound was inflicted by Camilla's henchman, whose invariably red clothes refer to the injury, and who represents the sexualised and negative double of the heroine. On the other hand, this ostensibly painful suture session is depicted in a way that clearly *suggests* a sexual intercourse with sadomasochistic connotations (and replaces the real intercourse that never takes place): Blomkvist stands behind Salander who is leaning forward and is seen moaning in close-up at each inserted staple. At the end of the film, it is only once Salander has gotten out of the rubber coating she was trapped in, revealing the now-healed wound on her back, that the heroine can finally put her sister in check, before the latter kills herself. In other words, Lisbeth's expiatory evacuation of her (hetero)sexual wound forms the central condition for neutralizing the film's toothed vagina: the invariably red dressed, sexualized and venomous sister who runs the crime syndicate that threatens to destroy the world. Of course, the discursive use of this symbolism could be explained by the fact that this adaptation is signed by Fede Álvarez, who directed *Evil Dead*. But that would be without taking into account this symbolism's presence in other successful productions. For example, by 2019, wound 'heat-sealing' had opportunely become Rey's celebrated new power in *Star Wars: The Rise of Skywalker* (2019), be it the three lacerations that invaginate the giant snake/penis's body she encounters underground (34:00) or the cut on Kylo Ren's side after their duel (1:022:00).[16] Rey not only closes orifices; she *erases* them.

The return of the repression of the fetishized repressed

The ambitions of this chapter have remained relatively modest and its objective primarily descriptive: the aim was to highlight, through the study of the narrative path to heroism of a few main female characters in contemporary cinema, the variety of uses of the toothed vagina motif in a broader discursive economy, designed to (de)construct powerful and autonomous heroines. These women do not destabilize masculine hegemony, insofar as they have renounced a sexuality that, in all likelihood, continues to condense the real or imagined concerns associated with independent femininity in the current patriarchal imagination.

Naturally, there is still much to be done in order to understand the relationship between these films, the various pleasures they convey, their use of this motif in relation to their representation of female heroism and the historical context in which they play a role. This difficult work seems even more necessary and pressing since the research that has examined these phenomena has mainly done so, following Creed's work, from a psychoanalytical perspective that has generally left the question of the historical determinations of these discourses in abeyance. Of course, as Carol Vance already pointed out in *Pleasure and Danger: Exploring Female Sexuality*, 'material change' has historically almost always favoured 'women's autonomy in general (wage labour, urbanisation, contraception, and abortion)' and allowed them 'to be sexual in more visible and daring ways' (Vance, 1984: 1). Regarding this assessment, not only does recent research on women's sexuality attest to an increase in their freedom, particularly in urban areas (Cattan and Leroy, 2016: 80–9), but, as I have argued elsewhere, the past two decades have also been marked by the emergence of a new set of technologies and techniques that, at least in terms of cinematographic imagination, have found their echo in a large number of productions. These productions appear designed to reaffirm the superiority of male heroes over machine women symbolizing sexual and political empowerment (Courcoux, 2018).

However, without wishing to over-speculate, perhaps there is a deeper reason for the re-emergence of this motif and the extremely violent treatment to which it is subjected. A large number of 'postfeminist' film heroines of the late 1990s and 2000s could indeed be described as 'phallic' women, both powerful and reassuring, whose supposedly 'castrated' dimension had been repressed through fetishistic strategies

(McRobbie, 2009: 83–7). These characters include Jordan O'Neil (Demi Moore) in *G.I. Jane* (1997), Trinity in *The Matrix*, Erin (Jessica Biel) in *The Texas Chainsaw Massacre* (2003), the Bride (Uma Thurman) in *Kill Bill: Vol. 1* and *Vol. 2* (2003–4), the heroines of *Charlie's Angels* (2000–3), Selene in the *Underworld* franchise, Lara Croft (Angelina Jolie) in *Lara Croft: Tomb Raider 1* and *2* (2001–3) and Alice (Milla Jovovich) in the *Resident Evil* franchise (2002–16). According to several analyses, the workings of this disavowal were often based on the fetishistic eroticization of these heroines' bodies through the use of tight suits, frequently made of latex, which emphasized their voluptuous forms. As Brown notes in this regard, 'uniforms as fetishistic costuming may sexualise the action heroine but they also ground her power within larger systems of paternal law' (2015: 81). However, the thesis defended by Creed in her book, and in particular in the chapter she devotes to the toothed vagina, is that film scholars have commonly neglected the castrating dimension of female characters in horror cinema. She posits that it is for the same reasons that Freud himself reduced it in his theorization of fears associated with female sexuality:

> Freud does not consider the other possibility that it is man who constructs woman as a castrator and that he has displaced his anxiety on to woman … Freud avoids confronting the possibility that man's fear of sexual intercourse with woman is based on irrational fears about the deadly powers of the vagina, especially the bleeding vagina. Rather than consider man's dread of the imaginary castrating woman, Freud takes refuge in his theory of woman's castration. (Creed, 1993: 121)

Following Creed's line of argument, we can hypothesize that both the fetishization and sexualization of the women fighters of the 1990–2000s participated, on the discursive level, in the same imagino-symbolic logic described by Creed: disavowing the castrating potentialities of these women through a fetishistic representation of their bodies and attributes, in order to underline their 'penis envy' hiding their 'lack' of one. As such, the proliferation of the toothed vagina and its repression in contemporary films could be considered as the 'return of the repressed' of a collective imaginary,[17] which, like Freud according to Creed, had first preferred to consider the growing power of women as an expression of a desire to fill their lack and to appropriate a power that wishfully would be man's own. However, as the events of 2017 seem to suggest, the containment power of such a strategy has not proven sufficient. Contemporary films now seek to exorcise/externalize the fear of the increasing power of women (white and heterosexual) in a form hitherto less recognizable: the fear of a bloody vagina, which, in the current cinematic imagination, seems to continue to stand for the physiological site to which men reduce/enlarge women's power.

Evidently, in these contexts, the castrated woman and the castrating woman stand for the 'two sides of the same coin'. But their historical succession mode, by which the castrated woman gives way to the castrating woman as the prevalent expression of male anxieties, is certainly not arbitrary. This succession could indeed very well be the symptom of a form of strategic exhaustion in the face of the perception of ever more powerful young women. This is particularly clear if one considers Jacques Lacan's commentary on Freud's fearful dream called 'Irma's Injection'. After associating Irma's throat with 'the terrifying anxiety-provoking image, to this *real Medusa's head*', Lacan points out that Freud's anguish finds its origin in the unconscious move from the mouth to the female genitals:

> The revelation of this something which properly speaking is unnameable, the back of this throat, the complex, unlocatable form, which also makes it into the primitive object par excellence, the abyss of the *feminine organ* from which all life emerges, this *gulf of the mouth*, in which everything is swallowed up, and no less the image of death in which everything comes to its end. (Lacan 1991: 164; emphases added)

This decisive shift, which correlates the female throat to death via the anxiety-provoking image of the vagina, is undoubtedly the one that, whether in Freud or on American screens, is most symptomatic of what we can call, after Lacan or in line with Kristeva's conception of the abject, 'the revelation of that which is least penetrable in the real, of the real lacking any possible mediation, of the ultimate real, the object of anxiety *par excellence*' (Lacan, 1991: 164). Hopefully, History – provided that there will be more research devoted to these phenomena – will tell us whether the debates and reflections that marked the turn of the 2020s have led to an audiovisual and semantic creativity that is sufficiently fruitful to overcome these anxieties and the lack of mediation that characterizes them, so as to renew and expand the terms that govern our gender relations.

Notes

1 For an account that differs from the prevailing optimism in the media that has been associated with the return in fashion of certain trends in feminism and points to the 'instrumentalisation' of the climate of fear on American campuses, see Kipnis (2017).

2 Regarding the audience's actual composition for these films, see Dika (1990: 87) and Nowell (2011).

3 I'm putting *Teeth* aside because, in addition to its post-feminist discourse, the film belongs to a group of productions that predate the emergence of the new heroines I want to study. Moreover, this film, which is mainly known to horror specialists, was neither a critical nor a financial success. See Henry (2014: 57–78).

4 Kasdan, Abrams and Arndt (n.d.: 45).

5 Ibid., 43.

6 Ibid., 47.

7 This sexually threatening imagery is indeed part of a long-standing iconographic and symbolic tradition, which, since the beginning of the saga, has endeavoured to assuage the masculine fear of castration by using numerous motifs: most notably, images of severed arms and the avatars of the vagina dentata that threaten Luke Skywalker and Han Solo. Examples include the trash compactor in *Star Wars* (1977), the giant alien worm in *The Empire Strikes Back* (1980) and the Sarlacc in *Return of the Jedi* (1983). The types of fears expressed in *Return of the Jedi* as elsewhere in the saga are extremely gendered. It is indeed significant that the only monster

Princess Leia kills (by strangulation) is Jabba the Hut, a sort of huge penis with a big mouth. This symbolic economy was noted by essayist Peter Biskind:

> Leia, suddenly sexualised in her revealing Barbarella outfit, must be rescued not only from Jabba but from her own sexuality. … The Jabba episode culminates in an explicit *vagina dentata* fantasy, as Luke and his pals have to walk a phallic gangplank into the pullulating maw – festooned with long, curved teeth – of the giant Sarlacc in its 'nesting place'. A more nightmarishly explicit image of threatening female sexuality would be hard to imagine. (2004: 129)

8 Kasdan, Abrams and Arndt (n.d.: 37).

9 This scar prefigures here in a threatening way the imposing scar visible, as a castration sign on the face of his mentor, on Supreme Leader Snoke (Andy Serkis).

10 Kasdan, Abrams and Arndt (n.d.: 106).

11 Unlike its remake, Raimi's film makes the theme of mating quite explicit through the recurring call of the voice saying to Ash: 'Join Us.'

12 In the original film, the medallion is not a symbol of brotherhood but of chaste love, offered by Ash (Bruce Campbell) to his girlfriend Linda (Betsy Baker) at the beginning of the narrative. In this respect, it is interesting to note that it is thanks to this medallion, and so to the reaffirmation of the superiority of love over the hysterical body, that Ash finally manages to destroy the Book of the Dead.

13 The thematic as well as iconographic similarities between the two productions seem so obvious that, in his review of *It: Chapter Two*, Peter Debruge (2019) calls '"Stranger Things" – a shameless "It" knockoff that improves on King's novel'.

14 See King (1980: 1000, 1134).

15 Palmer and Fukunaga (2016: 6, 36, 88).

16 Symbolically, the valorization of this kind of power is all the more striking after *Star Wars: The Last Jedi* has insisted on Rey's ability to explore and open up obstructed cracks throughout its narrative, especially during the film's final rescue scene of the Resistance on planet Crait.

17 It could be argued that this is a conscious use of the toothed vagina trope by professionals familiar with Freudian theories and writings on the subject and that there is therefore nothing really repressed about it. But

this self-awareness, even if it could be attested, doesn't say much about the function assigned to this figure, its modes of reception, its effects or even its meanings. Nor does it imply a stimulating understanding of those writings, as Maxime Cervulle has shown. Finally, one can argue, following Christian Metz and Jane Feuer, that reflexivity or even playfulness have never guaranteed a distancing effect and that, on the contrary, they may well favour more intense forms of spectator immersion. See Cervulle (2009: 35–49) and Courcoux (2018: 276–9).

Works cited

Álvarez, Fede, and Rodo Menez (2011), *Evil Dead, based on The Evil Dead, by Sam Raimi,* 20 October, draft.

Biskind, Peter (2004), *Gods and Monsters: Movers, Shakers, and Other Casualties of the Hollywood Machine*, New York: Nation Books.

Brown, Jeffrey A. (2011), *Dangerous Curves: Action Heroines, Gender, Fetishism and Popular Culture*, Jackson: University Press of Mississippi.

Brown, Jeffery A. (2015), *Beyond Bombshells: The New Action Heroine in Popular Culture*, Jackson: University Press of Mississippi.

Cattan, Nadine, and Stéphane Leroy (2016), *Atlas mondial des sexualités. Libertés, plaisirs et interdits*, Paris, Éditions Autrement.

Cervulle, Maxime (2009), 'Quentin Tarantino et le (post)féminisme. Politiques du genre dans Boulevard de la mort', *Nouvelles Questions Féministes*, 28.1: 35–49.

Clover, Carol J. (1987), 'Her body, himself: Gender in the slasher film', *Representations*, 20, 'Special Issue: Misogyny, Misandry, and Misanthropy': 187–228.

Courcoux, Charles-Antoine (2018), *Des machines et des hommes. Masculinité et technologie dans le cinéma américain contemporain*, 'préface de Raphaëlle Moine', Chêne-Bourg, Georg.

Creed, Barbara (1993), 'Medusa's head: The vagina dentata and Freudian theory', in *The Monstrous-Feminine: Film, Feminism, Psychoanalysis*, 105–21, London: Routledge.

Debruge, Peter (2019), 'Film review: "It: Chapter Two"', *Variety*, 3 September. Available online: https://variety.com/2019/film/reviews/it-chapter-two-review-1203321205/.

Dika, Vera (1990), *Games of Terror: Halloween, Friday the 13th, and the Films of the Stalker Cycle*, Fairleigh: Dickinson University Press.

Gates, Philippa (2011), *Detecting Women: Gender and the Hollywood Detective Film*, Albany: State University of New York Press.

Gill, Glen Robert (2019), 'Re-envisioning myth in *Star Wars: Episode VII: The Force Awakens*', *Journal of Religion and Popular Culture*, 31.1: 3–15.

Henry, Claire (2014), 'The postfeminist trap of vagina dentata for the American teen castratrice', in *Revisionist Rape-Revenge: Redefining a Film Genre*, 57–78, New York: Palgrave Macmillan.

Kasdan, Lawrence, J. J. Abrams and Michael Arndt (n.d.), *Star Wars: The Force Awakens*, final script.

King, Stephen (1980), *It*, iBooks edition, New York, New American Library.

Kipnis, Laura (2017), *Unwanted Advances: Sexual Paranoia Comes to Campus*, New York: HarperCollins.

Kristeva, Julia (1982), *Powers of Horror: An Essay on Abjection*, trans. from French by Leon S. Roudiez, New York: Columbia University Press.

Lacan, Jacques ([1978]1991), *The Seminar of Jacques Lacan: Book II. The Ego in Freud's Theory and the Technique of Psychoanalysis 1954–1955*, trans. Sylvana Tomaselli, New York: W. W. Norton.

McRobbie, Angela (2009), *The Aftermath of Feminism: Gender, Culture and Social Change*, Los Angeles: Sage.

Nowell, Richard (2011), *Blood Money: A History of the First Teen Slasher Film Cycle*, London: Continuum.

Palmer, Chase, and C. J. Fukunaga (2016), *It*, based on the novel by Stephen King, current revisions by Gary Dauberman, 3 November, draft.

Vance, Carole S. (1984), 'Pleasure and danger: Toward a politics of sexuality', in *Pleasure and Danger: Exploring Female Sexuality*, 1–27, Boston: Routledge & Kegan Paul.

Williams, Linda (1984), 'When the woman looks', in Mary Ann Doane, Patricia Mellencamp and Linda Williams (eds), *Re-Vision: Essays in Feminist Film Criticism*, 83–99, Frederick, MD: University Publications of America.

Williams, Linda (2001), 'When women look: A sequel', *Senses of Cinema*, July. Available online: http://sensesofcinema.com/2001/freuds-worst-nightmares-psychoanalysis-and-the-horror-film/horror_women/ (accessed 24 January 2020).

11

Can women be superheroes? Reflections on American cinema and beyond

Yvonne Tasker

The cultural and commercial prominence of the superhero film within American cinema is a marked feature of the twenty-first century, exemplified by the intensive promotion and international success of films such as *The Avengers* (2012) and *Guardians of the Galaxy* (2014). Despite the many available female characters in the Marvel and DC comic book lexicon, female characters have occupied a marginal position within this boom in American superhero cinema. Heroic women are typically present at the margins, as with Storm in *X-Men*, or Sue Storm/Invisible Woman in *Fantastic Four*, often featuring more memorably in villainous roles, as with Mystique in several of the *X-Men* films. Both *The Avengers* and *Guardians of the Galaxy*, in common with other multi-protagonist action films, feature a sole female member of the heroic team in the form of Natasha Romanoff/Black Widow (Scarlett Johansson) and Gamora (Zoe Saldana), respectively; both are effectively supporting or secondary characters in the larger generic space of superhero action and male melodrama. This is not unfamiliar territory for feminist cultural critics; we often find ourselves looking precisely in the margins in order to analyse the intricacies of gender representation. That logic is further heightened when we explore the figuration of women of colour in these cultural spaces.

As explored in Kristy Guevera-Flanagan's feminist documentary *Wonder Women! The Untold Story of American Superheroines* (2012), the marginalization of female superheroes and female characters more generally is not a new or isolated phenomenon. Rather, it speaks to a pattern of exclusion that can be understood in relation to wider issues of gender and racial inequalities within Western visual culture. Indeed, the long-delayed appearance of Wonder Woman as a character within a live action film is in many ways emblematic of the difficulty Hollywood cinema has had with imagining the female superhero as a significant symbolic, and indeed commercial, proposition. The commercial success of *Black Panther* (2018) in this context is also telling; with its roster of strong Black female characters, the film underlines the stories that are typically absent from superhero action. The commercial and critical success of Patty Jenkins's *Wonder Woman* (2017) similarly provides a fascinating site for reflection. As I will explore in more detail, the long-anticipated *Wonder Woman* builds on the supporting role played by Gal Gadot in the rather less well-received study in melancholic masculinity, *Batman v Superman* (2016). Her move from the margins to the centre of the fiction is, I argue, suggestive in the context of a film culture that has tended to regard the female hero as a risky commercial proposition.

This chapter explores the question posed in the title – 'Can women be superheroes?' – discussing the ways in which superhero cinema has tended to limit female agency on screen. There is, I propose, a short answer to this question: yes, but. My argument is presented in the spirit of this qualified positive, elaborating on both the 'yes' and the 'but' to suggest something of the power and limitation of superhero cinema as a site that reproduces and, at times, challenges conventional gender scripts. In the first part, I discuss the gendered dimensions of superhero cinema in relation to fantasy genres broadly understood, providing a critical frame derived principally from film (rather than comics) studies. Superhero films effectively couple the comic book universe – with its backstories, evolving characterization and bold design – with conventions and styles that have evolved through the Hollywood action cinema over decades and which have intensified in the twenty-first century. In the second part, I explore superhero gender scripts via a comparative analysis of Marvel's Thor and DC's Wonder Woman.

Noting that both are associated with an iconography of classical culture by way of the Italian peplum and the Hollywood epic that followed it, I discuss the ways in which these figures are framed in relation to themes of generational conflict, redemptive sacrifice and a nostalgic sense of moral simplicity evoked by the quasi-classical costumes and settings. My argument then takes a particular, and hopefully productive, route into this body of films in relation to the position occupied by women both on the margins and at the centre.

Female superheroes in cinema: Generic frames of action adventure and fantasy

Although they by no means predominate, female superheroes are nonetheless familiar figures in comics. Perhaps the most established and best known of comic books' female superheroes is Wonder Woman, a character who first appeared in print in 1941. As has been regularly observed, Wonder Woman was conceived as a character within the particular context of the Second World War, a patriotic vehicle – her costume evoking the stars and stripes – reputedly intended to both mobilize and celebrate women's war work in the United States. Wonder Woman's history both as a character and in terms of popular cultural reception is complex and I do not have space to do it justice here. Crucially, though, despite an extremely successful television series starring Linda Carter, *Wonder Woman* (1975–9), and the commercial/critical success of the *Superman* series of films starring Christopher Reeves (1978, 1979, 1983, 1987), Wonder Woman did not make the transition to live action cinema for over seventy years. Such an absence surely indicates an industry ambivalence about female heroes within popular cinema. The transition of other female characters to cinema, such as Storm (who debuted in comic books in 1975 and first appeared on screen in *X-Men* in 2000) or the assassin Elektra (appearing as a character in 1981 and in the film *Elektra* over twenty years later in 2005), seems to underline that industry uncertainty.

The iconic history of DC Comics' Wonder Woman, and her long delayed transition to live action cinema, provides the context for Guevera-Flanagan's documentary *Wonder Women!*, mentioned above. The film explores and aims to contextualize the cultural uncertainty around female action which frames this chapter, framing this as an 'untold' story. The documentary opens with a vox pop: men and women of different ages and ethnicities struggle to name a female superhero with the sole exception of Wonder Woman. This sequence gives way to a montage which draws together a number of film and television representations of strong women; these are not superheroes as such, but rather action heroines. In evoking films such as *Aliens* (1986) and television series such as *Xena: Warrior Princess* (1995–2001) and *Buffy the Vampire Slayer* (1997–2003), Guevera-Flanagan's film visually traces a lineage familiar within feminist scholarship on popular culture.[1] Not only have feminist critics had much to say on these figures, but we have become more adept at exploring the significance of supporting characters, and even figures in the background, as well as the protagonist. Such an approach has been vital for opening up perspectives on representations of race and popular culture, with women of colour more often cast in supporting than lead roles.

It is of course the very cultural and commercial visibility of superhero cinema which makes it matter as a site through which to consider conventional gendered hierarchies. As will already be clear, I am conceptualizing superhero films as the most recent and high-profile instance of the familiar, globally present film tradition of action. It has been argued that the overarching theme of action is that of transition, of becoming powerful. Lisa Purse elaborates this understanding of action's core theme when she writes,

> Action films trade in spectacles of physical mastery, in fantasies of empowerment … Action bodies, with their capacity to escape physical constraints, to subject environments, people, and more abstract entities like institutions and unruly criminal organisations to their physical mastery, offer fantasies of empowerment that allow us to

> rehearse our own dreamed-of escapes, our own becoming-masterful, in a fantasy context, allow us to 'feel' this mastery for ourselves through our sensorial connection with the body of the hero. (2011: 45)

These tropes of transition, power and difference – which Purse is careful to explore in relation to spatial as well as embodied aspects of the film image – are given new emphasis in superhero cinema via the border crossing of heroic (and villainous) figures who embody a transgression of boundaries such as human/animal, human/alien, living/dead. Wonder Woman's spectacular leaps and displays of strength offer one instance of the superhero character exceeding human limits. Another is Mystique's shift-shifting in the *X-Men* series, her natural state a blue almost-reptilian skin which she is capable of modifying to take on the appearance of other characters at well. Wonder Woman is a god, Mystique a mutant. Elsewhere in superhero cinema, tropes of bodily or genetic modification, whether by accident (Spider-Man, Captain Marvel) or design (Captain America), speak to both science-fiction and horror conventions.

In contrast to Mystique, the bodily integrity of Wonder Woman represents a distinct articulation of the superhero; her immense power and the film's visual emphasis on agility and constancy is framed by the use of location shooting as well as digital effects work for the battle sequences. The particular relationship of superhero films to fantasy, to the construction of worlds in which physical limits and cultural norms are overcome, is, I would argue, particularly resonant for questions of gender representation. Given that superhero action is fantastical, scenarios in which the hero's moral and physical qualities are exaggerated and the limiting aspects of Western culture are to the fore, where better to stage the possibilities of a female hero? Hollywood cinema has tended to struggle with the concept of the female action hero, however. As I have argued elsewhere (Tasker, 1998), Hollywood action and adventure has tended to treat the female hero with caution; culturally and commercially she is taken to be a risky proposition, a figure whose very existence requires lengthy sequences of exposition and explanation.

This is not to say that American cinema has excluded the female hero altogether, as authors such as Rikke Schubart (2007) have elaborated in some detail. Indeed, through Hollywood's history, including the silent period, adventurous or heroic female figures have appeared across action genres. Some adventure narratives feature female protagonists, as with *Anne of the Indies* (1951) in which Jean Peters plays pirate Captain Anne Providence. In female-centred films, romance plots may play a larger part, but the basic narrative structure is unchanged: adventure allows for growth and personal development amidst the battles and spectacle. In the second part of this chapter, we will see this logic of personal development at work in both *Thor* and *Wonder Woman*. In *Anne of the Indies*, Providence will ultimately forego her plans of vengeance and sacrifice herself for her beloved LaRochelle (Louis Jourdan), suggesting both adoption of contemporary codes of femininity and a contrived morality around piracy (which is shown not to pay). *Pirates of the Caribbean* (2003) serves as a later example of the subgenre in which the female lead is an active participant in the adventure. Whether it is the 1950s or the 2000s, however, female characters in adventure narratives are more often found awaiting rescue than initiating action.[2] Arguably, the most high-profile cinematic adaptations of female action through recent decades are not from comic books at all but from the world of gaming – the figures of Lara Croft of the *Tomb Raider* franchise and Alice in the *Resident Evil* series being highly visible examples – or fiction for young people (*The Hunger Games*). It would be rash to suggest that the world of gaming is more welcoming to women or to female characters than the cinema, and yet superhero cinema tends to confirm the sorts of gender hierarchies which have been consistent features of the genre.

The stultifying work of conservative gender scripts is evident in two films centred on female superheroes, neither of which fared well either critically or commercially, in turn feeding a received wisdom as to the viability of female-fronted films of this type. Presumably aware of their atypical female leads, both *Elektra* (2005) and *Catwoman* (2004) devote considerable time to 'explaining' female violence and power, effectively postponing action. While origin stories are key to superhero fictions, these titles betray an inability to handle that balance (a contrast, as I'll argue, to the thematic continuity between origin story and action in *Wonder Woman*). The framing of female violence through backstories that legitimate such unusual gender behaviour in genre terms is a familiar element of commercial cinema. Whether she seeks justice for herself or her family, to protect a child or surrogate child or to continue the legacy of her father, women's violence – and hence their role in action scenarios – is routinely hedged with explanation.

It is perhaps no surprise, then, that strong women who are physically capable and significant in narrative terms are present yet oddly peripheral to superhero cinema. An illustration of this logic is provided by the shifting presentation of Pepper Potts (Gwyneth Paltrow) in the *Iron Man* films. She is repeatedly cast as a woman in peril (being rescued in all three films), while serving a key narrative role as assistant (retrieving information on Stark's behalf, for example), before being recast as quasi-action figure in *Iron Man 3* (2013). Indeed, her power to protect Stark in the film's climax stems – perversely – from her very status as woman in peril: the film's villain has subjected Potts to the same process he has used to enhance his own body, bestowing on her strength and regenerative abilities. Since these powers will ultimately prove fatal, she must subsequently be cured, restored to a peripheral role.[3]

Earlier on I suggested that feminist writers must perforce examine marginal, supporting or peripheral figures in order to understand more about the gender culture of the blockbuster. I'd add that this examination needs to be contextualized, by factors such as industry conservatism which the phenomenal success of both *Wonder Woman* and *Black Panther* cannot easily undo. Until the release of *Captain Marvel* in 2019, the high-profile Marvel movies focused almost exclusively on male characters. *The Avengers* films do of course feature a prominent female character in the form of Natasha Romanoff/Black Widow, a superspy with no superpowers albeit possessing precisely the sorts of enhanced capacity for action familiar to action audiences; that is, improbably tough without being actually superhuman, Romanoff is able to deceive and manipulate others in pursuit of knowledge. Introduced in *Iron Man 2* (2010) as S.H.I.E.L.D.'s undercover operative within the Stark Corporation, Romanoff is smart, sexual and skilled in combat. In *The Avengers*, Romanoff enacts feminine vulnerability to secure intelligence on a number of occasions, employing her skills first against a clownish set of goons, then to bring in Bruce Banner without him transforming into the Hulk and later to secure information from another deceptive and articulate figure, Loki. Black Widow is introduced in a position of seeming danger: bound to a precariously poised chair she is being interrogated, a scene of violence interrupted by a phone call from S.H.I.E.L.D.'s Phil Coulson. Romanoff's cool assertion that she is 'working' – verbally inverting the assumed power relations of the scene – is followed by a sequence in which she easily overcomes her captors, using her body and the chair to which she is bound to physically assert her superiority.

Writing in the late 1990s, I argued that Hollywood cinema persistently equated the working woman with sexual performance, conflating 'women's bodies, sexuality and work' (1998: 5). Such logic is clearly evident in the Black Widow sequence to which I refer above. Yet it also enacts the action trope of becoming-powerful which Purse argues is so central to the genre, an initial impression of vulnerability supplanted by violence and decisive physical authority. In line with the intensifying character of challenge and performance which characterize the genre, by the time of the final battle scenes in New York, Black Widow demonstrates an extraordinary athleticism, leaping and back-flipping on and off alien vehicles. While all this is prefigured in the sequence that introduces her character, with her impressive fighting skills, Black Widow's incorporation into the Avengers team renders her more than human (although not, of course, superhuman). This is the visual and thematic terrain of contemporary action cinema: action bodies that perform extraordinary feats when necessary, movement through space, violence as source of both narrative and aesthetic pleasure, and the celebration of mastery that is in the process of being forged.

Black Widow is a fascinating figuration of the contradictory position of women in superhero action. She is a core member of the Avengers team while remaining a supporting character (*Black Widow*, a film based around her character was released in 2021). Aligned to S.H.I.E.L.D. and thus to the mechanisms of the state, Black Widow opts to set aside her former allegiances in *Captain America: The Winter Soldier* (2014). Black Widow's backstory in espionage (as revealed in *Avengers: Age of Ultron* (2015)) involves the erasure of self, a trope familiar within fantasy worlds populated by modified and mutated beings. Controversially at the time of its release, *Ultron* featured Black Widow implicitly defining herself as monstrous since she cannot have children, female agents being sterilized as part of their training. Black Widow's origin story belongs in a different genre it seems; an emphasis on sexuality frames her as a seductive spy, while her costume evokes action and combat. For all this, Black Widow is a substantive character within the Marvel films, her pragmatism and humanity functioning as a counterpoint to superhero posturing.

It is indicative, given how rarely women are to be found at the centre of the frame as the protagonist of superhero action, that Wonder Woman first appears in the DC film series as a supporting character. Early trailers for *Batman v Superman: Dawn of Justice* (2016) barely acknowledged the character's presence – she is of course not mentioned in the title. In the film itself, Wonder Woman is a mysterious figure who remains on the periphery of the unfolding action for much of the film's running time. Disguised, hesitant about involvement, initially fleeing when her identity seems about to be revealed, Wonder Woman leaves the history books and makes an explosive entry into battle in the film's finale where she fights alongside Batman and Superman to the amazement of both. With Gal Gadot's portrayal one of the few elements of the 2017 film welcomed by critics, the figure of Wonder Woman increased in prominence and visibility, in turn generating expectations around the solo film. Indeed, the commercial and critical success of Patty Jenkins's subsequent *Wonder Woman* – in contrast to other recent DC films which reviewers have labelled as laboured and leaden – neatly upends the commercial logic whereby titles centred on female characters are regarded as risky.

Surely, then, the production and success of the 2017 film *Wonder Woman* provides an emphatic answer to the question posed in my title, even as its very atypicality adds a resounding 'but' to the affirmative? In what follows, I explore the significance of Wonder Woman's appearance in relation to female superheroes and American cinema through a comparative analysis with the Marvel hero Thor. I situate Wonder Woman in relation to Thor rather than Batman or Superman, the male heroes alongside whom she appears in both comic books and cinema, in order to underline a shared iconography drawn from cinema and television engagements with the classical world of myth. In turn, the comparison brings into view the ways in which *Wonder Woman* successfully presents a female superhero at the centre of its action, unlike the Marvel films.

Gender and the mise en scène of classicism: Wonder Woman and Thor

The revelation of the identity of Wonder Woman in *Batman v Superman* is an intensely mediated moment involving images within images. Diana Prince's secret identity is revealed through archival traces, visually reconstructed by Bruce Wayne as he juxtaposes two contemporary recordings – one captured on the street, another via an ATM – with a fading black-and-white photograph, dated 1918. This image, redolent with the iconography of the First World War, provides the bridge between *Batman v Superman* and *Wonder Woman*, the latter featuring a scene detailing this photographic plate being made in the wake of a battle. The narrative of *Wonder Woman* proceeds from the mystery surrounding the figure of Diana Prince (and indeed this photograph), elaborating the origin story of her powers and how she became involved in human affairs. That origin story is framed by the Diana Prince persona as she appears in modern-day Paris; juxtaposed with the glass pyramid identifying the Louvre, Diana is figured as a sophisticated metropolitan woman, associated with Europe rather than the United States. Her movements within the frame are measured, her expression ambiguous. *Batman v. Superman* saw Bruce Wayne discover Diana Prince in the archives; she is now, it seems, a curator.

In this opening sequence, the arrival of a briefcase from Wayne Enterprises visually escorts the viewer to Diana, neatly acknowledging Bruce Wayne's discovery of her existence, though not her secrets. Now positioned as both past and present, archival presence and contemporary curator – she is pictured in the museum against a backdrop of ancient artefacts of war such as chest plates and swords (Figure 11.1) – Diana's voice-over reflects mournfully on what she has learnt about the human world. The briefcase is shown to contain the original photographic plate of the fading image revealed in *Batman v Superman*. The fragility and age of the glass and the fact that Diana herself has not visibly aged suggests that she exists outside time. An accompanying brief note speaks of Wayne having 'found the original' and hoping to one day hear her story. Diana's reflections do indeed present that story, although for the audience rather than Wayne; her recollections take us first to Themyscira, the island of the Amazons, exploring and explaining her

Figure 11.1 Diana Prince/Wonder Woman (Gal Gadot) appears as a curator associated with ancient artefacts of combat in *Wonder Woman* directed by Patty Jenkins © Warner Bros 2017.

entry into the world of men and her subsequent seeming withdrawal from it.

The introduction of Diana Prince then foregrounds the secrecy, and indeed the sadness of her modern-day identity. Contrast this to the cinematic appearance of superhero Thor. In the pre-credit sequence of *Thor* (2011), the superhero/god/king in waiting crashes to earth and is struck by astrophysicist Jane Foster's van as she, together with her assistant Darcy and colleague Dr Erik Selsvig, is monitoring atmospheric disturbances in New Mexico. As with Wayne's wish to hear Diana Prince's story, Jane's mystified question, 'Where did he come from?', provides the trigger for the film's action with Odin's voice-over intoning the mythical history of Asgard to, it is revealed, his young sons Thor and Loki. This encounter in the desert (and Jane's question about Thor's origins) is repeated with more detail later in the film; we now know that Thor has come from the heavens, expelled by his father Odin as a result of youthful arrogance. Rather than Diana Prince's mediations on her past via the photographic place, the culmination of this reprised sequence of arrival in *Thor* takes the form of comic – almost slapstick – humiliation as a raging Thor is felled with a Taser wielded by Jane's assistant Darcy.

Jane Foster's question – 'Where did he come from?' – opens up chronologies of gender and cinema heroism. Despite the humour at his expense, the cinematic articulation of Thor in recent Marvel films speaks to superhero action's dependence on conventional, and even conservative, gender scripts. The films may gently mock the hero whose masculinity is simultaneously other-worldly and distinctly old-fashioned, yet Thor as played by Chris Hemsworth is also presented as a heroic warrior and a site of sexual spectacle. In asking whether women can be superheroes in American cinema, we can productively reflect on the different construction of male and female heroism; while the female hero has proved challenging to American cinema, the male hero of superhero cinema is now such a familiar figure that he is subject to pastiche (as in *Thor*). Thor serves as a vehicle to consider superhero masculinities on film and a useful contrast to Wonder Woman, not least since both characters are godlike heroes who exercise their powers in behalf of humanity.

Both Wonder Woman and Thor are visually presented through the generic frame of the quasi-classical, gladiatorial imagery of the sword and sandal film. As I'll argue, this nostalgic evocation of an earlier period of film production contextualizes the ways in which these figures both perform and undercut conventional gender scripts, whether by humour (Thor) or the intense melodrama of battle (Wonder Woman). Derived from Norse mythology, Thor represents an obvious interface with the sword and sandal legacy of European peplum and US epic adventure cinema. The subgenre makes use of classical imagery and physical spectacle, with exaggerated gender types as one component of the film fiction (Steve Reeves as Hercules, or Arnold Schwarzenegger as Conan the Barbarian, for example). The Italian peplum and the Hollywood sword and sandal films it fed into showcase a quasi-classical male heroism centred on the spectacularized body of the star. Indeed, as a comic book character Thor first appears in 1962 at precisely the mid-century point when Italian peplum and Hollywood historical epics were flourishing. In contrast to the Second World War origins of Wonder Woman, then, the comic book origins of 'The Mighty Thor' are framed by the hyperbolic display and preoccupation with reworking classical and mythological themes evident in 1960s popular culture.

As a number of critics have observed, that legacy was revitalized by the commercial success in 2000 of Ridley Scott's *Gladiator*, which provided a frame for the Marvel series. Thor is the protagonist of three films: *Thor*, *Thor: The Dark World* (2013) and *Thor: Ragnarok* (2017) in which he is explicitly positioned within a futuristic gladiatorial arena, pitched against the Incredible Hulk. If Thor the comic book character first appeared in the heyday of the peplum and historical epic, the films I address here are framed through the reworking of that mode of cinema first in the Conan films, but most particularly in *Gladiator*. As Robert A. Rushing writes, 'Ridley Scott's classical epic *Gladiator* opened in 2000 to widespread popular and critical success', a cultural visibility and status rather different to peplum precursors (2016: 25).

Drawing attention to the earnest delivery and masculine melodrama evident in Scott's film, Rushing goes on to argue that '*Gladiator*'s melancholy proved to be powerfully influential in the contemporary peplum' (ibid., 26). Purse also draws this connection, suggesting that '*Gladiator*'s massive popularity was a key factor in the resurgence of the historical epic in films like *The Last Samurai* (2003), *Troy* (2004), *Alexander* (2004) and *Kingdom of Heaven* (2005)'. Like Rushing, Purse indicates how much these contemporary pepla articulate forms of cinematic masculinity. For Purse, each of these films 'was in its own way narratively preoccupied with the passing of this particular brand of heroic masculinity, even as they celebrated it' (2011: 97–8).

Combining other-worldly and nostalgic imagery, the Thor films foreground the mythical origins of the comic book character. Indeed, they also play on a link to films and television series based in the classical world. Thor's costume and that of his comrades – Sif and the Warriors Three – include elements of metal and leather, suggesting the classical stylings of the peplum and of television series such as *Hercules: The Legendary Journeys* (1995–9) and its spin-off success *Xena: Warrior Princess*. This iconography is also exploited in *Wonder Woman* with the young Diana located in a magical land of Amazons; fathered by Zeus, Diana is a figure associated with classical myth. In the highly technologized fictional world of the superhero film, both Wonder Woman and Thor are situated at a remove from technologies of communication or weaponry (sword and hammer over laser and gun), and thus from modernity. It is the imagery of the peplum, as rearticulated in films such as *Gladiator* that is preeminent in Thor. Similarly, *Wonder Woman* revels in classical imagery while distancing its hero from human warfare that is figured as both industrialized/ mechanized and, at the same time, savage or primitive. A nostalgic evocation of simplicity associated with the visual repertoire of what we can term 'pastness' is, as I will elaborate below, important albeit in different ways to the cinematic representation of both characters.

Thor handles the archaic classical pastness of its hero by situating him as overtly other-worldly; Thor is not 'from here' in multiple senses. Thus, while in *Thor* and *Thor: the Dark World* the hero evokes something of the melancholy melodramatic masculinity of *Gladiator*, in the ensemble films *The Avengers*, *Avengers: Age of Ultron* and *Avengers: Infinity War* (2018), Thor's other-world strength is situated within a team of enhanced fighters, casting him as a conventional straight man against other characters' verbal banter.[4] Chronologically, the appearance of Thor within Marvel films is first signalled at the end of *Iron Man 2* with a post-credit teaser revealing S.H.I.E.L.D. Agent Phil Coulson's discovery of Thor's hammer. The Marvel films have typically emphasized the difference of Thor even in a world of superhero action, extraordinary powers and fantastic costumes in which action takes place across diverse worlds and fantastic landscapes. While Thor becomes intimately connected to Earth, he is a man out of place (from another world) and time (he is old-fashioned). His language and behaviour are archaic and prompt responses from diegetic audiences ranging from laughter to fear, puzzlement and confusion.

Thor engages in a form of visual nostalgia; that nostalgia is applicable equally to Thor's old-fashioned language and gender behaviour, his courtship of Jane Foster characterized by asexual formality. Diana Prince, too, is framed in *Wonder Woman* as a figure from a radically different place, a difference given a temporal dimension via the use of classical imagery and mythological themes. Wonder Woman is characterized as a serious, even stern, presence in a human society that is marked by cynicism and banter, on the one hand, and brutal violence, on the other. While Thor's archaic language is a source of humour when juxtaposed to a contemporary context, Diana Prince's earnest pronouncements produce a more complex tone and texture around the hero out of time. Diana is naïve, shocked by death and violence yet capable of wielding immense power. Her counterpart and love interest, Steve Trevor, appears worldly, knowing but also determined to play his part – and ultimately to die – in the 'war to end all wars'. Unsurprisingly, it is in relation to codes of sexual propriety that *Wonder Woman* adopts a more humorous tone in its framing of Diana Prince as a woman out of time/place. Not only is she oblivious to gendered codes of dress and behaviour, Diana responds emotionally and spontaneously to sensual pleasures such as the sight of a baby or the taste of ice cream. In a department store she mistakes corsetry for armour and inquires how women can fight in the constricting costumes deemed appropriate for the day.

There are also intriguing connections between the narrative presentation of the two superhero characters, each inscribed in relation to a familiar trajectory of generational conflict and personal growth. Thor commences the 2011 film as an impatient king in waiting; by its end he acknowledges that he still has much to learn about kingship, accepting the authority and wisdom of his father Odin. Moreover, Thor is established at film's end as a figure bound to Earth via bonds of friendship for humans and romance (his love for Jane Foster). His desire to protect Earth and its inhabitants is as significant as Thor's responsibilities towards Asgard. The film's narrative takes the familiar form of a redemptive personal journey, a maturation in which Thor learns painful lessons in kingship. In the film's first act, Thor recklessly seeks out confrontation with the frost giants, a race previously conquered by his father Odin and with whom Asgard is now at peace. As a result of this wilful violence, Odin strips Thor of his powers and casts him out. Exiled on Earth, the weakened Thor must learn lessons as to the importance of order and peace – that is, when violence is and is not necessary – before he is restored, chastened, to his former position.

Thor demonstrates arrogance and poor judgement in seeking out conflict. In casting his son out, Odin angrily describes him as 'a vain, greedy, cruel boy', clearly indicating that he is not yet a man and that this will be a film concerned above all with themes of masculinity. Narratively, this is framed through a formulation of worthiness which must be earned/learned. On Earth, Thor must grapple with his disempowerment even though he has greater physical strength than 'mortals'; during his period of exile Thor is hit by Jane Foster's truck twice, is tasered, sedated and physically restrained. These sufferings are framed by both melancholy masculinity (Thor's sense of loss) and by a prevailing sense of the ridiculousness of the man/God figure. However, it is Thor's willingness to sacrifice himself – effectively to accept defeat and death – which redeems him and saves the day. A spectacular restoration of Thor's powers ensues as hammer and armour replace jeans and T-shirt. This sequence evokes both the seriousness and the comedic elements of Thor, the spectacle of male power rightly restored as seen through the adoring/amazed eyes of onlookers. Rushing argues that the peplum body is set up to be admired; such a construction is cheekily acknowledged in Jane Foster's words – 'Oh. My. God.' – a humorous pun condensing her delight in the hero's restoration, his physical embodiment and his status as a god. Thor's physique continues to trigger both admiration and humour as in the quip in *Infinity War*: 'It's like a pirate and an angel had a baby.'

Like Thor, Wonder Woman is a god who is ultimately pledged to protect humankind. Hers too is a tale of maturation and violence. *Wonder Woman* frames Diana's backstory as that of a girl/woman yearning to become a warrior and subsequently discovering her powers before entering and acting within the human world (referred to as 'the world of men', a phrase that knowingly plays on the use of the term 'men' to signal all peoples). From her childhood, Diana is fascinated by the training of the amazons, desiring to learn how to fight. Her mother seeks to shield Diana from her identity, refusing to countenance her training. We are given to understand via conversations to which she is not privy that Diana is special and that there is a secret relating to her powers and fate. This becomes clear to Diana in training and is used with glee later when she smashes her way up a tower wall to claim the treasured relics of sword, lasso and shield. Diana explicitly rebels against her mother's strictures, first by training in secret and then by vowing to leave the island with Steve Trevor. Unlike Thor, however, and in line with Diana's earnest desire to protect the innocent, her rebellion and departure is ultimately a sanctioned one. No petulant battle of generations is staged here since a resigned Hippolyta gives her permission for the earnest Diana to follow her instincts. While Thor is deemed unworthy by Odin and his hammer is taken from him, Hippolyta bestows on Diana a headpiece worn by her sister Antiope, urging her daughter to do it justice. This gift is accompanied by a warning: 'Be careful in the world of men Diana; they do not deserve you.'

Both Diana and Thor are positioned as mythological figures who are rendered sympathetic, less godlike via encounters with the human world. Both need to learn, and they are transformed by experience, love and loss. However, while Thor is positioned as an arrogant man-boy who must be humbled, Diana's development has to do with an understanding of complexity and power. It is humanity who do not deserve her; unlike Thor, Diana has nothing to prove. Her view of the world is, however, shown to be naïve, lacking in nuance as her mother Queen Hippolyta predicts. Equally, however, a sense of naïve hope is to some extent narratively justified as Diana's climactic battle with Aries ultimately leads to a cessation of violence. While Thor is raised as a king in waiting, Diana is not made aware of her powers, protected from her difference. She herself is the 'god-killer', the powerful weapon that she mistakenly believes to be her venerated sword. Her full power and potency is released by loss as Steve Trevor sacrifices himself to avoid the death of thousands.

Gadot's portrayal of Wonder Woman turns on her physical embodiment of a familiar character and the evocation of her love for Steve Trevor. This articulation of the female hero is very far from the knowing sexuality of Black Widow discussed above. Rather Diana Prince's other-worldliness is figured as melodramatic intensity of the kind more often associated with men in action scenarios. It is this characteristic that comes to the fore in a powerfully intense sequence which depicts Wonder Woman at the front line of the war, finally revealing rather than hiding herself in the human world. Putting on the headpiece which her mother had presented to her and casting aside her cloak to reveal her superhero guise in a succession of shots focused on shield, armour and lasso, Diana climbs up a wooden ladder to move determinedly into the no man's land between the trenches. The elongation of actions through editing and the measured, slowed pace echoes the visual conventions of war cinema, a genre which often employs slow motion at moments of tension and imminent death. Visually as well as narratively, this sequence emphasizes the hero as

Figure 11.2 Wonder Woman stands tall in No Man's Land, in *Wonder Woman* directed by Patty Jenkins © Warner Bros 2017.

different from the soldiers with whom she fights. As they crouch low, she stands upright, a mid-shot of Wonder Woman alone in no man's land (Figure 11.2), her flesh and costume bright against the dull brown tones of the mud, succeeded by a shot centred on a single bullet racing towards her; when she does crouch down it is to deflect the combined fire of machine guns, the trace of the weapons serving to centre her in the frame. Image composition, action shots and slow motion all work to underline Wonder Woman's warrior status and her rage.

These sequences, showcasing as they do Wonder Woman's iconic costume, also work to showcase the body of the heroine, underscoring her power and beauty. Wonder Woman's costume went through multiple iterations in the comics. Here the classical styling of the epic is clearly invoked. Purse writes that '*Gladiator* marked an emphatic return to the explicit spectacularisation of the male body that was a key characteristic of the action films of the 1980s' (2011: 97). As played by Hemsworth, Thor serves as both a site of spectacle organized around the male star body (with an insistent visual emphasis on the sculpted torso) and as a comedic figure of masculine identity, a straight-man foil in a playful genre. Thor's other-world persona, as a god-cum-strongman is valorized in earnest manner; yet it is also played for comedy via surreal encounters with humans (such as his attempt to purchase a horse in a pet shop in *Thor*, or brief journey amongst commuters on the

London Underground in *Dark World*). Thor's arrogance/self-belief is a recurrent source of comedy even while he remains a credible hero. I am not arguing that the humour surrounding Thor involves any complex critique; indeed, quite the opposite. Thor is a superhero god, a character who acquires maturity and insight; while the thrust of the narrative is that physical strength requires wisdom and judgement, the redemptive sacrifice that precedes the restoration of Thor's powers is, as it were, played straight.

The legacy of the peplum and historical epic is encapsulated in a look, what Purse in a different context refers to as 'square-jawed heroism' (2019). The strength and resilience of the heroes is associated with the texture of sculpted bodies, conceptualized by Rushing as 'haptic peplum' (2016: 6). The epic provided a context for male bodies on display with its ritualized and often sanitized scenes of violence. Thor looks to and reframes (rather than reworks) that visual repertoire. The Thor films draw on a rich set of generic intertexts to locate the masculine male hero; the relative paucity of such intertexts through which to imagine and reimagine the female hero is a key factor for the, often awkward, way in which she is presented. It is surely noteworthy, then, that Wonder Woman too makes use of classical imagery and mythological themes, most obviously in the sequences set on Themyscira. Indeed, the recycling of classical images via Xena suggests that *Wonder Woman* does have generic and visual intertexts on which to draw.

Becoming a man – a common enough theme in and beyond American cinema – is, of course, a gendered narrative trope. That becoming a woman signifies so differently lies at the root of American cinema's ambivalent embrace of the female hero. Action cinema offers a generic frame which facilitates narratives of power. Yet these overarching narratives can be inflected in diverse ways, a diversity evident within the cycle of superhero films that has developed in the 2010s. Diana Prince's discovery of her powers is framed through a desire for peace, Batman develops himself and his strength within a search for technologized vengeance, and the Marvel god/superhero Thor follows a trajectory in which the hero becomes a man by understanding the importance of peace and the limits of power. Each uses mise en scène in distinct ways, with the iconography and battle-scarred landscapes of the First World War – a stark contrast to the brightness of Themyscira – playing a particularly prominent part in the visual composition of *Wonder Woman*. It is above all the characterization of Wonder Woman as determined to act, to intervene rather than watch, that is the most striking aspect of her heroic characterization. In common with male superheroes such as Thor, Wonder Woman evokes lightness through leaps, bounds and images of flight, while strength is signalled through a command of weaponry such as sword and shield. She is figured as both mythological – the film's statuesque poses evoking classical imagery are enhanced by the use of slow motion – and yet deeply empathetic for the plight of those caught up in war.

Wonder Woman ends with the costumed heroine launching herself from atop a building – hurtling towards the camera/audience in flight, she enacts a recognizable superhero pose. This moment suggests a character who has embraced her superhero identity. Even so, in the subsequent film in which the character appears, *Justice League* (2017), Wonder Woman continues to adopt a low profile, hiding from any public gaze for the majority of the film. We might contrast this public reticence on the part of Wonder Woman to the assurance of Thor. The latter is seen, for example, posing for a selfie with young women on the streets of New York in *Thor: Ragnorok*. Of course, this is in part a function of the contrast between the radically different tone of Marvel and DC versions of the superhero film. The celebratory and comically nostalgic tone of *Captain Marvel* (2019), the first film in the long running Marvel series to centre on a female character, is interesting in this context. We might postulate that the contrast between the reticence of Wonder Woman and the comic ease of Marvel characters such as Thor, Iron Man and Captain Marvel (or indeed the emphasis on sexualized performance that characterizes Black Widow), is indicative of the atypical approach taken by *Wonder Woman* in its cinematic presentation of such an iconic character.

Postscript

It may be rather perverse to expect to find female superheroes in the cinema, given that the medium is seemingly so insistent on keeping strong women at the margins. In this account I've framed superhero cinema in terms of action and fantasy, drawing on both current and earlier cycles. This isn't an exhaustive approach and there is certainly more that can be said about the visual and sonic dimensions of these films. *Wonder Woman* is in many ways an exceptional superhero film; it uses the narrative patterns and imagery of the genre – along with modes such as the melodramatic war films – to centre a female hero. My interest here has been to look more broadly at the differences – and similarities – by which heroic men and heroic women are figured in recent superhero cinema. Asking whether, how and when women can be superheroes in American cinema highlights the continued work of gendered hierarchies that are encapsulated in the provisional answer with which I started this chapter: yes, but …

Notes

1 On film, see e.g. Barbara Creed's influential study *The Monstrous Feminine: Film, Feminism, Psychoanalysis* (1993); on television, see Amanda Lotz's exploration of action shows in her *Redesigning Women: Television after the Network Era* (2006).

2 Indeed, as Marianne Kac-Vergne (2016) notes, the visibility of both the *Alien* and *Terminator* series of films, so much discussed within feminist scholarship, 'often obscures the fact that women rarely play more than a bit part in science fiction films centred almost exclusively on male heroes'.

3 Potts takes an active role in the climactic battle of *Avengers: Endgame* (2019), a film that belatedly showcases some of the many female characters in Marvel comics.

4 Indeed, Thor's absence from *Captain America: Civil War* (2016) is sufficiently significant that it is extra-textually marked, generating a series

of promotional skits featuring the character's supposed timeout with Australian mate Darryl. See e.g. https://www.youtube.com/watch?v=bPNBKT6JLSU. On the melodramatic masculinity of *Gladiator*, see Fradley (2004).

Works cited

Creed, Barbara (1993), *The Monstrous Feminine: Film, Feminism, Psychoanalysis*, London: Routledge.

Fradley, Martin (2004), 'Maximus Melodramaticus: Masculinity, masochism and white male paranoia in contemporary Hollywood cinema', in Yvonne Tasker (ed.), *Action and Adventure Cinema*, 235–51, London, Routledge.

Kac-Vergne, Marianne (2016), 'Sidelining women in contemporary science-fiction film', *Miranda*, 12. Available online: http://journals.openedition.org/miranda/8642.

Lotz, Amanda D. (2006), *Redesigning Women: Television after the Network Era*, Urbana: University of Illinois Press.

Purse, Lisa (2011), *Contemporary Action Cinema*, Edinburgh: University of Edinburgh Press.

Purse, Lisa (2019), 'Square-jawed strength: Gender and resilience in the female astronaut film', *Science Fiction Film and Television*, 12.1: 53–72.

Rushing, Robert A. (2016), *Descended from Hercules: Biopolitics and the Muscled Male Body on Screen*, Bloomington: University of Indiana Press.

Schubart, Rikke (2007), *Super Bitches and Action Babes: The Female Hero in Popular Cinema, 1970–2006*, Jefferson, NC: McFarland.

Tasker, Yvonne (1998), *Working Girls: Gender and Sexuality in Popular Cinema*, London: Routledge.

Tasker, Yvonne (2015), *The Hollywood Action and Adventure Film*, Malden, MA: Wiley-Blackwell.

Index